SHAPERS
—— OF THE ——
GREAT DEBATE
—— ON ——
JACKSONIAN
DEMOCRACY

SHAPERS
— OF THE —
GREAT DEBATE
— ON —
JACKSONIAN DEMOCRACY

A BIOGRAPHICAL DICTIONARY

Paul E. Doutrich

Shapers of the Great American Debates, Number 3
Peter B. Levy, Series Editor

Greenwood Press
Westport, Connecticut • London

Library of Congress Cataloging-in-Publication Data

Doutrich, Paul E.
  Shapers of the great debate on Jacksonian democracy / by Paul E. Doutrich.
    p. cm. — (Shapers of the great American debates, ISSN 1099-2693)
  Includes bibliographical references and index.
  ISBN 0–313–31576–0 (alk. paper)
  1. United States—History—1815–1861—Biography—
Dictionaries. 2. Politicians—United States—Biography—
Dictionaries. 3. Social reformers—United States—Biography—
Dictionaries. 4. Intellectuals—United States—Biography—
Dictionaries. 5. United States—Politics and government—1815–
1861. 6. Federal government—United States—History—19th
century. 7. Jackson, Andrew, 1767–1845—Influence. I. Title. II. Series.
  E339.D68 2004
  973.5'092'2—dc22   2003061812

British Library Cataloguing in Publication Data is available.

Library of Congress Catalog Card Number: 2003061812
ISBN: 0–313–31576–0
ISSN: 1099-2693

First published in 2004

Greenwood Press, 88 Post Road West, Westport, CT 06881
An imprint of Greenwood Publishing Group, Inc.
www.greenwood.com

Printed in the United States of America

The paper used in this book complies with the
Permanent Paper Standard issued by the National
Information Standards Organization (Z39.48–1984).

10 9 8 7 6 5 4 3 2 1

This book is dedicated to my students
and especially to my two most important students,
Adam Jason Doutrich
and
Danielle Rene Doutrich Condly.

CONTENTS

WRITERS AND REFORMERS

SERIES FOREWORD

American history has been shaped by numerous debates over issues far ranging in content and time. Debates over the right, or lack thereof, to take the land of the Native Americans, and the proper place and role of women, sparked by Roger Williams and Anne Hutchinson, respectively, marked the earliest years of the Massachusetts Bay Colony. Debates over slavery, the nature and size of the federal government, the emergence of big business, the rights of labor and immigrants, were central to the Republic in the nineteenth century and, in some cases, remain alive today. World War I, World War II, and the Vietnam War sparked debates that tore at the body politic. Even the Revolution involved a debate over whether America should be America or remain part of Great Britain. And the Civil War, considered by many the central event in American history, was the outgrowth of a long debate that found no peaceful resolution.

This series, *Shapers of the Great American Debates*, will examine many of these debates—from those between Native Americans and European settlers to those between "natives" and "newcomers." Each volume will focus on a particular issue, concentrating on those men and women who *shaped* the debates. The authors will pay special attention to fleshing out the life histories of the shapers, considering the relationship between biography or personal history and policy or philosophy. Each volume will begin with an introductory overview, include approximately twenty biographies of ten to fifteen pages, an appendix that briefly describes other key figures, a bibliographical essay, and a subject index. Unlike works that emphasize end results, the books in this series will devote equal attention to both sides, to the "winners" and the "losers." This will lead to a more complete understanding of the richness and complexity of America's past than is afforded by works that examine only the victors.

Taken together, the books in this series remind us of the many ways that class, race, ethnicity, gender, and region have divided rather than united the inhabitants of the United States of America. Each study reminds us of the frequency and variety of debates in America, a reflection of the diversity of the nation and its democratic credo. One even wonders if a similar series could be developed for many other nations or if the diversity of America and its tradition of free expression have given rise to more debates than elsewhere.

Although many Americans have sought to crush the expression of opposing views by invoking the imperative of patriotism, more often than not Americans have respected the rights of others to voice their opinions. Every four years, Americans have voted for president and peacefully respected the results, demonstrating their faith in the process that institutionalizes political debate. More recently, candidates for the presidency have faced off in televised debates that often mark the climax of their campaigns. Americans not only look forward to these debates, but they would probably punish anyone who sought to avoid them. Put another way, debates are central to America's political culture, especially those that deal with key issues and involve the most prominent members of society.

Each volume in the series is written by an expert. While I offered my share of editorial suggestions, overall I relied on the author's expertise when it came to determining the most sensible way to organize and present each work. As a result, some of the volumes follow a chronological structure; others clump their material thematically; still others are separated into two sections, one pro and one con. All of the works are written with the needs of college and advanced high school students in mind. They should prove valuable both as sources for research papers and as supplemental texts in both general and specialized courses. The general public should also find the works an attractive means of learning more about many of the most important figures and equally as many seminal issues in American history.

Peter B. Levy
Associate Professor
Department of History
York College

ACKNOWLEDGMENTS

There are many people who have provided invaluable assistance to me on this project. First and foremost is my good friend and colleague at York College of Pennsylvania and the series editor, Dr. Peter Levy. I am incredibly fortunate to work with him on a daily basis. I am also fortunate to have the friendship and encouragement of several other colleagues. Dr. Philip Avillo, my former department chair, finagled some reduced teaching loads for me without which this book would still be a work in progress. Dr. Mel Kulbicki, my current chair, has provided much appreciated enthusiasm and encouragement during the past year. On a grander scale, I consider myself truly blessed to work in such a friendly, supportive environment as exists throughout York College of Pennsylvania. In addition to the scholars with whom I interact daily, there are two others who have played a particularly important role in shaping me intellectually. Dr. Lemuel Molvinsky, who directed my master's program at Penn State University, awakened me to the magic of doing and teaching history. For that I will be eternally grateful. Dr. Lance Banning, my doctoral director, taught me how to be a scholar.

As is indicated in the dedication, there are many students who have provided me with the inspiration, curiosity, and energy needed to tackle this project. The list includes but is not limited to Dr. Paul Newman, Stacy Doll, Stephanie Delong-Smith, Brian Moore, the three amigos (Matt Ruckdeschel, Zack Oberrath, and Jeff Ostendorf), Jake Raymond, Stacy Drega,

Darcie White, Eloise Bernthaizel, Joe Felice, Rich Apgar, Yvette "Thelma" Ganoe, Karen "Louise" Thoman, Kathryn Smith, Nicole Snyder, and Tom Sheeler.

On a more personal note, my two children, Adam and Danielle, have provided me with more inspiration and joy than they'll ever know. I only hope they are a tiny bit as proud of this work as I am of them. And finally, Annie Ward, whose humor, encouragement, and interest in my work and myself has fortified me.

AN INTRODUCTION TO JACKSONIAN AMERICA

The Jacksonian era began well before the election of Andrew Jackson in 1828 and reflects more than simply the issues and policies advocated by Jackson and his Democratic supporters. The era instead entailed profound change within American civilization. It became the bridge between the Enlightenment ideals upon which the nation was founded and the tensions that erupted into civil war seventy years later. The era was flavored by an unstoppable push westward, a rapidly expanding population, a burgeoning economy, and far-reaching social change. Likewise, in addition to Andrew Jackson there were many figures, both political and otherwise, who were instrumental in guiding the nation. Some, like Henry Clay, Daniel Webster, and John C. Calhoun, have been subjects for much scholarship over the years. However, there are others, including Martin Van Buren, Thomas Hart Benton, William Lloyd Garrison, and Ralph Waldo Emerson, who are often relegated to secondary roles. In fact the American experience during the period was influenced by a dynamic corps of determined individuals pursuing their own unique visions for the nation's future.

In many ways the Jacksonian era began after the controversial election of 1824. Though Andrew Jackson lost the contest, the issues and sectional interests that emerged during the campaign set the stage for the debates that marked the next two decades. The winner, John Quincy Adams, was the first president from a blossoming new generation of leadership. He and his cohorts had grown up during the Revolutionary War years but had not participated in the war. Instead they were nurtured by heroic stories about the war and the idealistic goals of the founding generation. Portraying the War of 1812 as the final defense of American independence, they saw that war as their chance to contribute to the revolutionary saga. Afterward they gladly accepted the responsibility of implementing their understanding of the founding generation's philosophical principles into the practical, day-to-day operation of the nation.

After the War of 1812, several factors encouraged American expansion. The most obvious was the burgeoning population. During the first two decades of the century the population almost doubled, growing from 5,308,843 people in 1800 to 9,638,453 in 1820. Over the next twenty years the number would again almost double, rising to 17,069,453 (U.S. Bureau of the Census 1800, 1820, 1840). An evolving nationalism further fed Americans' hunger to develop the vast lands west of the Mississippi River. Acquired through the Louisiana Purchase, the region had begun to attract population before the war. However, with the British threat removed and only sporadic Native American resistance, the land became a magnet for new settlers. After twenty years in which only two states—Ohio in 1803 and Louisiana in 1812—were added to the Union, six were admitted between 1816 and 1821—Indiana in 1816, Mississippi in 1817, Illinois in 1818, Alabama in 1819, Maine in 1821, and Missouri in 1821. The creation of new states, however, did little to satisfy the demands of a restless population. Territories in both the upper Midwest and lower Mississippi Valley had to be organized to administer the swelling numbers of inhabitants. Farther west, a corps of rugged adventurers pushed into the Rocky Mountains and beyond. Prowling the Missouri River region for beaver pelts, these "mountain men" further awakened Americans to the potential bounties first described by Lewis and Clark. In the far west, John Jacob Astor was busily building a diverse commercial empire that established him as one of the nation's wealthiest men.

Land west of the lower Mississippi was of particular interest to many Americans. Although the demand for staple farm commodities, particularly corn and wheat, steadily built immediately after the war, it was cotton that drew thousands west. Since the late eighteenth century, cotton had been transforming southern agriculture from a mixed subsistence and cash crop system to predominantly commercial farming. The lower Mississippi River Valley offered ideal conditions for both cotton and the new southern economy. Unfettered access to the Gulf of Mexico and world markets only added to the potential. Succumbing to "Alabama fever," many young southern planters eagerly hiked west to acquire new land. Ambitious farmers with limited resources also recognized an opportunity to prosper as well as a chance to escape the planter aristocracy of the old South. Likewise, avaricious entrepreneurs throughout the nation understood that sizeable profits could be made by speculating on land in the lower Mississippi River Valley.

The effects of escalating cotton production were also felt in the Northeast. Paralleling the transformation of southern agriculture was the evolution of an American factory system. In the years immediately prior to and during the war, competition with British textile manufacturers was limited. Consequently American mills, stimulated by southern cotton production, grew rapidly. In 1813 a group of Massachusetts merchants, the Boston Associates, pooled their capital and developed a system of large-scale textile mills. This experiment became a model for other industrial adventurers. After the war, European producers attempted to flood American markets with high-quality goods at prices comparable to those of domestic manufacturers. To counter the effort, Congress, despite some opposition from southern planters, passed a moderate protective tariff in 1816. The legislation aided the expansion of cotton production from 400,000 bales in 1820 to over 1.3 million bales in 1840 and helped the American textile industry to grow at an unprecedented rate during the next two decades (Pesson, 110).

Urbanization in the North accompanied industrial growth. The demand for unskilled labor attracted farm families to mill towns and cities. After years of overuse and subdivision many New England farmsteads, by the early nineteenth century, were unable to sustain the families that had operated them. In search of an alternative livelihood, some New Englanders accepted employment in the new textile mills. Others adjusted by remaining in their homes and performing piecemeal production designed to provide materials to nearby mills. Additionally, after the War of 1812 a growing wave of European immigrants, especially Irish and Germans, supplemented the potential pool of native-born labor. For most, becoming part of the urban labor force included relocating to the immediate vicinity of the mill in which they worked. These factors combined to accelerate the evolution of an urban environment from Boston to Baltimore.

A revolution in transportation added fervor to the nation's expansion. Networks of modern, new roads linked farms and population in the trans-Appalachian region to markets in the East. Turnpikes covered by various surfaces accommodated far more traffic and commerce than their predecessors ever had. Beginning in the 1810s a glut of canals further enhanced Americans' ability to transport themselves and goods. A few attempted to copy New York's ambitious and very successful Erie Canal experiment. However, numerous shorter ones were dug that connected communities to larger markets. Canals provided relatively fast, inexpensive access to goods that had previously been prohibitively costly. Along many of the nation's rivers, steamboats also came to play a vital economic role. The ability to travel rapidly upstream had a profound effect upon river trade and helped transform river cities like Pittsburgh, Cincinnati, Louisville, and St. Louis into thriving regional centers. Likewise, because of their low draft the boats were able to ply many smaller and shallower rivers. This ever-evolving web of transportation provided Americans with a multitude of entrepreneurial opportunities never before available.

Under President James Monroe, the federal government responded to the nation's desire to expand. The administration, directed chiefly by Secretary of State John Quincy Adams, aggressively negotiated an agreement through which the United States acquired Florida as well as the Spanish claim to the Oregon Territory. For more than a decade, American settlers had coveted the panhandle of Florida as a natural extension of the Mississippi Valley. Likewise, the panhandle offered an important defensive buffer for New Orleans. At the other edge of the continent, Adams, among others, understood that though population had just begun to settle in the Northwest, the region possessed great potential. Eliminating the Spanish from the Oregon Territory enhanced the American claim and left only the British to contend with for control of the entire region. In other negotiations, the United States was able to secure fishing rights in the north Atlantic and formal recognition of a border with Canada from northern Minnesota to the Rocky Mountains. The agreement ended any threats that the British might challenge the northern limits of the Louisiana Purchase. Meanwhile, diplomatic relations with the emerging nations of Latin America offered new opportunities. Through the Monroe Doctrine, authored by Adams, the United States warned against European colonization in the Western Hemisphere. These negotiations and maneuvers provided additional momentum to the expansionist hopes of most Americans.

Expansion, however, entailed several potentially divisive issues. One debate involved the method through which federal land would be distributed. Many Americans, particularly in the Northeast, advocated a relatively slow and controlled allocation process, arguing that federal land ought to be sold at market value and in large tracts of 640 acres. This method would attract primarily speculators and groups of individual farmers. It would also generate significant revenues for the federal government. Supporters proposed that essential political, social, and economic activities would develop more quickly in these communities. Additionally, the settlements would probably reflect a somewhat homogeneous character thus limiting potential internal tensions. Meanwhile, the revenues generated from the land sales could be used, among other things, to assist in creating infrastructure between the new territories and eastern commercial centers.

There were others throughout the nation who backed a more aggressive method of land distribution. Upholding the Jeffersonian tradition, they described the nation as one that had been built upon small family farmsteads. Rather than closely administered growth, they sought loose land policies at a minimal cost. By providing inexpensive tracts of as little as forty acres to anyone willing to work them, the federal government would continue an important American tradition. Likewise, squatters should be provided with an opportunity to acquire the land they cleared and worked even though it had not been offered for settlement by the government. Such lenient land policies would strengthen the nation's foundation and further secure dominance west of the Mississippi.

One land issue about which virtually all Americans agreed was the fate of those Native Americans who occupied acreage in the path of the nation's expansion. After the War of 1812, most considered a removal policy the only effective way to deal with the indigenous population. This policy was aggressively pursued during Andrew Jackson's presidency, and even John Quincy Adams generally agreed that removal was in the best interest of all involved. Like most of his countrymen, he believed that Native Americans constituted an obstacle to the nation's destiny. After two centuries of unsuccessful alternatives and periodic confrontations, the only solution appeared to be separation of the two civilizations. Therefore, the Native American population east of the Mississippi would have to move west. Even those tribes, such as the Cherokee, who had adapted to American civilization were required to vacate their lands. The culmination of this process became known as the Trail of Tears. Though considered a tragic episode by contemporary Americans, at the time and throughout the rest of the century Jackson and his successors' very forceful Indian policy was applauded by most, especially those anxious to acquire western land.

Controversy surrounding the Second Bank of the United States (BUS) added to the debate about western settlement. At issue was the role that the BUS would play in providing credit for land acquisitions. In 1816, three years after the First Bank of the United States was shut down, Congress approved a twenty-year charter for the second bank. The new BUS was given authority to maintain monetary stability throughout the nation by overseeing the credit policies of state-chartered banks. As the nation's bank, the BUS accepted all payments made to the federal government, which required accepting notes from state banks. The BUS was, therefore, able to monitor the amount of credit notes that state banks issued. If a bank distributed significantly more credit notes than it could redeem in gold or silver (specie), the BUS could demand payment of the state's bank notes. A state bank that was unable to redeem its notes was forced to call in the loans it had made, often to individuals purchasing land. If the state bank was still unable to pay its notes, the bank's only remaining option was to close, taking with it depositors' money. In this manner, the BUS was able to limit speculative adventures by state banks while also maintaining an acceptable balance between credit and specie throughout the nation.

As had been the case with the first bank, there were many who opposed the new BUS. When they challenged the bank's constitutionality in *McCulloch v. Maryland* (17 U.S. 316, 1819), Chief Justice John Marshall ruled in favor of the BUS. However, the decision in some ways only generated more concern. The fact remained that the bank was a private monopoly able to dominate all other banks in the nation. As a semiprivate institution, the BUS was expected to earn profits for its wealthy investors. Its headquarters were in Philadelphia, not Washington, and it had branches throughout the country. By design the BUS was more powerful than any other financial institution in the nation, including the U.S. Treasury. It was also beyond most federal regulation because only five of its twenty-five directors represented the interests of the government. Opponents lamented that the BUS was simply a vehicle that enabled the rich to get richer by using federal revenues and tightly controlling the economy.

The Panic of 1819 confirmed what critics of the BUS already believed. In an effort to tighten local credit practices, the BUS during the summer of 1818 began to require that state banks redeem their notes in specie. Caught overextended and amidst falling European demands for American farm commodities, some banks were forced into bankruptcy. The falling commodities market sent land values tumbling. Land that had once sold for as much as $69 an acre fell to $2 an acre while cotton revenues in some areas fell by almost 50 percent (Boyer, 286–87). Those hit hardest by the decline were land speculators and western farmers who were unable to pay their bank debts. This in turn made it impossible for some state banks to redeem credit notes issued to the BUS. Forced into bankruptcy, many state banks took both their creditors and depositors down with them. In the long run, the BUS policy created more secure credit management. Initially, however, the policy caused great financial distress, especially in the Mississippi River Valley. Though there were several other factors responsible for the Panic, many, including Andrew Jackson who himself almost went bankrupt, blamed it on the BUS. The Panic, they claimed, was merely a way for wealthy eastern investors to control western expansion and prosperity. Despite restoring economic stability and providing a solid base for significant growth, the BUS remained a very controversial issue throughout the era.

The first expansion-related crisis came in 1819 when Missouri applied for statehood. At the time there were eleven free states and eleven slave states. Not only would admittance provide an advantage to one side or the other but, as the first state from the land acquired by the Louisiana Purchase, Missouri would serve as a model for all future states from that region. Tensions built when New York Congressman James Tallmadge attached an amendment to a bill formally defining Missouri. The Tallmadge amendment sought to prohibit any new slavery in Missouri and gradually emancipate those slaves already there. Defeated in Congress, the proposal set off a rancorous debate that some feared might create a formal separation between the North and South. Northern congressmen protested that by counting slaves for legislative purposes, even at the three-fifths ratio as was done elsewhere, slave states gained an unfair advantage in Congress. Allowing slavery in Missouri ensured that the institution would continue unabated into the foreseeable future. The South retaliated that because there had been slavery in Missouri even before it was organized as a territory, it should be permitted to become a slave state. They complained that slave opponents were denying the people of Missouri sovereignty by attempting to end slavery legislatively through the federal government. When in 1820 southern congressmen refused to admit Maine to the union as a free state, the battle intensified.

Fortunately Henry Clay, employing all his skills as a statesman, was able to negotiate a compromise. Maneuvering through objections on both sides, he proposed that Missouri be accepted into the Union as a slave state. To placate the North, he also called for a line to be extended along 36°30" line of latitude west through the Louisiana Purchase lands. Slavery would be permissible south of the line but prohibited north of it. Finally, Maine was to be admitted as a free state, thus maintaining the balance between slave and free states. Although the Missouri Compromise was not completely satisfactory to either side, it did help to temper somewhat the slavery issue until the 1850s.

Questions about the constitutional rights of the states further complicated the slavery controversy. In 1824 Congress passed a modest tariff designed, in part, to protect American industry from foreign competition. In reaction, the South Carolina legislature formally resolved that a protective tariff was unconstitutional because it benefited northern industry at the expense of southern agriculture. Even though two other states, Virginia and Georgia, passed similar resolutions, the opposition remained essentially symbolic until 1828. In that year, a far higher tariff was passed by Congress. Part of an effort to undermine President John Quincy Adams, the tariff generated an immediate storm of protest in the South. Leading the charge was South Carolina. In a carefully reasoned statement anonymously written by John C. Calhoun, *The South Carolina Exposition and Protest*, Calhoun argued that the state had a right to nullify any federal legislation that was not in the best interests of its constituents. The *Exposition* went on to propose that the state also had the right to secede from the Union if the national government persisted in enforcing legislation that had been nullified by the state. In debates over the next four years, opponents of the tariff reasoned that if the federal government could regulate the economy through a tariff it could also regulate slavery.

Andrew Jackson brought his own fire to the tariff controversy. Though generally considered a states' rights supporter, Jackson, upon his election, stood by the tariff as a way to pay off the national debt. As the debate grew, he came to see the southern opposition as a challenge to his government as well as a personal affront. Finally in early 1833, armed with recent federal legislation that empowered him to use the military, Jackson prepared to impose martial law in South Carolina and force the state to obey the tariff. Many feared that such an action would create an armed conflict.

Fortunately, Henry Clay was able to engineer an acceptable compromise that called for reducing the tariff over a ten-year period. The compromise eased the immediate problems but did little to soothe the sectional animosity that had been generated during the confrontation.

Amidst the growing tensions about nullification, the state's rights debate played out on another front as well. In 1830 Daniel Webster and South Carolina Senator Robert Hayne became embroiled in a fierce debate. The argument initially involved federal land policy but was quickly transformed into a question of states' rights. Hayne, with coaching from Calhoun, defended the "Carolina doctrine" of state sovereignty and nullification. Webster countered in a spellbinding oration asserting that the federal government represented the interests of all Americans. In a memorable closing statement he proclaimed: "Liberty and Union, now and forever, one and inseparable." In the end both sides claimed victory, thus strengthening the philosophical foundation for both arguments.

Along with the tariff, state's rights advocates questioned whether the national government had the constitutional authority to fund internal improvements with federal revenues. After the War of 1812 some of those, including President Madison, who had consistently opposed internal improvements at federal expense, agreed that such government initiatives were necessary. The grand success of the Erie Canal further demonstrated the advantages of providing public support for transportation. However, strict constructionists holding fast to traditional Jeffersonian principles refused to budge. To counter the opposition, supporters linked improvements to the national defense and were able to gain the approval of a somewhat skeptical President Monroe. Additionally, an 1824 Supreme Court decision, *Gibbons v. Ogden* (22 U.S. 1), affirmed the power of the national government to regulate transportation within the states. As a result, some of the revenues collected by the Tariff of 1824 were assigned to be used for internal improvements. Critics, nevertheless, lamented that yet again the power of the state had been subordinated to that of the national government.

Coupled with opposition to President Jackson, the debates about the BUS, the tariff, and internal improvements provided a foundation for a new political party, the Whig Party. Formally established in 1834, the Whigs grew out of a reaction to Jackson's extensive use of his presidential authority. Some in Congress complained that the president's apparent disregard for the system of checks and balances usurped the Constitution. His veto of the bill rechartering the BUS in 1832 in particular drew together formidable opponents. Henry Clay and Daniel Webster immediately emerged as the new party's leaders. Pulling together diverse factions ranging from former Federalists and National Republicans to southern planters and western speculators, the two Whig leaders crafted a broad nationalistic party platform around policies Clay labeled "the American System." The

Whigs' basic premise was that the national government should actively encourage economic development. This included creating a new central bank similar to the BUS, legislating protective tariffs, and pursuing internal improvements. In an era of expanding democracy and declining voter limitations, Whigs also proposed that the government had an obligation to balance individual rights and social responsibilities. Essentially optimistic and progressive in its perspective, the Whig philosophy appealed to many Americans.

The Panic of 1837 provided Whigs with an opportunity to lead. Just weeks after Martin Van Buren succeeded Jackson in the presidency, the nation was struck by a severe economic decline. Although tumbling cotton markets and a European depression contributed to the problems, the primary source of the Panic was Jackson's economic policy. Since the demise of the BUS, spiraling speculation on western lands, risky investments, and the overextension of credit by state banks drained the nation's available specie. Conditions deteriorated in mid-1836 when the Jackson administration announced that it would accept only specie in payment for federal land purchases. In reaction, land sales plummeted. Nervous investors soon began to liquidate their various holdings, which created a run on many banks. Amidst the troubles, the New Orleans cotton market collapsed, setting off a chain reaction that quickly spread throughout the nation. Banks closed, farm land was forfeited, shops and factories shut down, and unemployment soared. In 1839 a second economic shock wave plunged the nation to almost total financial collapse. Through the difficult times, Martin Van Buren refused to provide relief. Instead his solution was to protect the nation's revenues in an independent subtreasury and to let the states and communities deal with the problems as they saw fit.

Victory at the polls, however, did not guarantee success for Whigs. Passing over Clay in favor of Indian fighter William Henry Harrison, the party was confronted by its own ambiguous stand on various issues. The problems became obvious after Harrison's death just four weeks into his presidency. John Tyler, an anti-Jackson Democrat, had been placed on the ticket to attract other southern anti-Jackson Democrats. Unfortunately his stand on most important issues, including the tariff and states' rights in general, collided with those of many Whig's leaders, especially Henry Clay. As a result, little was accomplished during Tyler's presidency.

The pursuit of reform was not limited to the political arena. During the era, a corps of influential activists promoted improvement within American society. The efforts took many shapes, but each in its own way attempted to perfect American civilization. Likewise, Jacksonian reform focused upon the individual and the premise that perfection within society could be achieved through personal commitment. Virtually all aspects of modern life were scrutinized by concerned and eager reformers. The results came through a range of approaches. Spiritually, various utopian experiments and evangelical crusades stirred the passions of many. New philosophical understandings further challenged the nation's collective intellect. A social purity movement that addressed the evolving socioeconomic realities associated with both urbanization and industrialization generated an anti-prostitution movement, a temperance crusade, and an ever more aggressive anti-slavery campaign. Initial efforts to transform public education and a reassessment of women's role in society began to reshape the family. By redefining the way Americans saw themselves and their world, these reform efforts profoundly affected life within the nation.

   In the 1840s the quest for domain, the pursuit of reform, and emerging sectional interests merged with the annexation of Texas. For twenty years, the region had been a priority for expansionists. By 1835 the number of transplanted Americans in the region had grown to almost 35,000, outnumbering the Mexican population by 7 to 1 (Almonte, 210–11). Unwilling to adjust to obvious cultural differences, the burgeoning American population confronted the Mexican government that administered them. The tensions culminated in 1836 with a successful independence movement. Immediately the Republic of Texas's first president, Sam Houston, pursued annexation by the United States. Though President Jackson coveted the region, he feared the potential ramifications of annexation and left the decision to his successor. Plagued by economic problems, Martin Van Buren shared Jackson's concerns and avoided action on Texas. The Harrison and Tyler administrations that followed also sidestepped the Texas issue until Tyler's final days in office. Responding to President-elect James Polk's campaign pledge to annex Texas, Tyler maneuvered congressional approval for annexation just three days before the new president took office. The action, as many expected, led to war with Mexico from May 1846 until September 1847, through which the United States acquired vast new acreage in the Southwest.

   The war with Mexico ended the Jacksonian era. Afterwards, slavery became the overriding debate facing the nation. Many of the other issues that had confronted Jacksonian leaders were no longer relevant. The BUS was gone and most agreed to replace it with an independent subtreasury. Debate about the tariff no longer divided the nation. Likewise, disputes about how to administer land sales were resolved. However, slavery and the related states' rights question separated Americans as never before. Of particular concern was the dilemma concerning slavery in the lands acquired from Mexico. Anti-slavery proponents were impatient with efforts to contain the institution, something they had expected decades earlier. Instead, Americans held a million more slaves in 1845 than they had a quarter of a century earlier. Anti-slavery advocates feared that the annexation of Texas was simply part of a strategy to perpetuate the institution. The South, on the other hand, was convinced that unless slavery was allowed in new territories, anti-slavery forces would soon pass legislation to eliminate the institution. These questions had gained significant momentum during the Jacksonian era and would encompass the next generation.

Though Jacksonian leaders, like the previous generation, allowed the slavery issue to fester, they did significantly change the course of the American experience. By adapting the founding principles to accommodate their vision of the future, they provided profound prospects for social, economic, and political growth. At the heart of this was an emerging concept of nation. Unlike most of their predecessors, Jacksonians came to recognize the benefits of a strong central government. They also understood that democratic reforms, particularly in terms of enfranchisement, enabled an ever larger number of citizens to actively participate in and contribute to the development of the nation. The results included a market revolution that provided vast new opportunities. Likewise, a wide range of internal improvements facilitated by government brought Americans unprecedented mobility. This encouraged a nation of entrepreneurs to acquire new lands while at the same time pursuing new manufacturing and commercial endeavors. European immigration accelerated both agricultural and industrial progress. Urbanization and the beginning of modern American cities also accompanied the expansion. In adjusting to change and as a way to maintain a necessary equilibrium within society, various agencies of reform were devised and institutionalized. The collective product of these Jacksonian era initiatives was the beginning of modern America.

METHOD FOR ORGANIZATION OF BIOGRAPHIES

The biographies that follow describe eighteen of the era's most important leaders. They have been organized into three groupings—Democrats, Whigs, and Reformers and Writers—which reflect the basic philosophy and political perspective of each grouping's subjects. The Democrats are presented first because, despite some ideological diversity, they had the greatest tangible impact on and clearest vision for Jacksonian America. The party in its initial decades differed from the stands it became associated with after the Civil War. Rather than identifying with organized labor and advocating various federally funded and administered social programs, Jacksonian Democrats were unwavering expansionists, their nationalism was tempered by regional concerns, especially western concerns. They were generally states' rights advocates who opposed a centralized bank and a rigidly managed national economy. Three served as president, the most successful of which was, of course, Andrew Jackson. In many ways, it was the reaction to the Democrat's policies that generated both Whig and Reform leaders during the era.

The Whig biographies describe six of the most influential opponents of Democratic policies. Headed by Henry Clay and Daniel Webster, these leaders coalesced into a new national political party, the Whig Party, midway through the era. Guided by personal ambition more than a unified political ideology, their individual stands on most issues, aside from a disdain for Jackson and his party, varied more than did those of the Democratic leaders. Nevertheless, the Whigs were generally nationalists who advocated a central bank, a tariff to protect nascent industry, and an economy directed by the national government. Though they too were expansionists, they called for a more tightly administered and pragmatic march West than did most Democrats. Although three of the Whigs rose to the presidency, none could be described as successful in that office.

The biographies within the Reformers and Writers section are about seven activists who in various ways promoted social change by questioning the conventional attitudes of Jacksonian America. The subjects range from transcendentalist philosopher Ralph Waldo Emerson to evangelist Charles Grandison Finney. Their appeals included a challenge to the traditional role of women in Jacksonian America as well as a demand to abolish slavery. By intuitively tapping into the mood and imagination of the country, one of the era's writers, James Fenimore Cooper, was able to create the first truly American literary role model. Through their efforts, the writers and reformers helped to frame the issues that became the focus of political debate during the era and beyond. In so doing, their impact upon the nation proved to be as profound as was that of the political leaders.

BIBLIOGRAPHY

Juan N. Almonte, "Statistical Report on Texas," *Southwestern Historical Quarterly* 28, no. 3 (January 1925): 210–11; Gilbert Hobbs Barnes, *The Antislavery Impulse, 1830–1844* (New York: Harcourt, Brace & World, 1964); Paul Boyer et al., *The Enduring Vision* 2d ed. (Lexington, MA: D.C. Heath and Co., 1993), 286–87; Robert F. Dalzell, Jr., *Enterprising Elite: The Boston Associates and the World They Made* (Cambridge, MA: Harvard University Press, 1987); George Dangerfield, *The Awakening of American Nationalism, 1815–1828* (New York: Harper & Row, 1965); Richard Ellis, *The Union at Risk: Jacksonian Democracy, States' Rights and the Nullification Crisis* (New York: Oxford University Press, 1987); Daniel Feller, *The Jacksonian Promise: America 1815–1840* (Baltimore: Johns Hopkins University Press, 1995); Ronald Formisano, *The Transformation of the Political Culture: Massachusetts Parties, 1790s–1840s* (New York: Oxford University Press, 1983); William Freehling, *The Road to Disunion: Secessionists at Bay, 1776–1854* (New York: Oxford University Press, 1990); David S. Heidler and Jeanne T. Heidler, *Old Hickory's War: Andrew Jackson and the Quest for Empire* (Mechanicsburg, PA: Stackpole Books, 1996); Michael Holt, *The Rise and Fall of the American Whig Party: Jacksonian Politics and the Onset of the Civil War* (New York: Oxford University Press, 1999); Paul Johnson, *A Shopkeeper's Millennium: Society and Revivals in Rochester, New York, 1815–1837* (New York: Hill and Wang, 1978); John M. McFaul, *The Politics of Jacksonian Finance* (Ithaca, NY: Cornell University Press, 1972); Marvin Meyers, *The Jacksonian Persuasion* (Stanford, CA: Stanford University Press, 1957); Edward Pessen, *Jacksonian America: Society, Personality, and Politics* (Urbana: University of Illinois Press, 1969); Merrill Peterson, *The Great Triumvirate: Clay, Webster, and Calhoun* (New York: Oxford University Press, 1987); Robert Remini, *Andrew Jackson and His Indian Wars* (New York: Penguin Putnam, 2001); Robert Remini, *Andrew Jackson and the Course of American Freedom, 1822–1832* (New York: Harper & Row, 1981); Robert Remini, *The Election of Andrew Jackson* (Philadelphia: Lippincott Press, 1963); Arthur Schlesinger, Jr., *The Age of Jackson* (Boston: Little, Brown and Co., 1945); Charles Sellers, *The Market Revolution: Jacksonian America, 1815–1846* (New York: Oxford University Press, 1991); and Harry L. Watson, *Liberty and Power: Politics of Jacksonian America* (New York: Noonday Press, 1990).

THE DEMOCRATS

ANDREW JACKSON
(1767–1845)

Few Americans have been celebrated in myth or in legend as has Andrew Jackson. President, warrior, frontier hero, entrepreneur, ardent expansionist, demagogue to some and defender of democracy to others, Jackson became the most celebrated figure of his generation. To a nation passionate about expansion and future but intent upon maintaining traditional values, Jackson was ideally suited as the icon of the era. Regardless of whether he was a visionary leader or simply an autocratic reactionary, his significance to America's history is undeniable.

Andrew Jackson grew up in the Carolina backcountry. His parents, Andrew and Elizabeth, were Scots-Irish immigrants who left Ireland to escape increasingly difficult social and economic conditions. They arrived in Charleston, South Carolina, in 1765. Hiking northwest into the backcountry along the South Carolina–North Carolina border, they carved out a farmstead in the Catawba River Valley at the edge of British settlement. The region, known as the Waxhams, was characterized by small, isolated farmsteads; rugged living conditions; and an ongoing struggle with local Indians. Unfortunately, Jackson's father did not survive the struggle for long. He died in January 1767, two months before his son was born.

Life in the Carolina backcountry was a challenge under any circumstances, but for a widow with three young children there were additional perils. Weeks before Andrew was born, his mother and two older brothers went to live with her invalid sister and brother-in-law on their nearby farmstead. It was there that Andrew was born and spent his childhood. During those years, his mother did the domestic chores for her sister's family. In exchange, Andrew and his brothers remained with the family. Young Andrew was an unruly, ill-disciplined, cantankerous child. In an environment that bred rambunctious behavior, he earned a reputation for being particularly impetuous and mischievous. He spent much of his time prowling through the woods, racing horses, and scuffling with anyone who confronted him. His formal education amounted to little more than learning how to read and write.

The American struggle for independence had a profound impact on Andrew Jackson's life. During the late years of the war, British armies regularly tramped through western Carolina, bringing some of the war's most fierce fighting to the region. Jackson and his brothers were part of a colonial militia unit that in early 1781 was captured by British troops. Badly scarred by an royal officer's saber, Jackson escaped his British captors but never forgave them. His brothers were not as fortunate. One died in battle and the other died from smallpox while a prisoner. Compounding Jackson's sorrow, his mother also died from smallpox contracted while attending her son.

After the war Jackson, only fifteen years old, was tormented by his loss. For several years he led an aimless existence. Buoyed by a small inheritance, he rambled through Charleston gambling, drinking, and fighting until his money was spent. He then returned to the Waxhams where he lived briefly with a succession of relatives. As ill behaved and combative as ever, he wore out his welcome quickly.

With the war over, westward expansion once again offered opportunities for those bold enough or desperate enough to pursue them. Andrew Jackson in the mid-1780s was both bold and desperate. Penniless and friendless, having alienated most of his relatives, he moved to Salisbury in central North Carolina with the intention of becoming a lawyer. In Salisbury he apprenticed for a prominent local lawyer. The relationship, however, did not work out. Amidst growing tavern bills, gambling debts, and constant confrontations, Jackson, after a year, agreed to finish his training elsewhere. Six months later, in 1787, he was granted permission to practice law.

Jackson came to Nashville in 1788. At the time the community was little more than a frontier fortification. Only nine years earlier, the region's first American settlers had established themselves at the site then known as French Lick. A year later, with French help, Fort Nashborough was built to secure the location from the British and their Native American allies. After the war a growing number of settlers came looking for farmland and acreage that could be quickly and profitably resold. The area seemed perfectly suited for both endeavors. The soil was rich and the growing season long with ample rainfall. Located on the Cumberland River, the emerging community also appeared well situated to become a regional commercial center and a hub for travel into the southern Mississippi River Valley.

Nashville was incorporated as a town in 1784, but life remained rugged. Fort Nashborough's palisades encircled much of the settlement into the nineteenth century. At the time of Jackson's arrival, town residents occupied primitive log cabins with few luxuries. The local population was rowdy and free spirited, and community services, including law and order, were virtually nonexistent. Beyond the town, roads were simply footpaths through the wilderness. The Cherokee, who had unknowingly ceded huge acreage to speculators, roamed freely through much of the surrounding woodlands, and hostilities between natives and settlers remained commonplace. Nevertheless, for some, especially land speculators, the town was becoming a bonanza.

Andrew Jackson found fortune and fame in Nashville. For him, the absence of lawyers offered abundant opportunities. Land speculators needed legal help legitimizing claims. Land disputes required sanctioned advocates. A scarcity of justices of the peace, county court administrators, and judges hampered the region's growth. Expanding commercial activity generated another area of enterprise for those trained in the law. Because the demand for lawyers far outdistanced the supply, lack of formal legal training, skills, or experience were inconsequential to success in the courtroom. A license was all that the courts required, and Andrew Jackson met the requirement.

Jackson flourished almost immediately upon arriving in Nashville. With a long backlog of cases flooding the court's docket, he had all the work he wanted. Eager and willing to handle whatever cases that came his way, his client list grew rapidly. Within several months he had become involved in almost half the suits that the local courts heard. His activity brought financial rewards, but he sought more. Early on he set his sights upon the status and security of a judgeship. A step toward that goal came just a year after he arrived in Nashville. He was appointed attorney general for the community. As a prosecutor, Jackson quickly established a reputation for law and order. He also allied himself with the local commercial community by immediately enforcing dozens of writs against delinquent debtors.

Two people were instrumental in Jackson's continued rise to prominence. One of them was his future wife, Rachel Donelson Robards. Soon after coming to Nashville, Jackson boarded with the Donelsons. The family was among the first to settle in Tennessee, and Judge Donelson was one of the territory's largest landholders. Upon meeting the family, Jackson was instantly entranced by the judge's daughter, Rachel. Though she was already married, the two developed a close friendship. Rachel's husband, Lewis Robards, soon became suspicious of the budding relationship and took Rachel to live in Kentucky. Alarmed by rumors that Robards was abusing his wife, Jackson rode off to rescue Rachel. After bringing her back to Nashville, he and Rachel began a serious courtship that ended in marriage.

Unfortunately, though they both believed that Robards had obtained a divorce, in fact, it was another two years before he did so. Rachel, therefore, was still married at the time of her marriage to Jackson. Once the divorce was confirmed, another marriage ceremony was quietly performed. In the short run the episode ended satisfactorily for Jackson. He had Rachel and was a member of one of the more prominent Nashville families. In the long run, however, the episode became the source of scandal and bitter political attacks that tormented both he and Rachel.

Aside from Rachel, Jackson's most important supporter was William Blount. A friend of Judge Donelson, Blount was a shrewd land speculator and the territory's first governor. With his support, Jackson was reappointed as attorney general and a short time later became judge advocate of the county militia. A few years later, in 1796, he served as one of five county representatives to the state's first constitutional convention. Riding Blount's coattails, Jackson was elected as the state's first congressman and a year later, when Blount was expelled from the Senate, Jackson was appointed to fill the Senate term. Distrustful of a federal government directed by men he considered unprincipled opportunists and uncomfortable amidst eastern society, he resigned from the Senate after less than six months in office. Upon his return to Nashville, Jackson was rewarded by the Blount regime with the judgeship he had long sought.

For the next six years, Jackson traveled the region as a circuit court judge. Understanding life on the frontier, he established a reputation as a fair judge who did not tolerate rancor. At the time, backwoods judges were not expected to instruct juries or provide instructions about the law. Rather they were to oversee court procedures and render decisions. Jackson was well suited for such responsibilities. His decisions were usually brief, lacked technical elements, and sometimes were grammatically flawed but rarely were they challenged. His stern courtroom manner and fiery temper left no question about his authority. Those bold enough to question his decisions paid the consequences. On one occasion, a bully cursed Judge Jackson and brazenly stomped out of his courtroom. When the local sheriff failed to retrieve the man immediately, Jackson had himself deputized, then marched through to the village and up to the pistol-wielding bully. Threatening to shoot the man, Jackson brought him back to the courtroom and sentenced him. Outside the courtroom Jackson was drawn to the conviviality of taverns, cockfights, and horse races. Though uncouth by eastern standards, he in many ways epitomized frontier civility.

In 1801 Jackson left the judiciary. Despite having no military experience, he was elected major general of the Tennessee militia, the state's highest military post. The position brought Jackson significant new political power. As commanding officer of the state's militia, he became a necessary ally for elected officials. Land speculators anxious to acquire and develop Native American lands also relied upon Jackson's cooperation. Tennessee lay at the threshold of the unsettled lower Mississippi Valley. Though after 1801 the United States had undisputed title to the region, the threat of European occupation remained constant during the early nineteenth century. Likewise, the Native American population that had occupied the valley for centuries was not ready to accept the authority of the United States. Andrew Jackson understood that control of the lower Mississippi River Valley was crucial to the immediate security and future growth of his state as well as the nation. As major general of the Tennessee militia, he made the defense of the region a primary objective. During the next two decades, Jackson used his position at the head of the Tennessee militia to fortify his political status and earn him the reputation as a frontier hero.

One of those who recognized Jackson's prominence was Aaron Burr. Shortly after killing Alexander Hamilton in a duel, Burr sought Jackson's assistance in a scheme that became known as the Burr Conspiracy. With Jackson's military support, Burr hoped to sever off a portion of the lower Mississippi region and establish his own government. Wise enough to remain uncommitted, Jackson convincingly denied any role in the scheme after Burr's capture.

Jackson established his reputation as a military leader during the War of 1812. Early in the war the Creek Indians, buoyed by a successful campaign in the upper Mississippi Valley, hardened their resistance to American settlement in the lower Mississippi. In August 1813, they attacked an American outpost, Fort Mims, in northern Alabama, killing all within the fortification. In retaliation, Jackson and his militia launched a series of attacks throughout the region. After three months of fierce and bloody fighting, the general was able to subdue his enemy. Ruthless in battle, Jackson proved to be a capable tactician and uncompromising commander. A year later he again demonstrated his military capabilities against the British in New Orleans. Leading a ragged army of 5,000 volunteers, Jackson, despite being outnumbered three to one, relentlessly sliced through a well-positioned British army to win the most significant American victory of the war.

Jackson's Indian fighting continued after the war. As the military commander in the lower Mississippi region, he dominated postwar settlements with Native Americans, presiding over about half himself. Imposing rigid restraints, he accepted no resistance to his administration. Even Native American populations who had supported the United States during the war were required to forfeit large tracts of land and submit. Jackson's totalitarian policies soon bred new hostilities. Responding to the problems, in 1818 the general initiated an aggressive campaign to subdue all recalcitrant natives within the region. Armed with somewhat ambiguous instructions from President Monroe, he extended his campaign into Spanish territory in east Florida. He justified his actions by claiming that Native Americans were launching attacks from east Florida. Additionally, according to the general, runaway slaves were organizing in east Florida to assist the natives. Jackson spent the summer of 1818 prowling through northern Florida and doing battle with whomever resisted his authority. Among those who fell were three British trappers.

Jackson's excursion into Florida engendered the possibility of war with both Spain and Great Britain. So concerned and angry was President Monroe that he threatened to allow the British or the Spanish to seize the general. Fortunately for Jackson, Secretary of State John Quincy Adams had a better plan. Adams brilliantly negotiated the acquisition of Florida from Spain and, in so doing, enhanced Jackson's reputation as a conscientious American warrior.

With the transfer of Florida to the United States came the need for someone to head a territorial government. Jackson was an obvious choice and in 1821 he resigned from the army to become Florida's first territorial governor. Interpreting the offer as a repudiation of his military conduct, he attempted to govern Florida in much the same fashion that he had commanded his army. It was a choice that Jackson soon regretted. Within weeks he had again alienated the Spanish, this time by having the former governor arrested. Defying the territory's new federal judge, he refused to release the Spaniard. Meanwhile, employing patronage extensively he filled his administration with loyal supporters who encouraged unsavory land speculation. Jackson's autocratic rule and defiant demeanor angered Monroe and alienated various prominent members of Congress, most notably Henry Clay. By the end of 1821, Jackson had had his fill of Florida and resigned, thus saving Monroe the embarrassment of removing him.

Upon returning to Nashville, Jackson intended to become a gentleman cotton farmer. He and Rachel moved out of the log house where they had lived for almost twenty years and moved into a new, brick home that better reflected the general's status. The house remained his home until it burned down in 1834. It was then that he built the grand Greek Revival home that he called "the Hermitage."

In retirement Jackson soon found himself drawn back into politics. In late 1822, recognizing his status as a national hero, opponents of Tennessee's governor, William Carroll, began promoting Jackson as the state's candidate for the 1824 presidential election. Though they doubted that the nomination would amount to much, they discovered that Jackson had support not only in Tennessee but also throughout parts of the nation. Seizing the moment, Jackson's supporters convinced the state's legislature to elect him to the Senate as a stepping stone to higher office. Somewhat reluctantly, the general agreed to postpone his retirement and serve a term in Washington.

Once Jackson was in the Senate his supporters, whom he called "the Junto," began a letter-writing campaign in support of his presidential candidacy. Led by John Eaton, the Junto presented Jackson as an alternative to the corruption and opportunism that had evolved within the national government. He was portrayed as a continuation of the "Republican" virtue and idealism that characterized the founding fathers. His military service was likened to that of George Washington. Meanwhile, in the Senate Jackson worked at dispelling his image as an uncouth, fiery backwoodsman. He was conciliatory toward his critics, courteous to opponents, and courtly at all times. Early in the election year, Jackson's candidacy remained a long shot but he had caught the interest of several influential congressmen. He also benefited from the skillful management, particularly in Pennsylvania, of his supporters.

In 1824 the relative political unity that had characterized the previous eight years disintegrated as a proliferation of candidates maneuvered to succeed Monroe. Most were offered as favorite-son candidates with little support beyond their state borders. However, by the fall four had emerged as front-runners. Three of the four held prominent offices and had extensive experience in the national government. John Quincy Adams was secretary of state, William C. Crawford was secretary of the treasury, and Henry Clay was speaker of the House of Representatives. The fourth candidate was Andrew Jackson. Though he had minimal experience in government and had taken no stand on the controversial issues of the day, he was embraced by many throughout the country. Small farmers saw him as an opponent of the Bank of the United States (BUS). Advocates of states' rights assumed he opposed the national government's authority, and southern slaveholders recognized him as one of their own. Jackson's candidacy gained additional momentum when Crawford was debilitated by a stroke.

The election of 1824 was one of the most memorable in American history. Each of the four candidates reflected specific regional interests and each garnered significant popular votes. Surprising to many, Jackson received a plurality of the vote. Adams was his closest opponent with Crawford and Clay finishing third and fourth. Because none of the four had received the necessary electoral votes, the election went to the House of Representatives. There most recognized that Clay, who was constitutionally ineligible for election because he came in fourth, could determine the winner. Jackson and his supporters were particularly concerned because Clay on numerous occasions had portrayed the general as a military chieftain unfit for the presidency. Rumors about a bargain between Adams and Clay further alarmed the general's supporters. When Clay cast the Kentucky vote for Adams despite the state legislature's instructions to vote for Jackson, charges of a deal grew. Clay's nomination as secretary of state immediately after Adams was elected seemed to confirm what became known as "the corrupt bargain." In reality there was never any question about who Clay would support. Although he and Adams had personal differences, Clay respected Adams and saw him as a worthy successor to Monroe. Nevertheless, the cry of corrupt bargain hung in the air throughout the Quincy Adams presidency.

Jackson's supporters began preparing for the 1828 election almost as soon as the 1824 election ended. Just weeks after Adams's inauguration, the Tennessee legislature again nominated the general as its presidential selection for 1828. There were others in the country who also began lining up behind the general. Most important among them was New York Congressman Martin Van Buren. In 1824 Van Buren had begun to build a political coalition around William Crawford. Embracing the traditional Jeffersonian principles of states' rights and limited government, the coalition sought to challenge the emerging centrist policies and economic nationalism of John Quincy Adams and Henry Clay. A shrewd political observer, Van Buren recognized that the issues his coalition embraced also appealed to Jackson's supporters. Additionally, he understood the significance of Jackson's hero status. Though the general lacked Crawford's political skills and experience, he seemed ideally suited to replace Crawford as the coalition's figurehead.

Under Van Buren's guidance, the efforts to create a Jackson coalition took several forms. At the local and state levels, a diverse collection of political committees, clubs, and organizations was stitched together. Often bypassing the ruling gentry, these organizations were designed to mobilize grassroots support. At the same time, Van Buren masterfully aligned northern congressmen who opposed Adams's brand of republicanism with pro-slavery representatives from the South. Jackson's supporters in Congress challenged and often bitterly denounced virtually every action taken by the Adams administration. A national network of more than fifty newspapers was also assembled. Media activities ranged from attacks on the Adams administration to a biography that portrayed Jackson as a modern-day George Washington. From these origins emerged a dynamic political base upon which the modern Democratic Party evolved.

Although well aware of the various maneuverings designed to promote his candidacy, Jackson remained somewhat aloof from the organization evolving around him. In October 1825, he resigned from the Senate, complaining about an intrigue that permeated the national government. Back home on his plantation, he sought to emulate George Washington's role as the nation's patriarch. Harnessing his famous temper, he continued to denounce the corruption that he claimed threatened American democracy. Instead, he called for a return to the principles upon which the nation had been founded.

The election of 1828 was a ruthless affair characterized by vicious personal attacks from both sides. Drawing upon popular patriot tactics common during the Revolutionary War years, Jackson's supporters, calling themselves Democrats, resorted to vitriolic rallies, speeches, symbols, and songs. They depicted Adams as an American aristocrat with no connection to the common person. Voters were constantly reminded about his corrupt bargain with Clay as well as his other alleged conspiracies against democracy. Adams was also accused of procuring young American women for the Russian czar. Countering the attacks, Adams supporters portrayed Jackson as a gambler, drunkard, duelist, and bully who was intellectually unfit for office. One campaign publication, known as the "coffin handbill," proposed that Jackson was responsible for the murder of six militiamen during the Creek War. Rachel Jackson's reputation was also challenged. She was labeled as a bigamist because she had remarried before divorcing her first husband. When she died from a heart attack shortly after the election, Jackson, who was devastated, blamed his political enemies, particularly Henry Clay.

Jackson won the 1828 election, polling almost 60 percent of the popular vote and 70 percent of the electoral vote. Several factors contributed to his resounding victory but none was more important than his public image. Americans were convinced that their new president was a fearless champion of the common person and an instinctive leader. He was a man of intense conviction who shared the public's growing disaffection for the political system. A rugged individualist possessing an egalitarian spirit, he seemed to embody the qualities that characterized the American nation itself. It was an image that was embraced by a constituency that included more than a million small farmers and laborers than in 1824.

When he came to the presidency, Jackson brought a new approach to government. He believed that his election was a triumph of democracy over aristocracy and therefore ushered in a new age of self-government. As he saw it, the nation in 1828 was locked in a struggle between an increasingly powerful, commercial elite and the hard-working masses. As president, it had become his responsibility to lead a crusade in defense of the common persons who had so overwhelmingly elected him. That included resurrecting the egalitarian ideals that had guided the founding fathers. Likewise, Jackson intended to re-create a simple method of government in which elected officials were more directly dependent upon the will of their constituents. Integral to that goal was the relationship between the state government and the federal government. Because the state could respond more immediately to its citizens, Jackson sought to fortify the states' authority. Though he claimed that his ultimate goal was merely to revive traditional Jeffersonian principles, in fact, Jackson introduced his own populist interpretation of American government.

Jackson as president attempted to run the government the way he had run his army. In so doing, he brought significant new power to the office and altered forever the relationship between the three branches of government. The nation's founding fathers, when creating the presidency, had been concerned about encouraging the rise of a powerful chief executive. Instead, since Washington's administration the legislature had been preeminent in directing the course of the nation. Jackson challenged that tradition. He contended that because he was elected by the entire constituency, he, not Congress, reflected the will of the people. He was, therefore, empowered by the people to define the issues and lead the government in pursuit of national goals. From Congress he demanded compliance. Those who opposed him, such as Henry Clay or Daniel Webster, were labeled obstructionists and potential subversives. If Congress passed legislation that did not conform to his goals, he had a responsibility to invalidate that legislation. Likewise, if the judiciary rendered a decision that in his opinion was not in the best interest of the nation, he was obliged to ignore executing the court's decision. This challenge to both the legislative and the judicial branches redefined the presidency and began the evolution of the modern American presidency.

A guiding principle of the Jackson presidency was the rotation of officeholders. Jackson believed that by regularly rotating officeholders, he could provide the common man with an opportunity to participate in the government that, in turn, would encourage democratic government. It was also a way to eliminate the "unfaithful and corrupt" from his government. He rationalized that rotating officeholders allowed his administration to better reflect the will of those who had elected him and enabled Americans to better understand the problems facing the nation. From a pragmatic political perspective, the rotation of officeholders helped Jackson fortify his own power as president. By rewarding supporters with positions ranging from the Cabinet to the Post Office, he filled his administration with loyal subordinates who were dependent upon his approval. Those appointees who questioned Jackson's policies or decisions could be immediately replaced. Jackson also assumed almost absolute power in removing appointees. Unlike his predecessors, he felt little need to get congressional approval when replacing a cabinet member. Denounced as despotic patronage by critics, Jackson's practice of regularly rotating administrators significantly strengthened the presidency.

Jackson's use of the veto further empowered the presidency. During his two terms in office, he vetoed more legislation than had all of his predecessors combined. Since the beginning of the national government, vetoes had only been used to invalidate legislation that the president considered unconstitutional. Jackson revised that tradition. He argued that he had a duty to use his veto powers whenever Congress passed legislation that he considered detrimental to the public's well-being. Not only was the constitutionality of legislation a reason for a veto, but so too were the political, social, or economic consequences of the legislation. Jackson's aggressive use of his veto powers required Congress for the first time to consider carefully the broad and varied interests of the president when enacting legislation.

Once in office, Jackson was immediately confronted with an issue that enabled him to redefine presidential authority. In 1828, shortly before the election, Congress had passed a particularly high tariff. The legislation provided protection for northern industry and commerce, but had the potential to severely limit southern agricultural exports. Led by the South Carolina state government, opponents of the tariff threatened to ignore the legislation within their states. Most thought Jackson as president would be an advocate for states' rights and would pursue tariff reduction. Instead Jackson eagerly anticipated the tariff revenues. Announcing that the tariff would enable his administration to pay off the national debt, he bridled southern opposition for a year. However, by 1830 a few southern leaders began demanding action on the tariff. Taking the lead in the protest, South Carolina refused to implement the legislation. The debate grew more intense with the publication of the *South Carolina Exposition*. The author, who remained anonymous, proposed that each state had the right to nullify the tariff as well as all federal legislation within the state if the state's legislature considered the federal legislation to be contrary to the best interests of the states' people.

Confronted by the threat of nullification, Jackson maneuvered cautiously and countered with a decidedly nationalistic response. He maintained that for the Union to be preserved, no state could have the power to annul federal legislation. The founding fathers had created the national government, in part, as a way to protect individual citizens from abuse by the state. If the state had the power to disregard federal legislation, then the federal government could no longer protect the individual. It was a compelling argument in favor of the national government's authority over the states.

As the controversy grew, the president's tolerance for his opposition waned. By 1832 he had come to see the issue as more than simply a debate about the tariff or a state's rights. Instead it had become a personal affront designed to embarrass him, discredit his presidency, and challenge his authority. With each new encounter, he became more hostile toward South Carolina's defenders. He was further infuriated upon learning that the anonymous author of the *South Carolina Exposition* was, in fact, his own vice president, John C. Calhoun.

Immediately after winning reelection in 1832, Jackson prepared to end the controversy himself. Upon quick congressional passage of the Force Bill, he threatened that unless South Carolina obeyed the tariff, he would lead the army into the state and impose martial law. The magnitude of the threat and potential for civil war alarmed the nation. Fortunately Henry Clay, one of Jackson's chief critics, was able to devise a last-minute compromise tariff that proved acceptable to both Jackson and the southern opposition. However, although the compromise resolved the tariff issue, it did not end the debate about state's rights.

Though he had staunchly defended federal authority during the tariff controversy, Jackson periodically reversed his stance to promote his policies. Such was the case with his Native American policy. Soon after he came into office, the U.S. Supreme Court rendered a decision that Jackson vehemently opposed. The case, *Cherokee Nation v. Georgia* (30 U.S., 1831), involved Cherokee tribes in Georgia who were ordered by the state to leave their land. The Cherokee challenged Georgia in the courts. In a controversial decision, U.S. Supreme Court Chief Justice John Marshall determined that peaceful Native Americans had a right to the land they occupied. Jackson was upset by the decision. Instead of obeying it, he imposed his own constitutional interpretation. He announced that in this case, the state's authority superseded that of the national government and that the national government had no responsibility for protecting the rights of peaceful Native Americans.

Jackson defended extending his authority into the judiciary's domain by claiming that he was simply carrying out the will of the American people. When he came into office, he had promised to move all Native Americans in the East to reserved lands west of the Mississippi River. As did most nineteenth-century Americans, Jackson believed that Native Americans were inherently inferior to European Americans and that the two civilizations could not coexist. Further, Native American settlement was an obstacle to the continued expansion of the nation. Thus, if Native Americans were to survive, they would have to move or be moved beyond regular contact with the European American population. Jackson demanded that the relocation of Native Americans, not the court's decision, was in the nation's best interest. The forceful removal of Native Americans that followed became known as "the Trail of Tears" and is one of the more tragic episodes in American history.

Jackson defended slavery in much the same manner that he justified his Native American policy. He believed that like Native Americans, slaves were the responsibility of the white population. A slaveholder himself, he expected masters to treat their slaves humanely and on at least one occasion threatened his own overseer with dismissal if he treated slaves poorly. Jackson blamed the growing tensions surrounding slavery on the anti-slavery movement. Abolitionists such as William Lloyd Garrison were, he believed, dangerously mistaken when they demanded the immediate end of slavery. Jackson was certain that most slaves were simply incapable of sustaining themselves in American society. After the bloody Nat Turner rebellion in 1832, he concluded that the anti-slavery movement had become a threat to the nation, and he used his power as president to curtail their activities. He instructed the Post Office to refuse to deliver anti-slavery literature and he endorsed the gag order that prohibited all debate about slavery in Congress. However, rather than curtailing abolitionist activity, Jackson's policies inadvertently encouraged the anti-slavery movement.

The Second Bank of the United States (also called BUS) was another target for Jackson. Congress chartered the bank in 1816 to provide stability for the American economy and to administer the nation's revenues. Jackson was concerned that the bank and its branches throughout the nation could control the American economy and undermine the government. Though five congressmen sat on its twenty-five-member board, the BUS was a private business. Its concern was the well-being of its stockholders, not the welfare of the nation. If BUS needed money, it was able to issue credit notes that, in effect, became currency. On the other hand, if tight credit was beneficial, the BUS could require the payment of notes already in circulation. Thus, the bank had the power to manipulate the American economy for its own purposes. As did many southern and western farmers, Jackson complained that the bank's policies were designed to benefit northeastern speculators at the expense of small farmers. He also contended that the BUS used its power to control elections. As evidence, he pointed to the 1824 election. He claimed that in New Hampshire, the BUS had effectively blocked his and fellow Democrats' election in favor of candidates who supported the bank.

In addition to his political concerns, Jackson's opposition to BUS was personal. During his early days in Tennessee, he had invested in land and commodities. To finance various endeavors, he had speculated on bank notes. On two occasions his ventures failed and left him almost penniless. Jackson blamed crafty eastern bankers for his problems. He also blamed the Panic of 1819, which had devastated the fortunes of many small farmers on ruthless BUS policies. An advocate of hard money, Jackson portrayed bankers in general and the BUS in particular as conniving opportunists who fed off the labor of the common person.

As president, Jackson waged a personal war against the BUS. In his first message to Congress, he announced that he considered the bank unconstitutional and that it had failed to establish a sound economy. Later he attacked it as undemocratic, warning that the freedom of each American required a separation of the government from the country's banks. Supporters of the BUS feared that because the bank's charter was scheduled to expire in 1836, Jackson, if reelected, would have an opportunity to put the bank out of business. Even if Congress approved rechartering, Jackson could veto the action and there appeared little hope of overriding a Jackson veto. Anticipating the crisis, supporters of the bank, led by Henry Clay and Daniel Webster, convinced the BUS president, Nicholas Biddle, to apply for rechartering in 1832, thus making the bank an important campaign issue. The strategy failed. As expected, Congress during the summer of 1832 approved rechartering but, convinced that the episode was simply another attempt by the BUS to control the government, Jackson boldly vetoed the legislation.

Jackson's veto did not end his assault. He instructed his secretary of the treasury to redirect the nation's revenues into state banks, referred to as "pet banks," which supported his administration's policies. The action violated the BUS's charter, which was valid for another four years. Jackson's opponents in Congress, led by Henry Clay, reacted by censuring the president but were unable to reverse his banking policy. Over the next three years, Jackson's decision to put the BUS out of business effectively destabilized the economy. Though he left office before the full effects were felt, his successor, Martin Van Buren, wrestled with the problems throughout his presidency.

Though he focused almost exclusively on domestic issues, there was one area of foreign policy in which Jackson took a keen interest. Acquisition of the Southwest in general and Texas in particular had been important to him long before he became president. An aggressive expansionist throughout his life, he considered the region integral to the nation's future. However, he recognized that there were several important considerations involved in annexing the Southwest. Mexico with the support of its allies, especially Great Britain, would probably go to war rather than lose its northern provinces. Likewise, annexation might ignite potentially explosive sectional tensions, including new debates about slavery and states' rights. Nevertheless, as president, Jackson did what he could to acquire the region and especially Texas.

Early in his presidency, Jackson assigned Anthony Butler to negotiate with the Mexican government. When traditional offers to purchase Texas failed, Butler, a man of dubious character, tried unsuccessfully to bribe Mexican officials. In 1835, Jackson replaced Butler with General Edmund Gaines and his army. Ordered to guard and protect the American border with Texas and American shipping in the Gulf of Mexico, Gaines attempted to bully Mexican officials much as Jackson had done to the Spanish in Florida. Meanwhile, Jackson quietly encouraged the growing insurgent movement in Texas but officially refused to assist the independence movement. Even as late as December 1836, almost a year after battles at the Alamo and Goliad, Jackson resisted acknowledging Texas independence because of the potential for war with Mexico. Finally, during his last days as president, he could resist no longer and formally recognized the independent Republic of Texas. It was an action that would have profound ramifications for the nation.

Jackson's last months in office were spent battling various illnesses. In November 1836, he collapsed for the second time in three years. Both seizures created grave doubts that he would survive his presidency. The source of the collapses remains unknown but Jackson was regularly plagued by severe headaches, chest pains, fevers, and intestinal problems that may have indicated kidney or heart ailments. His weary body was also riddled by ancient wounds. Abscesses caused by internal hemorrhaging further plagued him. On several occasions during his military career, he had received injuries that went unattended and tormented him throughout the rest of his life. For more than twenty years, his body carried at least two lead bullets. One particularly painful bullet, received in a barroom brawl with Thomas Hart Benton and his brother, had to be cut out shortly after Jackson became president. Gripped by long coughing spells, perhaps consumption, and by fevers and an assortment of debilitating pains, his health problems periodically threatened his ability to attend to his office. At the time that he vetoed the BUS rechartering, he was suffering from a fever that many did not expect him to survive. As with other challenges, Jackson overcame his infirmities by calling upon a great personal reservoir of strength and fortitude. However, as his presidency came to an end, his ability to overcome his many health problems had obviously ebbed.

Upon leaving office, Jackson returned to his farm, the Hermitage, outside Nashville. Modeling himself after Thomas Jefferson, he spent the last years of his life as a gentleman farmer managing his plantation. Though his spirit continued to hover over the Democratic Party, he remained apart from most public activity. His chief political concern during his retirement was protecting his legacy. On several occasions, he issued stern directives condemning contemplated revisions to his policies. His most aggressive statements involved the economy. Throughout the Panic of 1837 and the ongoing economic travails that plagued the Van Buren presidency, Jackson steadfastly warned about creating a central bank. He was also disheartened by his party's defeat in the 1840 election. With the Whigs in power, he lamented the return of what he considered government by cabal. Four years later the election of his young Tennessee protégé, James Knox Polk, gave Jackson some satisfaction. The annexation of Texas the following March further cheered him, though by that time his health was deteriorating steadily. Two months later, in June 1845, eight years after leaving office he died.

Andrew Jackson is generally remembered as one of the more productive presidents in the nation's history. He is an appropriate namesake for an era characterized by unbridled capitalism, individualism, and opportunism. His legacy rests primarily upon his aggressive governing style and his status as the symbol for a new age of American democracy. Parlaying his war hero status into the presidency, he became the people's champion. An unflinching nationalist, his policies were designed both to protect the nation and to promote opportunity for the middle and lower strata of American society. By portraying himself as a defender of the common man, he brought significant new power to his office. In so doing, he redefined forever the relationship between the executive branch and the other two branches of government. Jackson transformed the presidency into the nation's primary policy-making office. Foregoing the previous generation's altruistic philosophy, his autocratic approach to government grew from personal experiences and an unrelenting concern about aristocratic conspiracies. His reasoning was easily understood and his methods were applauded by much of middle-class America. Through the institutionalization of the political party, he brought new opportunity for Americans to influence the national government. Although he lamented partisan politics, Jackson was the catalyst in the emergence of the modern American political party system. Though his policies produced mixed results, his two terms as president serve as a crucial early step in the evolution of government in the United States.

BIBLIOGRAPHY

Lee Benson, *The Concept of Jacksonian Democracy* (Princeton, NJ: Princeton University Press, 1961); Andrew Burstein, *The Passions of Andrew Jackson* (New York: Alfred A. Knopf, 2003); Donald B. Cole, *The Presidency of Andrew Jackson* (Lawrence: University of Kansas Press, 1999); James Curtis, *Andrew Jackson and the Search for Vindication* (Lexington: University of Kentucky Press, 1976); David S. Heidler and Jeanne T. Heidler, *Old Hickory's War: Andrew Jackson and the Quest for Empire* (Mechanicsburg, PA: Stackpole Books, 1996); Richard B. Latmer, *The Presidency of Andrew Jackson* (Athens: University of Georgia Press, 1979); Marvin Meyers, *The Jacksonian Persuasion* (Stanford: Stanford University Press, 1957); Robert Remini, *Andrew Jackson* (New York: HarperCollins Publishers, 1966); Robert Remini, *Andrew Jackson and the Course of American Democracy, 1822–1832* (New York: Harper & Row Publishers, Inc., 1977); Robert Remini, *The Election of Andrew Jackson* (Philadelphia: Lippincott, 1963); Arthur Schlesinger, Jr., *The Age of Jackson* (Boston: Little, Brown and Company, 1945); and Harry Watson, *Liberty and Power: The Politics of Jacksonian America* (New York: Hill and Wang, 1990).

MARTIN VAN BUREN
(1782–1862)

Martin Van Buren was the preeminent political organizer of his era. A defender of partisan government, he took a primary role in the creation of the Democratic Party. Dubbed the "Little Magician" and the "Red Fox of Kinderhook," he was acknowledged as a cunning and skillful strategist by his peers. He began his political career in New York, where he devised the methods that he used to help plot Andrew Jackson's election in 1828. Advocating Jeffersonian principles, he pragmatically pursued political power as none before him had. During Jackson's presidency, he emerged as one of the most powerful figures in the administration, serving as both secretary of state and as vice president. By 1834 he had become the obvious choice to succeed Jackson. Elected president two years later, his one term in office was scarred by philosophical differences among Democrats and evolving political conditions associated with the Panic of 1837. Nevertheless, despite a generally unsuccessful presidency, it was Van Buren who in many ways created the tactics that characterized politics during much of the Jacksonian era.

Born in 1782, the same year as Daniel Webster, John C. Calhoun, and Thomas Hart Benton, Martin Van Buren spent his childhood in the village of Kinderhook, New York. His ancestors were farmers who had come to New York from Holland in the mid-seventeenth century. His father, Abraham, operated a tavern and farmed successfully enough to support his family though little else. When funds were available and family obligations allowed it, Martin attended the village academy. At fourteen he went to work in a local law office where, for the next five years, he served as a clerk. His employer, Francis Sylvester, one of the leading Federalists in the area, unsuccessfully tried to enlist the young man into the Federalist cause. Sylvester recognized his clerk's potential as a lawyer and encouraged him to complete his legal studies in New York City, advice that Van Buren followed.

In 1803 Van Buren was licensed and admitted to the New York state bar. Returning home to Kinderhook, he began a private practice, and for the next five years most of his energy was directed at building a successful law office. In the courtroom he was not considered a compelling orator. Instead he relied upon a masterful grasp of detail and analysis. Likewise, rather than presenting material in the robust, demonstrative fashion that characterized many of his peers, he used wit and subtle suggestions to make his points. Able to weave complex concepts into lucid, concise, easily understood arguments, he developed a reputation as an exceptionally capable lawyer.

From the time that he began working as a law clerk, Van Buren was engrossed by politics. Like his father, he was a Jeffersonian Republican who embraced a states' rights attitude. Local and state authority was at the heart of good government, according to Van Buren. He opposed both the First and Second Bank of the United States (BUS) and was wary of the wealthy commercial interests that he felt were trying to dominate the nation. Not completely opposed to a protective tariff, he believed that it should be used judiciously and kept low. Throughout his life, Van Buren adhered fairly consistently to these principles. However, political philosophy was not what intrigued him. Rather, his passion was the political contest. A pragmatist, he reveled at playing the game of politics and became an expert at it. Unlike some, he considered a well-organized, disciplined political party essential when promoting policy. The creation and operation of a political party were the activities that most motivated Van Buren.

As his law practice grew, Van Buren was able to become ever more involved in politics. Though frugal, he enjoyed the luxuries and lifestyle that his success as a lawyer and some wise investments provided for him. He was also a social climber who happily pursued the benefits of rising status. At the same time, his humble background enabled him to identify with the interests of common folk. These qualities facilitated his political endeavors. His wealth bought him time for politics, his practice produced professional respect, and his budding status brought him necessary contacts.

In 1808 Van Buren was appointed to his first political office: a judgeship for Columbia County, New York. A patronage position, the office was a reward for local service and an encouragement for future activity. During the next four years, he created a local organization that became an important political factor within the state. He also used his growing influence to win election to the state senate in 1812. Three years later, he was appointed New York's attorney general. In his rapid climb to power, Van Buren benefited from his service on behalf of DeWitt Clinton. The governor of New York, Clinton set his sights on the presidency in 1812 and Van Buren successfully directed his efforts in the state. However, within a couple of years the two men had parted ways and led opposing factions of the state's Republicans. The source of the split was in part personal and in part policy driven but ultimately enabled Van Buren, at least temporarily, to take charge of state politics.

Leader of the "Bucktail" faction of New York Republicans, Van Buren orchestrated an impressive victory over Clinton Republicans in 1820. Though Clinton narrowly remained governor, the state's Assembly was dominated by Bucktails who, as a result, gained control of thousands of patronage positions. Van Buren adroitly used the patronage to expand his Bucktail base throughout the state. Directed from the capital, he and his cohorts, referred to as the Albany Regency, built a wide-ranging network of loyal political operatives. By 1821 the Regency was so well entrenched that Van Buren was able to maneuver for himself selection to the United States Senate.

In Washington, Van Buren intended to use his position to strengthen his evolving state political party. However, he soon realized that the nation's capital during the Monroe presidency was characterized by a swirl of ill-disciplined coalitions all claiming to share a similar political philosophy. Slaveholding planters, anti-slavery merchants, proponents and opponents of the Second Bank of the United States, supporters of a strong central government, and ardent states' rights advocates, among others, all identified themselves as Jeffersonian Republicans. Van Buren also learned quickly that Washington was an isolated center of government far removed from his home state. Creating political order in one while maintaining control in the other would be difficult. However, because Washington was so far removed from state affairs, Van Buren concluded that tight party order and discipline at one level of government was essential to the other. Party organization within the national government was required for New York to maximize benefits from national policies. Likewise, political unity within the state was essential to demonstrate the state's influence on specific national debates.

Van Buren's first real opportunity to demonstrate the potential benefits of a coordinated national and state political organization came with the election of 1824. He planned to use New York's support to promote and perhaps elect Monroe's successor. Backing Secretary of the Treasury William C. Crawford of Georgia, Van Buren attempted to forge an alliance between New York and the South. With the exception of his pro-slavery stand, Crawford generally agreed with Van Buren on most major issues.

However, New Yorkers were not as comfortable with the southerner. After Crawford suffered a debilitating stroke, many voters as well as some within Van Buren's state party gave up on Crawford. Aggressive anti-Clinton maneuvers further alienated the New York constituency. Finally, Van Buren was outmaneuvered by Henry Clay and John Quincy Adams when the controversial election went into the House of Representatives. Most embarrassingly, in the House, New York's votes were delivered to Adams. The election ended with two of Van Buren's arch political rivals, Clinton and Adams, chosen as governor and president. Additionally, the political machine that he had worked so hard to create had broken down. Van Buren did learn at least one important lesson from the election. He came to understand that being aware and responsive to the constituency was as important to a political party as was internal organization.

Less than a year after the election, Van Buren was already preparing for the 1828 election. He began in New York by reorganizing the Albany Regency and restoring unity among his Bucktail faction. He also built partnerships with Thomas Ritchie, Virginia's political organizer, and Vice President John C. Calhoun. As it had been in 1824, Van Buren's goal was to create an alliance between New York and the South. Meanwhile he began assessing possible presidential challengers. The obvious choice was Andrew Jackson, but Van Buren had some reservations. The general had served only briefly, and unhappily, at the national level and his political stances were ill-defined. After a trip through the South, Van Buren came to recognize that Jackson, despite his limitations, was the person most likely to defeat Adams in the upcoming election. His military hero status inspired thoughts of George Washington. His backwoods persona added a common touch, and there were many Americans who felt that in 1824 Jackson had been the victim of a "corrupt bargain" between Clay and Adams. By 1826, Van Buren was fully involved in managing the Jackson candidacy. His plan was to run a campaign based on personality rather than issues. Stressing party loyalty and cooperation, Van Buren built an impressive grassroots organization to promote Jackson. Coupled with several ill-advised Adams policies, the campaign proved very effective.

Jackson's sweeping victory in 1828 elevated Van Buren to national prominence. Elected governor of New York, he resigned after only three months to become Jackson's secretary of state. The switch began a political struggle between Van Buren and Vice President Calhoun. The vice president believed that Van Buren was already maneuvering to become Jackson's successor, a role Calhoun had staked out for himself. During the next two years, Calhoun attempted to undermine Van Buren in several ways, but each time it was Calhoun who suffered. The most controversial issue involved the Tariff of 1828. Recognizing that Van Buren differed somewhat from Jackson, Calhoun pushed both men for a specific stance on the issue. However, Van Buren wisely deferred to Jackson, thus maintaining the president's support. Eventually Calhoun garnered Jackson's full wrath because of an anonymous tract he authored, the *South Carolina Exposition*, which challenged the president. In another episode Calhoun's wife, Floride, led a gossip campaign against Peggy Eaton, the wife of Jackson's secretary of war. Van Buren, a widower, befriended Eaton and won further appreciation from Jackson. On another occasion, Calhoun quietly orchestrated a newspaper campaign against Van Buren. An angry Jackson complained that the effort threatened Democratic unity. Finally, in 1831 Calhoun blocked the appointment of Van Buren as the American minister to England. The move backfired badly. Van Buren had reluctantly accepted the post as a way to restore harmony among Democrats. Calhoun's personal affront brought sympathy and respect to Van Buren from many within his party, thus almost assuring that he would replace Calhoun on the Democratic ticket in 1832.

Throughout Jackson's presidency, Van Buren served as one of several important advisors. However, realizing that the two men had some philosophical differences, Van Buren prudently limited most of his suggestions to the political ramifications of policy decisions. Of the major issues that confronted the Jackson administration, Van Buren took a strong stand on only the Maysville Road debate. Like Jackson, he considered the road a local rather than a national matter. On other issues, including the tariff controversy and the BUS recharter veto, Van Buren was decidedly more moderate than Jackson but did not openly disagree with him. Unlike Jackson, Van Buren was not completely opposed to the BUS. Instead he argued that the bank had superseded its appropriate authority. Van Buren also envisioned a larger role for the states but deferred to Jackson's decisions. During the tariff controversy, Van Buren initially proposed a gradual reduction but conformed to Jackson's rigid stand. Van Buren knew full well that Jackson would not tolerate open dissent, and therefore when the two did disagree he attempted to nudge Jackson gently rather than challenge him overtly. The tactic proved effective, thus expanding Van Buren's role in the Jackson administration.

On a personal level, Van Buren and Jackson initially were a bit wary of each other. In many ways they were opposites. Van Buren focused on details and was cautious and calculating. Jackson was a generalist, often impetuous, and far more interested in the big picture than intricacies. A larger than life military hero, he cast a compelling and even charismatic image, whereas physically Van Buren was ordinary and generally nondescript. Reflecting his New York lawyer/merchant background, he enjoyed the luxuries that came with his prominence. Jackson, the southern planter/speculator, spurned such extravagances. Nevertheless, despite their differences the two men came to appreciate and respect each other. Van Buren admired Jackson's conviction and bold approach to issues, and Jackson increasingly came to rely on Van Buren's astute political analysis. Both men considered loyalty an essential quality and, in their own ways, did not tolerate betrayal. Thus, regardless of some philosophical differences they developed a mutual esteem and were able to work together effectively.

When the time came for Jackson to designate a successor, there was little doubt who it would be. However, there were many Democrats who did not share Jackson's enthusiasm. Throughout the South, Van Buren's stand on the tariff and slavery were questioned. Westerners criticized his approach to Texas and expansion in general. He was also portrayed as an unscrupulous political schemer, something voters disdained. Ultimately Jackson interpreted the opposition as yet another plot to divide the party. With his full support behind his hand-picked protégé, he pushed Democrats to nominate Van Buren. In the election, despite some internal rifts, the Democratic Party was far better organized than the nascent Whig Party. Unable to settle on a single candidate, Whigs ran regional favorites with hopes of preventing an electoral victory. The strategy almost succeeded as Van Buren won by a surprisingly narrow margin.

The new president set out to restore harmony within his party and temper the partisan attacks that had characterized his predecessors' eight years in office. Replacing only two of six Cabinet members, Van Buren hoped to maintain continuity with Jackson's administration. He also reached out to southern Democrats, especially Virginians, who had questioned his candidacy. On several important issues, most notably annexation of Texas and the slavery debate, he sought to maintain the status quo and limit potentially divisive congressional debate.

Despite his efforts, there was one issue that Van Buren could not avoid. For over a year, economic conditions had been deteriorating. A primary source of the problem was the declining authority of the BUS. No longer dependent upon the central bank, state banks began issuing significantly more credit notes than they could redeem. Some soon went bankrupt, taking both creditors and debtors down with them. To halt risky speculation, the Jackson administration created the controversial Specie Circular. The legislation required payment in either gold or silver for the purchase of government land. Ending the use of credit for land sales, the policy soon shrank both state and national revenues. The Specie Circular also squeezed state banks for specie (gold and silver), thus further limiting most banks' ability to extend the credit needed to facilitate economic activity, including the acquisition of land. This, in turn, actually encouraged speculation. Strapped for specie, all but a handful of the nation's almost 800 banks chose to disregard the Specie Circular. Thus the frenzied use of credit continued unabated, pushing the nation toward a potential economic collapse. Compounding the problems were a declining cotton market and growing debts to British lenders. The end product was an uncontrolled economy spiraling downward.

The problems intensified in early May 1837. Deeply in debt, state banks throughout the nation began to close. This triggered reactions throughout the economy. Commodity prices plummeted as did the value of paper money. Debtors were compelled to pay off their obligations with the devalued money. Like banks, many businesses, unable to find or afford credit, were ruined. Unemployment rapidly spread to urban areas, especially northern textile mills. Meanwhile, growing numbers of farm families who defaulted on their debts were forced off their land. Within weeks, the nation was tightly gripped by the worst economic panic in its history.

Calling for a special session of Congress in September 1837, Van Buren began a three-year campaign to reform the nation's banking system. There were numerous proposed solutions for the troubled economy. On one side, led by Thomas Hart Benton, were fiscally conservative Democrats who advocated a rigid hard-money policy. Even before Van Buren came into office, they had warned that the economy was heading for a crisis. Although admittedly the exclusive use of specie would be painful initially, they contended that it offered the only real solution. Whigs agreed that a crisis was near but argued the solution was the creation of another Bank of the United States. They blamed the problems on Jackson's veto of the BUS recharter and his subsequent use of state banks to handle the nation's money. Meanwhile, Van Buren staked out a middle ground. Never an ardent opponent of the BUS, he accepted the institution's role in monitoring the nation's banks. On the other hand, he disagreed with the unchecked power that the BUS had acquired. His solution was to create an independent subtreasury that would assume the BUS responsibilities but would not have the political clout that the bank had wielded.

For Van Buren, the political ramifications of his plan were, in many ways, even more perilous than were the economic consequences. Implementation required delicate negotiations and maneuvering. Van Buren had to be careful not to alienate suspicious Jackson Democrats who had cautiously supported him in the past. Creating an independent treasury required revising a basic tenet in the Democratic philosophy that dated back to Thomas Jefferson. Likewise, Van Buren had to find a way to explain reforming Jackson's banking policies without tarnishing the general's reputation or bruising his ego. Opposition from ambitious Democrats like John C. Calhoun as well as the newspapers who supported them had to be neutralized. Of course, hungry Whig opposition would also have to be controlled. And through it all, Van Buren would have to maintain some base of public support. It was a mammoth political task. Fortunately Van Buren had some able assistance in Congress, most notably his New York protégé in the Senate, Silas Wight. After three years of intense and at times bitter debate, the call for an independent treasury was approved.

Van Buren's plan produced mixed results. On one hand, the act insulated federal funds from direct manipulation by speculators or by the government. In theory, this created fiscal and banking controls that protected the nation from risky monetary policies. On the other hand, the Independent Treasury Act (1840) also barred government reserves from being used to aid an economic recovery. Likewise, the Act neither encouraged the use of specie nor curtailed the use of speculative bank notes as was hoped. Consequently, it did nothing to tame what many considered the corrupting influences of business and industry. Among the primary beneficiaries were southern planters, but the policy did little to help the masses of small farmers that the Democratic Party claimed as its base of support. As a result, the act inadvertently aided the Whig Party and intensified the acrimonious partisan battles that characterized Van Buren's presidency.

As Van Buren wrestled with the bank crisis, another dark cloud gathered over his administration. In 1836 Texas won its independence from Mexico and immediately began efforts to become part of the United States. Despite his encouraging rhetoric, Jackson delayed officially recognizing the Republic until several days before leaving office. With Jackson gone, pressure to annex shifted to Van Buren. Texans clamored for territorial status with the promise of statehood soon afterward. There were also many throughout the nation, especially in the South, who supported the effort. Van Buren understood that annexation was an issue fraught with hazards. Because Mexico disputed the Republic's southern border, the president worried that annexation might lead to war. In light of the nation's economic problems, a war with Mexico was not something that he felt the United States could afford. Annexation would also require a potentially divisive debate about slavery. Van Buren steadfastly sought to avoid such a debate because he feared that it would split the Democratic Party and perhaps the nation as well. At the very least, it would shatter the fragile alliances that he so badly needed to achieve banking reform. Rationalizing that the annexation of Texas would abrogate an 1832 treaty with Mexico, Van Buren cautiously sidestepped the issue.

Problems along the Canadian border also plagued Van Buren's presidency. In 1837, pockets of disgruntled Canadians rebelled against their British administration. Some Americans along the border rallied to support the insurgents. In Buffalo a small force of New Yorkers organized by Canadian William Lloyd MacKenzie fortified Navy Island on the north side of the Niagara River and declared it an independent provisional government. In retaliation British authorities attacked and sank one of the rebel ships while it was docked on the American side of the river. In the melee, an American was killed and several others were injured. Meanwhile, questions about millions of acres along the unsettled border between Canada and Maine were also building. When Maine attempted to clear the region of Canadians in 1839, the British seized a force of the state's militia. With the potential for a bigger conflict growing, Van Buren acted decisively on both fronts. He sent General Winfield Scott to New York to restrain new assaults. At the same time, he initiated legislation that empowered the government to forcibly subdue attacks on Canada launched from American soil. To settle the problems in Maine, he appealed directly to the British prime minister. Calling for the immediate withdrawal of all forces from the disputed region, he proposed future discussions to determine a mutually acceptable border. Van Buren's efforts succeeded. Despite a few minor confrontations, tensions along the New York border eased. In Maine, a three-year process was begun that in 1842 culminated in a permanent border.

After four years in office, many of the factors that aided Van Buren's election in 1836 had eroded. Most importantly, the Whigs were not only united behind a single candidate but they were also well organized nationally and ready to do whatever was necessary to end twelve years of Democratic presidents. Their most effective issue was the ongoing economic problems and Van Buren's apparent inability to solve them. Also, in William Henry Harrison they had a candidate who reminded voters in many ways of Andrew Jackson. He was from the West, was a war hero, and claimed to be just an average "log cabin and hard cider" American. Van Buren, on the other hand, was portrayed as a spendthrift and dandy who craved personal luxuries at a time when most in the nation were floundering. Festering relations with Jackson further compromised Van Buren's popularity. Jackson had become an increasingly vocal opponent of his successor's bank reform. He also complained that the administration was neglecting the West. And, finally, he grumbled when Van Buren refused to replace his controversial vice president, Richard Johnson, with Tennessean James K. Polk. With wavering approval from Jackson, Van Buren could not count on solid support among Democrats. As a result, the Democratic Party in 1840, despite the president's efforts, was divided. Old and new leaders began maneuvering for prominence at Van Buren's expense. Although the Democrats unanimously renominated him, the party generally ran a lackluster, unenthusiastic campaign.

Weeks before the election, there was little doubt about the outcome. The Whigs, who were well organized, devised a new, aggressive, and effective style of campaigning. Rather than lofty rhetoric, the party resorted to a more emotional appeal. Managed by a cunning New Yorker, Thurlow Weed, the party presented its candidate, William Henry Harrison, as the plain-spoken champion of the people. Local rallies and celebrations were organized throughout the nation, and for the first time symbols, slogans, and a wide array of campaign souvenirs were distributed to promote the candidate. Further breaking from tradition, Harrison also went on the campaign trail delivering several speeches and, more importantly, mingling with the constituency. Never before had a presidential candidate actively promoted himself. The tactics transformed future campaign methods. Ironically, Van Buren, who twenty years earlier had revolutionized political organization, was the target of the new way of campaigning. Instead of adapting to the popular techniques, he and his Democratic supporters maintained standard election procedures. Consequently, the election was over long before voters went to the polls.

The defeat in 1840 ended Van Buren's career in elective office. Disappointed that he had failed to win reelection, he soon began laying the groundwork for another run in 1844. After a somewhat successful tour of the South in 1842, he appeared to be the Democratic frontrunner. However, obvious sectional interests, especially concerning slavery, states' rights, and Texas, had begun to divide Democrats. Control of the party was shifting to the South. Though he continued to remain silent on most potentially disruptive issues, Van Buren was unable to reestablish the alliances he needed to again capture his party. At the Democratic convention in 1844 few saw him as a viable candidate, and after the first ballot he was dropped from consideration. Eight ballots later, the party united behind James Knox Polk.

Always ready to maneuver politically, Van Buren in 1848 made one last attempt to win the presidency. Rebuffed once again by his party, he gathered dissatisfied castoffs from the two major parties in an effort to maneuver his way back into office. Running under the Free Soil Party banner, he attempted to build a coalition around the issue of slavery. Embracing the Wilmot Proviso, he called for a gradual end to the institution. Unfortunately, with no organizational structure and little more than a handful of zealous stump speakers, the campaign had no chance of success. It did, however, attract enough northern Democrats to insure a Whig victory for Zachary Taylor. Eight years later, Free Soilers provided part of the foundation from which the Republican Party emerged, but by that time Van Buren had returned to the Democratic Party. In 1852 he endorsed Democrat Franklin Pierce and in 1856 backed James Buchanan, though he was troubled by the accommodating stance both took toward the South and slavery. He spent his last years at his Kinderhook home writing his memoirs. He died in 1862.

BIBLIOGRAPHY

Donald Cole, *Martin Van Buren and the American Political System* (Princeton, NJ: Princeton University Press, 1984); James C. Curtis, *The Fox at Bay: Martin Van Buren and the Presidency, 1837–1841* (Lexington: University of Kentucky Press, 1970); John Niven, *Martin Van Buren: The Romantic Age of American Politics* (New York: Oxford University Press, 1983); Joel Sibley, *Martin Van Buren and the Emergence of American Popular Politics* (Lanham, MD: Rowman and Littlefield Publishers, 2002); and Major Wilson, *The Presidency of Martin Van Buren* (Lawrence: University of Kansas Press, 1984).

JOHN C. CALHOUN
(1782–1850)

A powerful leader and compelling orator, John C. Calhoun more than anyone else helped to light the fires that eventually exploded into civil war. He
began his long political career as an avowed nationalist who consistently
endorsed federal authority. However, his unwavering advocacy of the
South transformed him into an uncompromising sectionalist. Blessed with
a brilliant legal mind, he lay the intellectual foundations for the southern
defense of states' rights and slavery. Though a Jackson Democrat, he never
truly conformed to party leadership. Instead, he maintained an independence that enabled him to pursue more effectively southern interests.

John Caldwell Calhoun was born in 1782. He lived his first eighteen
years on the family's farmstead near Fort Ninety-Six in southwestern South
Carolina. His parents had migrated to the region from Virginia shortly after
the Seven Years War, and by the time John was born his father, Patrick,
had carved out a comparatively prosperous existence. Small compared to
the expansive plantations in the South Carolina tidewater lowlands, the
Calhoun farmstead was one of the more substantial within the western, or
upland, part of the state. It included several thousand acres and one of the
largest slave holdings in the region. During the mid-1770s, Patrick was
elected to the colonial legislature that declared South Carolina's independence. Although committed to the American struggle, the Calhouns, like
many uplanders, were suspicious of patriot leadership in Charleston. Instead the family remained on the periphery of the struggle as much as

possible. After the war, Patrick became an advocate of local autonomy and shared an anti-federalist concern about ratification of the Constitution.

The relative isolation of western South Carolina provided young John with few opportunities for formal education. His mother and a few itinerant schoolteachers who irregularly visited the area provided most of his learning. One itinerant who had a marked influence on him was Moses Waddel. After marrying Calhoun's older sister, Waddel opened a school fifty miles from the Calhoun plantation. John was one of the first enrolled but, unfortunately, when his sister died Waddel temporarily closed the school and moved away. Though the school had operated for only a year, Calhoun discovered a passion for reading, especially history and philosophy. However, the death of his father delayed any opportunities to pursue his newfound interests. Because his two older brothers had already established themselves elsewhere, the responsibility of managing the family holdings fell upon him even though he was only fourteen. For the next four years, farming was his priority.

After successfully operating the family farm and encouraged by his older brothers to pursue a profession, Calhoun was able to resume formal studies with Moses Waddel. For the next two years, he eagerly filled the voids in his academic background. Throughout his endeavors, he proved to be a proficient and conscientious student. So promising was his development that in 1802, upon Waddel's advice, he enrolled at Yale. Two important factors influenced Calhoun's decision to leave his home. The death of his mother in 1801 was traumatic for him, and he sought to escape constant reminders of her as well as those of his father and sister. Additionally, the reputation of Yale's dynamic new president, Timothy Dwight, attracted him to the school. Passing preliminary exams for advanced standing, Calhoun, at age twenty, left his rural home deep in the South Carolina uplands in favor of Yale and a cosmopolitan life in New England.

Despite feeling a bit out of place, Calhoun thrived at Yale. Though a few years older than most of his contemporaries, he was popular and became involved in various student activities. Likewise, many of his fellow students as well as college President Dwight and his staff advocated Federalist policies. Calhoun, as his father had, embraced the principles of limited government and staunchly supported Jefferson's administration. Calhoun's attitudes about slavery also set him apart. By the early nineteenth century, an anti-slavery movement was well entrenched in the Yale community. Calhoun, on the other hand, had grown up a slaveholder and defended the institution. A general cultural bias that often characterized relationships between New Englanders and southerners also periodically colored Calhoun's relationship with students and mentors. Nevertheless, he enjoyed his two years at Yale and further demonstrated exceptional intellectual promise.

Upon graduation from Yale, Calhoun returned home to pursue a legal career. However, after briefly serving an apprenticeship with a prominent Charleston judge, he became disillusioned and, along with a fellow apprentice, enrolled in Tapping Reeve's law school in Litchfield, Connecticut. Reeve had instructed James Madison as well as several notable Yale graduates. Calhoun spent the next two years studying with Reeve and his staff. In 1806 he returned to Charleston, completed his apprenticeship, moved back to his upcountry home, and established a practice in Abbeville near the family farm. Recognized for his clearly presented and logical arguments, he immediately attracted clients from throughout western South Carolina. Soon he was pleading cases as far away as Charleston. Despite his success, he became bored with his new career and began to set his sights on a career in public service.

Calhoun began his political career amidst America's building tensions with the British. In reaction to the Chesapeake Affair, he organized a particularly effective local protest. Combining his new activist role with his ever-growing legal one, he ran for and easily won election to the state legislature. Energetic and compelling, he immediately became a leader in the legislature. In 1808 his particular target was the Embargo of 1807. Like commercial interests all along the Atlantic coast, he lamented that the embargo was having a devastating effect upon Charleston. South Carolina farmers, many of whom depended upon international trade, were also being ruined. However, unlike Federalists in New England, Calhoun called for a more aggressive approach. Even in 1808 he saw the distinct possibility that the United States might again become involved in a war with the British. Rather than avoid such a conflict, he advised preparing for it. With his prominence in the state legislature, he won election to the U.S. House of Representatives in 1810.

Before traveling to Washington, Calhoun made another change in his life. For two years he had been casually courting his second cousin, Floride Bonneau Calhoun. They had met shortly before he graduated from Yale. Floride's mother was the wealthy widow of his cousin, John E. Calhoun, and had invited young John to visit the family while they were summering in Rhode Island. Upon returning to South Carolina, he continued to call upon the family regularly. Six years later, soon after Floride's eighteenth birthday, John formally made his intentions known. A tidewater heiress, Floride was a vivacious, intelligent young woman. Marriage to her brought John new social status as well as enough wealth that he was able to close his law practice in favor of gentleman farming and his political career. Soon after their marriage in early 1811, John purchased an 800-acre estate, called Bath, near Abbeville. The following October, Andrew Pickens Calhoun, the first of the Calhouns's four sons and two daughters, was born. Floride and their children became a great source of support and pride for John throughout the rest of his life.

There was never any doubt about Calhoun's early political allegiances.

As he had throughout his days at Yale, he remained a loyal Republican who looked to Thomas Jefferson as his ideological leader. Like Jefferson he considered farming to be the fundamental activity of American society. Most importantly, he believed that agriculture reinforced the virtues upon which America's democratic republic was established. Although advocating a mixed economy, he nevertheless considered commerce and industry to be merely supplemental endeavors helpful in promoting agriculture. For him the primary role of government, whether state or national, ought to be the protection and maintenance of American values and prosperity. This meant sustaining the natural order, including slavery, which had evolved in American society. To fulfill these responsibilities, he acknowledged that there are times when the national government must have powers beyond those of the state. However, he also held that the state must have specific powers to limit the national government's authority.

In Washington Calhoun immediately joined a group of young congressmen, led by Henry Clay, who reflected the interests and attitudes of a new generation. Early nationalists, they were eager to promote American interests, particularly internal improvements and western expansion. They supported the controversial Bank of the United States (BUS), contending that it could provide the nation with a predictable currency as well as economic stability. Likewise, they generally agreed that when employed judiciously, a protective tariff would encourage nascent northeastern manufacturing, thus creating new domestic markets for agricultural production, particularly cotton. Government-sponsored improvements to the infrastructure, especially road and canal building, would also facilitate commerce throughout the entire nation. As did Calhoun, they defended the right of the states to protect individual liberties. They were also slaveholders who had no moral qualms about the institution. Instead they saw slavery as a necessary source of agricultural labor and part of the natural order of American society.

Of all the issues that they embraced, the most important to Calhoun and his new colleagues was westward expansion. They believed that the future of the American people lay in the West. There, abundant resources, particularly farmland, would generate profound economic and demographic growth into the foreseeable future. However, even before Calhoun arrived in Washington, many complained that the British government had become the primary obstacle impeding American expansion. Authorities in Canada were accused of deterring American settlement by providing the indigenous population with weapons and military expertise. Coupled with the ongoing tensions in the Atlantic, the British North American policy had become intolerable to some Americans. Resorting to increasingly confrontational rhetoric, Henry Clay and his young cohorts were aptly labeled "War Hawks" by fellow congressmen.

From his first days in Congress, Calhoun aggressively asserted himself as a War Hawk leader. A member of the foreign affairs committee, he used his position to convince the nation that an armed struggle with Great Britain was unavoidable. He argued that Parliament had never completely accepted American independence. Therefore, a second war would become the concluding chapter in the American Revolution. Additionally, such a clash would unify the nation and regenerate the patriotic fervor that had characterized the 1770s. The impending conflict might also enable the United States to acquire new lands in Canada and perhaps eliminate the British from the continent altogether. On a personal level, he expected that a war would propel his career to new heights. Ambitious, willing to take on all opposition, and a skillful orator, he quickly emerged as one of the preeminent War Hawk leaders. Teamed with Henry Clay's razor-sharp rhetoric, Calhoun's eloquence had a significant influence upon his congressional colleagues and the nation.

The War of 1812 presented Calhoun with a difficult political challenge. Among the most aggressive proponents of declaring war, he was compelled to counter Federalist opposition to Madison's method of handling the war. On several occasions this drew him into spirited debates with a formidable young Massachusetts Federalist, Daniel Webster, concerning funding and manpower needs (Calhoun, 1: 255–56, 331–39, especially a speech in defense of Madison and criticism of Webster on October 25, 1814). At the same time, Calhoun himself questioned various wartime policies, including trade restrictions imposed by the administration. Likewise, with an eye on his own political future, he did not want to alienate potential New England constituents. Through it all, he emerged as a forceful advocate for strengthening the military (Calhoun, 1: 228, 277–82).

The election of James Monroe in 1816 fed Calhoun's political ambitions. While chairman of the foreign relations committee during the war, he had worked closely with Monroe who was Madison's secretary of state. Calhoun also supported Monroe rather than Georgia's William Crawford in the election. Acknowledging the support and Calhoun's growing political prominence, Monroe invited him to serve as secretary of war. Eagerly accepting the post, Calhoun launched a program of sweeping reforms within the department. His goal was to reorganize the military, which included reemploying civilian authority and modernizing the nation's defense. Streamlining the department's administration, he introduced a more effective method of supplying the military. At the same time, because he was still concerned about the British in Canada, he initiated the creation of a string of fortifications along the Atlantic coast and in the West. He was also successful at reestablishing a chain of command that he ultimately headed (Calhoun, 2: 16; American State Papers, 1: 627–35, 669–80).

Though generally an effective administrator, Calhoun's reputation was tarnished by several unsuccessful ventures. The most embarrassing was an effort to begin developing the upper Rocky Mountain region (Calhoun, 3:

60–61). For that purpose, the War Department sponsored an ambitious expedition to the Yellowstone River area. Unfortunately, Calhoun entrusted the adventure to the ill-prepared brother of a political crony. When the project failed, the secretary was showered with criticism from political adversaries as well as unhappy fur trading companies. Dubious investments by his chief clerk and a series of questionable real estate agreements by his department further stained Calhoun's record as secretary of war (*Washington Gazette*, 24 February 1820; *Annals of Congress*, 1594).

Shortly after assuming his new post, Calhoun was confronted with a crisis. Andrew Jackson, acting upon ambiguous instructions from Monroe, pursued Native Americans into Spanish Florida. Convinced that British spies in Florida were instigating native attacks north into the United States, Jackson captured and executed two British trappers. Calhoun was not upset that Jackson had waged an undeclared war against the Native Americans. Like many Americans, Calhoun demonstrated little empathy for native civilization and actively sought to remove them from east of the Mississippi River. However, he was deeply concerned that by invading Spanish territory and assaulting British subjects, Jackson risked a war with both nations. In several emotional debates with Secretary of State John Quincy Adams, Calhoun advised President Monroe to placate England and Spain by recalling and formally censuring Jackson. Fortunately, Adams prevailed and subsequently made one of the more brilliant maneuvers in American diplomatic history. Aggressively negotiating with the Spanish, he defended Jackson and was able to acquire from Spain both Florida and the Spanish claim to the Oregon Territory. Although the debates between President Monroe, his secretary of state, Adams, and secretary of war, Calhoun, during late summer 1818 were not secretive, Jackson did not learn about Calhoun's stance until years later (Adams, 32, 108–15).

As early as 1821, Calhoun made known his intentions to succeed Monroe. Once the political maneuvering began in earnest, his relations with other likely candidates, especially Secretary of the Treasury William Crawford, hardened. Crawford considered Calhoun his chief competition for the traditional southern support and subtly challenged him at every opportunity. Responding to the partisan attacks and evolving factionalism, Calhoun became ever more overt. However, the emergence of a surprise candidate, Andrew Jackson, ultimately doomed his efforts. When many of his Pennsylvania supporters joined the swelling Jackson tide and gave that state's nomination to the general, Calhoun recognized he had virtually no chance of winning the presidency in 1824. Instead he took solace in running for the vice presidency with the approval of the four leading presidential candidates.

Elected vice president by a comfortable margin, Calhoun, like many Americans, was disturbed by the apparent "corrupt bargain" that carried John Quincy Adams to the presidency. It was unacceptable to him for a candidate who received less than one third of the total popular vote to win the election. He worried that the electoral college was at odds with democratic government. To correct the problem, he joined the call for a constitutional amendment that would reform or perhaps even abolish the electoral college. From a more immediate perspective, he feared that the election reflected an ominous trend by endorsing an excessively nationalistic agenda promoted by Adams and Clay. As he saw it, such policies would hasten and make permanent an evolving shift in power to northeastern commercial and industrial interests. As evidence, he cited the Tariff of 1824. Although he had supported tariffs in the past, he complained that the 1824 tariff protected northeastern interests at the expense of southern and western agriculture (*Annals*, 1st. sess., 686–87, 2207, 2208, 2361). The burgeoning northeastern population further heightened Calhoun's concerns. With additional population came additional congressional representation. After the 1820 census, pro-tariff states gained twenty-four new representatives, whereas free trade states gained only six. He feared that if the trend continued, it would undermine a balanced national government and imperil southern society. In reaction Calhoun, who had traditionally agreed with nationalistic programs, began to revise his political philosophy. By 1828 he was well on his way to becoming the nation's leading sectionalist and preeminent defender of the South.

Soon after the 1824 election, Calhoun began laying the groundwork for a future run at the presidency. However, he quickly recognized that there was little hope of defeating Andrew Jackson in 1828. The lingering bitterness from the 1824 election made Jackson the obvious front-runner. Martin Van Buren's skillful management added to Jackson's advantage. By uniting various factions that opposed Adams, Van Buren had begun molding a new political party, the Democratic Party, to promote the general's candidacy. Even constituencies that had been loyal to Calhoun lined up behind Jackson. Rather than challenge the rising tide of the new political party, Calhoun chose to join it. Although he had reservations about Jackson's competency as president, some of the new party's stands on issues, including the tariff and states' rights, better reflected his views than did the programs of Adams and Clay. Also, Jackson claimed that he would serve only one term. Calhoun reasoned that if he supported Jackson in 1828, Democrats might support him in 1832. Carefully weighing his options, Calhoun, midway through the Adams presidency, formally switched his allegiance to Jackson.

Added to the Jackson ticket through Van Buren's deft maneuvering, Calhoun won reelection as vice president in 1828. However, immediately after the election, a rift between himself and Jackson developed. The source of the problem was the Tariff of 1828, which opponents labeled "the Tariff of Abominations," that was passed nine months prior to the election. As did many southern congressmen, Calhoun reluctantly accepted the exceedingly high tariff because he thought that it would help elect Jackson and that, once in office, the new administration would lower the tariff to a level beneath that of the earlier tariff in 1824. However, after coming to the presidency, Jackson announced that the revenues generated by the tariff would help pay off the national debt and therefore he would not seek a quick tariff reduction. Southern planters became enraged. Some began to organize a formal protest, channeling it through state officials. Calhoun, who at heart was a planter himself, sympathized with southern planters. Throughout the Adams presidency, depressed conditions plagued cotton growers. At the same time northern industry, protected by the tariff, boomed. He proposed that the source of the problem was the current tariff. Calling it unfair, he warned that it also reflected a subtle long-term policy to subordinate southern agriculture to northern industrial interests. He worried that ultimately the economic and political balance, which had characterized the nation since its inception, would be undone and that division, possibly entailing an armed conflict, would become inevitable. To avoid this fate, he reasoned that the Tariff of 1828 had to be repealed. However, unlike some of the more adamant tariff opponents, he called for negotiations rather than confrontation.

Implicit in Calhoun's opposition to the tariff was a defense of slavery. He worried that those who supported the tariff were the same people who wanted to eliminate slavery. President Adams was philosophically opposed to slavery. Other influential officials including Henry Clay, a slaveholder himself, and Daniel Webster advocated gradually eliminating the institution. Even more troubling was the building momentum of an abolitionist movement, led by Benjamin Lundy and William Lloyd Garrison, which demanded an immediate end to slavery. Calhoun staunchly maintained that without slavery, traditional southern society could not survive. Slavery provided an irreplaceable source of labor and, in his opinion, was a benevolent way for the South to maintain its sizable but inherently inferior black population.

Amid the growing protest, Calhoun accepted an invitation by the South Carolina legislature to write a list of grievances against the tariff. Published anonymously shortly after the 1828 election, the document became known as the *South Carolina Exposition*. Calhoun hoped that it would provide the protest with a solid philosophical and legal foundation while at the same time tempering the tariff's more aggressive opponents. He began by proposing that the nation was involved in a struggle between the agrarian producers, or "Operatives," and industrial interests, which he labeled "Capitalists." The tariff issue was part of a Capitalist effort to subordinate Operatives and create a ruling elite similar to European aristocracies. The key to his argument was an understanding that each state had to have the authority to nullify federal legislation within that state, otherwise self-serving Capitalists could use their wealth to gain control of the federal government. Once in power, Capitalists could compel each state to enforce federal legislation, such as a protective tariff, that was detrimental to the state's citizens. This, in turn, would lead to complete Capitalist control of government. Rather than a sectional defense, Calhoun hoped that his theory of nullification would provide a way to maintain a balance between the nation's predominant economic interests. Instead it served as a compelling argument for state's rights and established him as the South's chief defender rather than as a national leader (Calhoun, 13: 457–60).

Though Calhoun eventually acknowledged his authorship, the *Exposition* was initially published anonymously. On one hand the vice president was concerned that his work might alienate influential future supporters, thereby preventing him from succeeding Jackson. Just as importantly, he was concerned that it might enrage Jackson. Well aware of the president's notorious temper and his reputation as "the Dean of Duelists," Calhoun wanted to avoid an ugly physical reprisal. At the same time, he felt obligated to defend his state's interests. Fortunately although Jackson suspected for a long time that the vice president was the author, by the time he was certain Calhoun had left the administration.

Floride Calhoun also played a role in fraying relations between her husband and Jackson. A popular Washington socialite, she joined several cabinet members' wives in shunning Peggy Eaton, the wife of Secretary of War John Eaton. Vicious rumors about Peggy's past, and stories about her first husband's suicide as well as her courtship with John Eaton, marked her as untouchable in Washington society. Jackson, on the other hand, empathized with Peggy because she reminded him of his recently deceased wife, Rachel. On several occasions early in his first term, he angrily chided Calhoun and cabinet members about the matter. However, the rebuke had little effect. Among Peggy's harshest detractors, Floride continued to avoid the Eatons. Meanwhile, Calhoun was caught in the middle and the President heaped special blame on him.

The Hayne-Webster debate in early 1831 accelerated the breach between Calhoun and Jackson. By injecting slavery into the debate, Hayne added new furor to the nullification controversy. Many suspected, and rightfully so, that Calhoun had quietly helped Hayne prepare his challenge to the Jackson administration. Later, after rhetorically jousting with Jackson at a Democratic dinner, Calhoun became more overt in his opposition. At the same time, Van Buren shrewdly isolated the vice president politically. Faced with either losing his base of support in South Carolina or his place in the Jackson administration, Calhoun left no doubt about where he stood. During the summer, he drafted an address that echoed his earlier anonymous *South Carolina Exposition* statement, formally declaring his stand on nullification. In late 1831 he severed his ties to the Jackson administration completely, announcing that he would not support the president's reelection. Further demonstrating his independence a few months later, he cast a tie-breaking vote in the Senate that denied Jackson's nominee, Martin Van Buren, an appointment as the American minister to Great Britain.

With his political future in jeopardy, Calhoun sought to fortify his leadership in South Carolina. By 1832 the tariff controversy that he had helped to initiate was rapidly spinning out of control in his home state. Radicals had used talk about secession to help gain influential state offices. Calhoun attempted to temper extremists by arguing that a state's power to nullify federal legislation rendered secession unnecessary. For the first time, he also enthusiastically embraced a strict interpretation of the Constitution because it ensured a balance between state interests and national authority. Outside South Carolina, he was labeled as a sectionalist. However, within the state his stand successfully countered opposition. Carefully maneuvering, he was selected to serve again in the U.S. Senate; thus he was able to reassert his leadership.

Resigning as vice president, Calhoun returned to the Senate in December 1832. There his first order of business was to find a satisfactory end to the five-year-old tariff controversy and the nullification debate. Making the task even more daunting was passage in early 1833 of the Force Bill, which authorized Jackson's use of the military to compel state compliance with the tariff. As many of his state constituents prepared to do battle against the U.S. Army, Calhoun urgently worked for a peaceful resolution. Joining Henry Clay, he helped to craft a compromise tariff that would reduce rates over ten years, eventually bringing the tariff back to its pre-1824 level. Because it was designed to generate revenue for the national government rather than to protect a sector of the economy, Calhoun was able to convince state leaders to go along with the compromise. However, though the immediate crisis was resolved and a potential military confrontation avoided, the equally threatening question about state's rights remained an open issue.

Though he remained a Democrat, Calhoun often sided with the emerging Whig Party on important issues. A long-time proponent of internal improvements at government expense, he allied with Whigs in supporting the Maysville Road proposal as well as other transportation projects. He also supported the Second Bank of the United States and during the rechartering controversy joined Clay, Webster, and other Whigs in opposing Jackson's veto. Although not particularly passionate about rechartering, he did lead criticism of Jackson's use of "pet banks" after the veto. Likewise, he remained a notable critic of Jackson and his administration in general, again providing valuable support to the Whigs. At the same time, he was as wary of Clay as he was of Jackson. Because he considered the Kentucky senator to be the ultimate political opportunist, Calhoun carefully assessed any support he might provide Clay's party and generally tried to stake out a middle ground between Clay and Jackson.

The issue that became Calhoun's focus was slavery. After the Missouri

Compromise, he grew increasingly concerned that there was an evolving campaign to end slavery. The tariff controversy confirmed his fears. During the debate, he came to believe that an alliance between industrial interests and anti-slavery forces had been forged to subordinate southern agriculture by eliminating slavery. The swelling abolitionist movement, Nat Turner's bloody slave rebellion, and a call to prohibit the slave trade in the District of Columbia provided further evidence that the institution was under a direct attack. To thwart the effort, he mounted an aggressive defense that included strong support of a state's exclusive right to legislate slave policy. He argued that the national government had no constitutional authority to abolish slavery. Instead the Constitution protected slavery by protecting each citizen's property. He also proposed that in a capitalistic economy, slavery in one form or another was inevitable. As practiced in the South, he believed, it was humane because master and slave were mutually dependent and ultimately both benefited. On the other hand, northern industry was developing a more insidious and inhumane form of slavery. Though unskilled workers in the North were considered free, Calhoun claimed that, in fact, they were virtually enslaved. Northern laborers, employed only when work was available, were compelled to fend for themselves periodically each year. Meanwhile, southern slaves were provided with the essentials of life regardless of annual work cycles. Additionally, in the North a growing pool of labor, spurred by an influx of impoverished European immigrants, created bitter competition for employment. This helped to keep wages low and produced a permanently destitute unskilled laboring class. Likewise, northern laborers were completely dependent upon their industrialist employers even though the industrial class was free of any accountability to the working class. Calhoun's compelling socioeconomic theory, his thorough knowledge of constitutional law and interpretations, as well as his exceptional debating skills and unflinching support established him as one of slavery's most effective defenders.

The Panic of 1837 enabled Calhoun to reestablish his leadership within the Democratic Party. Since Jackson's BUS veto, Calhoun had warned that the nation's system of currency and credit was unsound. The collapse of the cotton market shortly after Van Buren came into office confirmed Calhoun's predictions. To manage the crisis, the new president proposed the creation of a subtreasury. Calhoun immediately endorsed the idea and became a particularly effective supporter. The proposal also enabled him politically to stake out a middle ground between Jackson Democrats who opposed bank reforms and Whigs who hoped to create a third Bank of the United States. Outmaneuvering opponents, he established South Carolina as a base of support for the plan. Likewise, his budding reputation as slavery's primary defender helped him line up other southern states. Recognizing Calhoun's growing influence, Van Buren understood that the senator's assistance was essential to the success of the subtreasury.

Calhoun's renewed allegiance to Van Buren and the Democratic Party came with consequences. Recognizing little chance that he might supplant Van Buren as the party's presidential candidate in 1840, Calhoun began preparing for the subsequent election. Van Buren's defeat in 1840 added momentum to his plans. Attempting to solidify and broaden his political base, he focused on several key issues. They included a defense of the recently instituted subtreasury against all Whig reprisals. He opposed a new tariff, instead advocating free trade, a stand that generated support in the South and in some northern regions. And, as always, he maintained a vehement justification of slavery and states' rights. On a more personal level, whenever possible he portrayed Henry Clay as the ultimate political manipulator and someone who could not be trusted. Clay's obvious quest for power, especially after Harrison's death, added credence to the charges. However, although the division among Whigs was heartening, the expanding list of potential Democratic candidates was not. To give additional impetus to his efforts, Calhoun resigned from the Senate in March 1843 and began molding a campaign organization. Although receiving nominations from the South Carolina and Georgia legislatures, his efforts were not as successful in other states. Portrayed as the leader of a planter oligarchy, he was undone by former President Van Buren in New York and Virginia. Likewise, his support in Pennsylvania and the northwest eroded as the Democratic convention approached. With his candidacy collapsing and Van Buren's growing, Calhoun wisely withdrew from the race.

Rather than actively continue his campaign, in March 1844 Calhoun became President Tyler's fourth secretary of state. Lacking much knowledge about American foreign policy, he nevertheless immediately found himself at the center of two interrelated and potentially explosive issues: annexation of Texas and relations with Great Britain. By 1844 the annexation, which Calhoun heartily supported, was in full motion. He argued that Texas would enhance American cotton markets and help to perpetuate slavery. However, opponents including Henry Clay and Martin Van Buren warned that the acquisition might involve a war with Mexico. Of particular concern was the position that Great Britain would take. With the two nations already wrestling for control of the Oregon Territory, the chances seemed good that Great Britain would join Mexico should there be a war. The old War Hawk Calhoun concluded that Great Britain was the primary source of America's tensions with Mexico. He believed that since the War of 1812, the British goal had been to control the American economy by dominating the cotton market. To further undermine American agriculture, Parliament was waging a subtle crusade against slavery. Calhoun's solution was to pursue annexation aggressively and to take a hard line when dealing with the British.

The election of James K. Polk in 1844 temporarily energized Calhoun. Still resentful about being outmaneuvered by Martin Van Buren, Calhoun helped to split the Democratic Party, thus preventing Van Buren from winning the nomination. For twenty years the two had competed for power, usually to Van Buren's advantage. With the loss, the New Yorker also lost his claim as leader of the party whereas Calhoun's position was strengthened. Polk, though initially an unlikely candidate, was a very acceptable one to Calhoun. He claimed to be an opponent of a protective tariff. He enthusiastically endorsed the annexation of Texas and a tough policy in the northwest, and he defended slavery. Additionally, his running mate, George Dallas, had been a strong Calhoun supporter, which gave Calhoun hope that he might be retained as secretary of state by the new administration. Polk's victory also threatened to end the career of another longtime adversary, Henry Clay, who had been the Whig's presidential candidate. With Clay and Van Buren in decline, Calhoun expected to have greater influence on the national government.

Calhoun's hopes sank soon after Polk came into office. He was deeply disappointed that he was not invited to remain as secretary of state and complete negotiations in Oregon. Likewise, Polk's position on several key issues, most notably a protective tariff, seemed to shift once he was in office. Accepting an invitation from the South Carolina legislature to return to the U.S. Senate, Calhoun in mid-1845 began organizing supporters. Opposing Polk's confrontational Oregon policy, he almost single-handedly convinced fellow congressmen to approve a compromise in the Northwest. Once again, he took the lead in defending slavery and attacking the ever-growing abolitionist movement. In an effort to enhance cotton profits, he also renewed his call for the federal government to facilitate internal improvements. Though his stands were designed to generate immediate results, they were also part of yet another long-term Calhoun campaign to win the Democratic nomination.

Calhoun's hope that he might ever become president died with his opposition to the Mexican War. Calculating that the American people would quickly resent the conflict's costs and carnage, he was one of only a few in Congress who denounced the war. At the core of his opposition was a growing distrust of Polk and his administration. In the months preceding the war, Calhoun warned that the impending conflict would invite European intervention and threaten American negotiations in the Oregon Territory. Once war was declared he embraced a traditional Jeffersonian philosophy, arguing that the president had exceeded his constitutional authority and pushed the nation into an offensive war. The goal was not to protect American interests but to conquer and confiscate Mexican land. A victory would destroy the nation's delicate sectional balance. Likewise, conquering such a large population opposed to slavery would aid the abolitionist cause. Therefore, in many ways the ultimate loser would be South Carolina and the rest of the Old South.

The Wilmot Proviso in 1846 heightened Calhoun's fear that the war was a step toward ending slavery. By prohibiting the practice from all territories acquired as a result of the war, the Proviso left no doubt about the federal government's power to legislate slavery. Leading the charge against the Proviso, Calhoun proposed several resolutions in the Senate. At the core of these proposals was a challenge to Congress's constitutional authority to exclude slavery from the territories. He argued that Congress was required to protect all citizens' property including slaveholders who took slaves into new territories. Not only was the Proviso unconstitutional but so too was any federal legislation, including the Missouri Compromise, which put limitations upon the institution. Likewise, popular sovereignty, an idea that some prominent politicians had begun to offer as a way past the slave debate, was also unacceptable because it again ultimately assigned the power to legislate the institution to Congress. Instead, Calhoun demanded that any restriction on slavery in new territories was unconstitutional.

Almost as troubling was the evolving political realignment that emerged after the war. Responding to the slavery question, both the Whig Party and the Democratic Party began reorganizing into northern and southern factions. Likewise, several new splinter parties formed soon after the war. Particularly alarming was the Free Soil movement that began taking shape in the new western states and territories. Concerned about possible competition from slaveholders, Free Soilers joined the call to limit slavery. Calhoun feared that the growing movement would soon enable anti-slavery proponents to dominate the slave debate. To maintain southern unity and protect southern interests, he began organizing a southern wing of the Democratic Party. Increasingly confrontational negotiations with anti-slave forces gave momentum to Calhoun's call for southern unity. The proposed admittance of California as a free state seemed an obvious step toward empowering the federal government to legislate slavery throughout the territories acquired from Mexico. Likewise, a renewed call to prohibit slavery in the District of Columbia alarmed Calhoun and his southern colleagues. In reaction they demanded a new, more stringent fugitive slave law. Calhoun was particularly abrasive in his attacks. In several incendiary speeches, he warned that the union of states would soon divide. Although preferring to maintain the Union, he applauded the call for a convention of slave states through which the South could begin preparing its own frame of government. He hoped that the convention, which was held in Nashville, would demonstrate southern resolve and push opponents of slavery to moderate their stand.

At the same time Calhoun was leading the defense of slavery, he was also battling health problems. For years tuberculosis had been slowly sapping his strength. By March 1850, his once commanding presence had been reduced to a gaunt and frail frame barely able to endure daily congressional sessions. In mid-March during a series of fiery sectional debates, he addressed his colleagues for the last time. Leaning upon a fellow senator for support, he mustered all his strength and once again masterfully chided anti-slavery forces for pushing the South to the brink of secession. His target was the proposed Compromise of 1850, which he railed, imploring fellow southerners to resist. He warned that if approved, the agreement would enable the growing northern majority to dominate the South. Despite his plea, the compromise narrowly won congressional approval. However, Calhoun's compelling admonishments further stoked sectional fires that made civil war inevitable.

Two weeks after the speech, Calhoun died. Despite his increasingly aggressive defense of slavery, he had throughout his life sought to maintain the union of states. As did Henry Clay and Daniel Webster, Calhoun had been able to promote his sectional views while at the same time restraining the more confrontational elements within his region. With his death, the one southern leader able to counter secessionist appeals was gone.

BIBLIOGRAPHY

John Quincy Adams, *Memoirs of John Quincy Adams*, vol. 4, (Philadelphia: J.B. Lippincott & Co., 1874–77), 32, 108–15; *American State Papers: Documents, Legislative and Executive*, vol. 1, (Washington: Gales and Seaton, 1832–1861), 627–35, 669–80; *Annals of the Congress*, 16th Cong., 1st sess., 686–87, 1594, 2207, 2208, 2361; Frederic Bancroft, *Calhoun and the South Carolina Nullification Movement* (Baltimore: Johns Hopkins Press, 1928); John C. Calhoun, *John C. Calhoun Papers*, vol. 1, (Washington: National Archives, National Archives and Records Service, 1954), 277–82, 331–39; John C. Calhoun, *John C. Calhoun Papers*, vol. 2, (Washington: National Archives, National Archives and Records Service, 1954), 16; John C. Calhoun, *John C. Calhoun Papers*, vol. 3, (Washington: National Archives, National Archives and Records Service, 1954), 60–61; John C. Calhoun, *John C. Calhoun Papers*, vol. 13, (Washington: National Archives, National Archives and Records Service, 1954), 457–60; Wilbur Cash, *The Mind of the South* (New York: Vintage Press, 1957); Richard Ellis, *Union at Risk, Jacksonian Democracy, State Rights, and the Nullification Crisis* (New York: Oxford University Press, 1987); Ernest Lander, *Reluctant Imperialists: Calhoun, the South Carolinians, and the Mexican War* (Baton Rouge: Louisiana State University Press, 1980); John Niven, *John C. Calhoun and the Price of Union: A Biography* (Baton Rouge: Louisiana State University Press, 1988); and Merrill Peterson, *The Great Triumvirate: Webster, Clay, and Calhoun* (New York: Oxford University Press, 1987); and *Washington Gazette*, 24 February 1820.

JAMES KNOX POLK
(1795–1849)

James Knox Polk was a man of strong personal and political convictions. Throughout his career in government, he consistently championed principles associated with Jacksonian democracy. Toiling in the shadow of Andrew Jackson, he provided a sharp contrast to his mentor in temperament and demeanor. Often criticized for being detached, judgmental, and aloof, he lacked the charisma and earthy appeal of the era's namesake. However, even more so than Jackson, he advocated populist causes. He was an astute political strategist who carefully plotted his own path from the Tennessee state house to the White House. As president, he was exceptionally hardworking and productive. An ardent expansionist, he added more than 1 million acres to the American domain and achieved what contemporaries considered to be the nation's "manifest destiny." It was also during his administration that the nation instituted a permanent independent treasury. Failing to anticipate the bitter debates that would divide the nation soon after he left office, Polk became the last true Jacksonian leader.

Polk was born on November 2, 1795, in Mecklenburg County, North Carolina. Of Scots-Irish decent, his ancestors had migrated to North Carolina from Pennsylvania and Maryland three generations earlier. They were among the first to settle in the region. Sustaining themselves by farming, the family became part of the area's early political leadership. During the Revolution, several members of the Polk clan played prominent roles locally. After the war, armed with land warrants, they began speculating on vast acreage in what would soon become Tennessee. James's grandfather was one of the first to claim and survey land west of the mountains though he continued living in North Carolina until 1803. Three years after the family patriarch moved west, James's parents, lured by stories of bountiful farmland and the promise of inexpensive acreage, relocated into the fertile Duck River Valley in central Tennessee. Settling approximately 100 miles south of Nashville, Polk's father, Samuel, established what became a prosperous farmstead. Benefiting from a resolution of land disputes with the Cherokee as well as the emergence of cotton farming, the Polk family immediately prospered in their new home.

The oldest of ten children, Polk suffered from chronically poor health. Small and weak, he was unable to carry out many of the tasks typically expected of a backwoods boy. As a result, he spent much of his youth in the family cabin with his mother. Jane Knox Polk was a pious Presbyterian who claimed to have descended from John Knox, a founder of the Presbyterian Church. She instilled in her son strong religious convictions and a work ethic that he carried with him throughout his life. Many of Polk's childhood infirmities stemmed from persistent stomach problems. When he was seventeen, during one particularly severe attack, he was taken to see renowned backwoods physician Ephram McDowell. Diagnosing the problem as a gallstone, McDowell, in what was at the time a very dangerous operation, removed the obstruction. Afterward Polk's strength grew and his chronic stomach problems ended.

Until he was eighteen, Polk received no formal education. However, the establishment of a town, Columbia, nearby and a Presbyterian church to serve it provided him with his first real academic opportunity. Older than most of his classmates but barely able to read or write, he had to work hard to make up for his deficiencies. It was a challenge that he eagerly tackled. Demonstrating an obvious ability to learn, within a year he had mastered the basic skills the school offered as well as the admiration of his instructor. So impressed was his father that he enrolled him in a more demanding academy fifty miles away in Murfreesboro. Again Polk proved to be both a capable and an exceptionally hardworking student. After two productive years in Murfreesboro, he set off for the University of North Carolina where he had an uncle who was an active and influential trustee. During his three years at the university, Polk matured significantly. Again, through hard work he was able to overcome his lack of academic skills and preparation. He also discovered his intellectual strengths. Joining a student literary society, he developed outstanding writing and debating skills as well as a new interest in politics. By the time he graduated from the university, he had grown into a confident, self-assured young man anxious to pursue a legal career.

Returning home, Polk wasted little time beginning his law studies. Moving to Nashville, he sought out Felix Grundy with whom he hoped to train.

Grundy had recently relocated to Nashville from southern Kentucky and was recognized as one of the foremost criminal lawyers in the West. Though he had given up his career in government not long before, he remained very influential within Tennessee politics. The combination suited the ambitious Polk perfectly. He also enjoyed the prominent clients and associates who regularly visited Grundy's office. A year into his legal studies, Polk took advantage of his mentor's contacts. At Grundy's invitation and maneuvering, Polk was hired as clerk for the Tennessee Senate, a post he held for four years. Though a part-time responsibility, the position paid well and provided contact with some of the state's political leaders. After his first term of clerking, he finished reading law with Grundy and was admitted to the state bar. In 1820, while retaining his post as senate clerk, he returned to Columbia to begin his own practice. Helped by his father, who had become prosperous growing cotton and speculating on land in western Tennessee, the young lawyer briefly settled into a comfortable practice.

From his vantage point as the senate clerk, Polk was able to plot a formal entry into elective office. In 1822, responding to the growing economic uncertainties that fed the state's shifting political tides, he set his sights upon a seat in the lower house of the Tennessee legislature. Running against a popular incumbent, his chances initially appeared slim. However, by aggressively and energetically campaigning, he steadily cut into his opponent's lead. As election day approached, Polk stepped up his activities, employing all the campaign tactics and rough arts associated with a frontier campaign. Winning by a surprisingly large margin, he immediately established himself as a promising young star within Tennessee politics. Because he was well educated, from a prominent and prosperous local family, armed with numerous influential contacts, and ambitious, there was little doubt about his potential.

Polk's marriage to Sarah Childress a year after his election further enhanced his political potential. Sarah was from a prominent Murfreesboro family. Her father was a prosperous merchant-speculator who had spared no expense when educating his daughter. Well read and knowledgeable in a variety of subjects, she was equally adept at traditional domestic tasks. Socially, her interests and skills complemented her husband's in many ways. Although Polk often appeared aloof and detached, his wife was a gracious and charming hostess. At ease in all sorts of gatherings and an animated conversationalist, she enjoyed the entertaining generally expected of a successful politician. She was also a Presbyterian whose strict religious convictions in many ways mirrored those of her husband. The Polk-Childress wedding was a grand celebration in Murfreesboro, and their life together was a happy one.

By the time he entered the Tennessee legislature, Polk's ideology was fully formed and changed little during his political career. As his father and grandfather had, he embraced many traditional principles of Jeffersonian democracy. At the core of his philosophy was an idealized vision of an agrarian nation. Polk extolled the virtues of the self-reliant farmer who toiled with few expectations aside from individual liberty. On matters of governmental authority he was a strict constructionist. He questioned whether government could assume responsibilities or assert power without a specific constitutional mandate. In considering the relationship between the state and nation, he envisioned two well-defined domains of authority. When those domains overlapped, he usually stood on the side of the federal government. For example, he held that with few exceptions, internal improvements were the responsibility of the state. However, federal authority was valid when a project enhanced the entire nation. He was also an advocate of tight fiscal policies. Taxes should be used exclusively to pay for the essential costs of government. Taxation for any other purposes, such as economic development, would invite corruption and encourage aristocracy. In terms of foreign policy, Polk endorsed noninvolvement whenever possible. He mistrusted all European nations, especially Great Britain, and feared that active participation in Latin America would eventually entangle the nation in a conflict. Instead, he preferred that the United States limit interaction with other nations to essential relations.

As a freshman legislator, Polk immediately established a reputation for independence. Expected to ally with a powerful faction of land speculators led by John Overton, a Jeffersonian Republican from Tennessee, he instead supported the reform opposition. On numerous occasions he also opposed his former mentor, Felix Grundy, who had been elected to the state Senate in 1822 and was part of the Overton coalition. Most notable was a controversy between the two men concerning lands in western Tennessee. Grundy favored recognizing old North Carolina land warrants that would benefit speculators. Polk disagreed, arguing that the warrants should not be honored. Instead, he proposed that the lands claimed by the warrants ought to be opened for settlement and that a portion of the proceeds should be used to fund common schools in the state. Ably countering Grundy's maneuvers, Polk marshalled enough support to carry his proposal. On another occasion, the two became embroiled in a debate about how state banks should pay notes that they had issued. Still gripped by the effects of the Panic of 1819, bankers sought to suspend the use of specie, or hard currency, when paying their notes. Grundy agreed, arguing that if specie payment were required then banks would be forced to foreclose upon many mortgages throughout the state. True to his fiscally conservative philosophy, Polk disagreed and engineered a compromise that phased in specie payments over a two-year period. Although not always as successful in his encounters with Grundy, Polk did not defer to his former benefactor and soon emerged as a spokesman for the state's small farmers and reform interests.

Buoyed by his burgeoning reputation in the state house, Polk, in 1825, set his sights upon a seat in Congress. Running against four others, he was a legitimate contender but not the initial front-runner. That distinction rested with Andrew Erwin, a crafty power broker who had assembled a solid base of support. Erwin recognized Polk's potential and skillfully exposed his opposition to federally funded internal improvements. Polk retaliated by vigorously assuring voters that he supported federal road-building projects, like a proposed road that would link Tennessee with New Orleans, when they benefited the nation as a whole. Tirelessly stumping throughout the district, Polk was able to shed the characteristically stiff and apparently distant demeanor that often estranged him from the rustic farm folk who populated the region. Though he only received 35 percent of the vote, it was enough to defeat his four opponents. The hard-fought victory further demonstrated his growing political prowess.

Polk came to Washington shortly after the disputed election of 1824. Like many others, he believed that a corrupt bargain between Henry Clay and John Quincy Adams had been cut to deny Jackson the election. Wary about a perfidious eastern conspiracy, Polk, from his first days in Congress, was part of the Democratic efforts to undermine the Adams presidency. Most importantly, he was a longtime admirer and supporter of Andrew Jackson. Since his childhood he had known the general, and both his father and uncle considered Jackson to be a close friend. When the general was first mentioned as a presidential candidate, Polk split with his allies in the state house and supported him. Likewise, he supported Jackson's nomination to the U.S. Senate. Beyond their personal relationship, Polk shared many of Jackson's political attitudes. Both embraced traditional Jeffersonian values. Both distrusted banks. Both claimed to represent the interests of the small farmer and the West. Both saw a clear distinction between state and federal authority. And both were expansionists.

During his first two terms in the House of Representatives, Polk was among a group of Jackson loyalists who consistently opposed the Adams administration. At the core of his differences was a basic philosophical disagreement. The president envisioned a powerful national government with sweeping authority. Polk saw a more balanced distribution of power and scoffed at the president's ambitious proposals, including his call to create a national university and a national observatory. Likewise, he protested the administration's efforts to open Tennessee's western district to speculative ventures. As he had during his debates with Grundy, Polk again maintained that the western land was the state's domain and a portion of the proceeds from land sales should be used to fund common schools. Polk also opposed Adams's foreign policies. He feared that Adams and his secretary of state, Henry Clay, were secretly conspiring to tighten the commercial binds between the United States and Great Britain. Concerning Latin America, Polk, who opposed the Monroe Doctrine that Adams had authored, warned that the administration was overextending American authority. When Adams sent representatives to negotiate with Latin American nations at the Panama Congress, Polk complained that the effort would entangle the United States in local Latin American affairs. Only on internal improvements did Polk's opposition waver. Because of campaign promises he agreed with a few, but certainly not all, of the administration's road-building initiatives.

Polk worked to elect Jackson in 1828. Convinced that the general had won four years earlier, he, as did many Americans, saw the election as a reaffirmation of American democracy. Afterward, he served Jackson faithfully and usually without question. When dissension between Calhoun and Van Buren threatened to polarize the administration, Polk cautiously chose a difficult middle course between the two factions. Although not breaking from Calhoun and his defense of states' rights, neither did he actively oppose Van Buren. Instead, Jackson's interests guided him. Likewise, despite Sarah's disdain for Secretary of War John Eaton's wife Peggy, Polk maintained the civility toward the Eatons that Jackson expected. In the House of Representatives, he often spearheaded administration initiatives and led attacks on those who opposed the president. Though he had a few minor philosophical differences with the president, he put them aside in favor of Jackson's policies. On several occasions, including the Maysville Road veto, he helped to write Jackson's messages to Congress. In return, Polk earned the president's full appreciation.

The Tariff of 1828 tested Polk's loyalty to Jackson. Unlike many of the president's supporters, he had voted against the tariff. He complained that it protected eastern manufacturers while unfairly burdening western agriculture. Additionally, he feared that the revenue it generated would enable the federal government to expand its authority by funding various programs that ought to be administered by the states. Jackson's decision to maintain the tariff until the national debt was paid disappointed Polk, but reluctantly he acknowledged the president's wishes. Wrangling between the president and South Carolina further irritated him, as did Jackson's insistence in 1832 that Congress pass the Force Bill. Polk worried that the bill would set a dangerous precedent and bring additional power to the national government. However, he again yielded to Jackson. Meanwhile, some in the administration, recognizing Polk's allegiance to the president, pressured him into leading an effort to legislate a compromise tariff. Though Henry Clay eventually took credit for the bill, it was Polk who initiated the legislation and pasted together much of the support necessary to pass it. Throughout the tariff ordeal, Polk, despite his personal convictions, attentively supported Jackson's policy and in so doing maintained the president's regard.

Although Polk differed with Jackson about the tariff, there was no disagreement about the Second Bank of the United States (BUS). Both men vehemently opposed the BUS. Both considered it an instrument through which eastern commercial and speculative interests were undermining democratic government. And both wanted the bank's powerful role in the economy ended. To accomplish their goal, Jackson maneuvered Polk onto the Ways and Means Committee that was investigating the BUS. Though the committee found no irregularities, Polk wrote a minority opinion that accused the bank of several improprieties. The report implied that if the bank was allowed to continue operating, its authority would soon rival that of the federal government. Using the report as a justification, Jackson vetoed the rechartering bill and ordered federal funds withdrawn. During the acrimonious discussions and eventual censure that followed, Polk steadfastly defended Jackson. The bank, he maintained, threatened American democracy and the president had wisely disabled it.

Polk benefited in several ways from Jackson's eight years in office. Most importantly, he had earned the full appreciation and esteem of the president. He had also emerged as a powerful Democratic congressman. In 1835 he was able to parley that status into election as speaker of the House. On the other hand, Polk had also pinned his political future upon the success of Jackson policies, especially his banking policy. As the economy began to falter in the mid-1830s, he became a target for anti-Jackson Democrats. When Jackson left office, the insulation from direct criticism that the president had provided was also gone, thus opening up Polk to ever more aggressive political attacks. Likewise, anti-Jackson newspapers throughout the country shifted their criticism to Polk among others still in government.

Jackson's retirement initiated an intense struggle within the Democratic Party. Polk aligned himself with Martin Van Buren, Jackson's hand-picked successor, and worked hard for his election. In return, the new president helped him retain his position as speaker. Despite the endorsement, many of Polk's Tennessee constituents, like many throughout the South, did not share his enthusiasm for the New Yorker. When the new administration, plagued by a collapsing economy, soon foundered, they joined the growing criticism of both Van Buren and Polk. The two men shared a similar understanding of the problems and generally agreed upon the solutions. However, their efforts to implement the necessary corrections were severely handicapped by political realities. Because Van Buren's chief benefactor, Andrew Jackson, staunchly opposed a central bank, the new president was unable to implement what he and Polk agreed the economy needed: an independent subtreasury. For two frustrating years, Polk unsuccessfully battled on behalf of Van Buren's policies but eventually concluded that his best option politically was to resign from Congress and run for governor.

Running an energetic and aggressive campaign, Polk in 1839 was able to overcome stiff opposition and narrowly win election as governor. He was also credited with enabling Democrats to regain control of the state legislature. However, his victory did not end the factionalism that had characterized Tennessee politics during the previous five years. Additionally, Polk's powers as governor were limited. Most importantly, he did not have veto power and had only minimal ability to create public policy. He was, therefore, in many ways dependent upon the state legislature and its various political alignments. As a result, many of his campaign promises went unfulfilled. Of particular concern were the banking reforms and road-building projects that he contended were necessary to reinvigorate the state's ailing economy. Although he was able to maintain his standing among Democrats nationally, even receiving serious consideration as a potential vice presidential candidate in 1840, he lost support within the state during his two-year term. In his reelection efforts, he was defeated.

Polk's first electoral defeat was discouraging but did not drain his political ambition. Instead he considered the loss to be part of the Whig wave that had swept the nation in 1840. He was confident that he could regain the governorship and in 1843 ran a long, vigorous campaign speaking in every corner of the state. His detailed policy statements and polished rhetoric provided a sharp contrast to the folksy, homespun style of incumbent Whig Governor James Jones. As he had two years earlier, Polk focused on the state's continuing banking problems and the rising national tariff. Wherever he spoke, prospective voters apparently embraced his proposals, thus buoying his hopes. Anxious to repudiate his defeat, Polk anticipated a decisive victory. However, that was not to be. When the votes were counted, Polk had lost again, by approximately 3 percent of the vote. Citing a surprisingly low voter turnout, he rationalized that his second loss was a product of an apathetic population. Dejected and sourly disappointed by the loss, he rallied his spirits, promising to continue fighting on behalf of Jeffersonian and Democratic principles.

Losing the 1843 state election was doubly upsetting to Polk because he had hoped to use his victory as a stepping stone to the 1844 Democratic vice presidential nomination. Still ambitious as ever, he nevertheless pushed ahead with his plans. Since 1841 he had been subtly promoting Martin Van Buren as the party's next presidential candidate and expected that Van Buren, in need of a southerner to balance the ticket, would select him as his running mate. Despite his recent defeats, Polk retained a solid base of support. In Washington his allies were able to maintain his standing among many Democrats. In Tennessee he had built an extensive organization and generally controlled the state's Democratic Party. Reflecting his control, state Democrats chose a slate of Polk delegates to the 1844 national convention in Baltimore. Polk could also count on the unflinching support of Andrew Jackson. Though in poor health and somewhat removed from the nation's daily political struggles, Jackson remained the Democratic Party's symbolic leader and he reminded fellow Democrats not to overlook Polk. As the 1844 election approached, Jackson actively lobbied to have his Tennessee protégé considered for the vice presidency.

By May 1844, when the convention met, Democrats were splintered into several factions. For four years various leaders, most notably Van Buren and Calhoun, had been maneuvering for the party's nomination. Van Buren was the front-runner, but because he appeared to oppose annexation of Texas and avoided the slavery question many southern Democrats rejected him. On the other hand, Calhoun's strident stand on slavery and states' rights as well as his opposition to a protective tariff alienated the North. When Van Buren's nomination fell short on the convention's first ballot, delegates began a frenzied search for an acceptable alternative. Into the swirl was placed Polk's name. At the insistence of Andrew Jackson, Polk a few weeks earlier had begun contemplating a possible presidential nomination and had enlisted some assistance just in case Van Buren's nomination fell through. Able to count on most of Van Buren's former supporters and acceptable to southerners, he immediately became a viable choice. With two capable floor managers manipulating delegates, Polk's nomination picked up some momentum. Jackson's endorsement and insistence that Polk was the candidate most able to maintain party unity further fortified his chances. On the ninth ballot, the convention agreed to make him their choice.

As expected, the Whig candidate in 1844 was once again Henry Clay. In many ways, he and Polk were at opposite ends of the political spectrum. Author of "the American System," Clay had historically advocated a protective tariff, government support for internal improvements, and the Bank of the United States. Polk had opposed these policies throughout his career. The election, however, focused on two other issues: expansion and slavery. Clay did all he could to avoid the issues, and when he did finally address annexation he became entangled in conflicting statements. Polk, on the other hand, left no doubt about where he stood on Texas or expansion in general. Not only did he favor annexation but he also proposed pressing American claims in the Oregon Territory. If necessary, he was ready go to war to pursue American interests in both Mexico and Oregon. A bit more subdued, his stand on slavery echoed Jefferson's attitude about the South's "peculiar institution." Intellectually he admitted many contradictions between slavery and a nation built upon individual freedom and equality. However, as a practical matter, slavery had been part of the American experience for two centuries and could not easily be eliminated. Likewise, the institution was essential to a significant portion of the American economy. He himself owned almost fifty slaves and considered them better off as slaves than they would be as free blacks. Clay also owned slaves but because of his need to appease northern Whigs sidestepped the issue whenever possible.

The campaign demonstrated Polk's well-honed skills as a political strategist. From his home in Tennessee, he carefully orchestrated support throughout the country and at almost every opportunity outmaneuvered

Clay. Both candidates employed all the devices and tactics expected of an aggressive campaign. Slogans, banners, songs, celebrations, and memorabilia were common. Newspapers throughout the country eagerly battled for one side or the other. However, unlike previous campaigns there was little name-calling and mudslinging. In the end, though he lost his home state, Polk carried three important northern states, Pennsylvania, New York, and New Hampshire, which enabled him to win a relatively comfortable electoral but narrow popular victory.

As president, Polk was an active and involved executive who modeled himself in many ways after his mentor, Andrew Jackson. Because he was the only federal officeholder elected by a national constituency, he assumed that both the responsibility and the authority of shaping policies rested with him rather than with the legislative branch. Although his forthright manner periodically alienated Congress, he demonstrated a keen political acumen when maneuvering proposals past opponents. Consistent with his strict constructionist philosophy, he opposed any policy, including a protective tariff, which he felt benefited one section of the country at the expense of another. On one occasion, he used his veto power to defeat a controversial road-building project that he considered regional rather than national. A frugal fiscal policy also characterized his leadership. As always he was unwilling to approve spending that might expand the responsibilities of government. In crafting policies he relied a great deal upon his Cabinet, though ultimately he accepted responsibility for all decisions. When dealing with his Cabinet, he was a stern taskmaster who demanded a great deal from his appointees. Sharing much authority with them, he became very involved in the daily operation of his government. Often working eighteen hours a day, he gained a reputation as a particularly hardworking executive. At the same time he maintained his solitary habits, spending many hours alone in his office. He usually avoided the pomp and circumstance often associated with the presidency, instead favoring a fairly rigid schedule of meetings, official visits, and time at his desk.

Texas dominated Polk's presidency. An ardent expansionist, he came into office having pledged to annex the Republic. Subscribing to the popular notion that the United States had a manifest destiny in North America, Polk agreed that Texas as well as the entire Southwest was an essential part of that destiny. Although he preferred to pursue expansion through diplomacy, his predecessor, John Tyler, by initiating the annexation process, had limited Polk's opportunities to negotiate. Nevertheless, soon after taking office he sent a mission to Mexico City with instructions to settle the boundary dispute between Texas and Mexico and to purchase New Mexico and California. The Mexican government, however, had already warned that it was prepared to go to war with the United States if Texas was annexed. Consequently, negotiations did not go well. Amid the fruitless talks, Polk anticipated hostilities and ordered Zachary Taylor to position his army along the Rio Grande, which he considered to be the southern border of Texas.

Meanwhile, Polk recognized that the United States' relationship with Great Britain in the Oregon Territory potentially jeopardized his diplomatic maneuverings with Mexico. During his presidential campaign, he had shrilly promised to defend the American claim to the Oregon Territory all the way to the Alaskan border. If necessary he was ready to go to war for the region. However, with wars looming against both Mexico in the Southwest and Great Britain in the Northwest, Polk chose to modify his demands in Oregon. Arguing that the northern portion of the territory was of little value, he agreed to divide the region in half. The compromise satisfied the British and freed Polk to deal more forcefully with Mexico.

In April 1847, Taylor reported that he had been attacked by Mexican troops. Two weeks later, Congress declared a war against Mexico. With the declaration, Polk assumed a heavy load of new responsibilities. Among them, military duties became his priority. Consulting with his Cabinet and the military, he began devising an American strategy. Throughout the war, he remained the nation's chief strategist. Integral to his plan was choosing an appropriate military leader to direct the untested, undermanned American forces. He found his leader in Zachary Taylor, though midway through the war he worried that Taylor was becoming a national hero much as Jackson had after the War of 1812. To dilute Taylor's postwar political potential, Polk replaced him with Winfield Scott, a general who had already established his political intentions. Polk also acted quickly to recruit men and raise the units deemed necessary to fight the war. Mobilizing American industry was another immediate concern. Just as it lacked manpower, so too did the military lack adequate equipment, munitions, weaponry, and other essentials. Likewise, the ability to move raw materials, finished goods, and men plagued American efforts during the early months of the war. Maintaining political support was yet another of Polk's important tasks. Initially a frenzied public embraced the conflict but significant opposition, especially throughout New England, emerged within several months. Working long hours, Polk diligently responded to these new chores.

While overseeing the military, Polk also directed the nation's diplomatic ventures. These efforts included encouraging a second war front in California by actively promoting an insurrection. Once a rebellion was underway, Polk provided the transplanted Americans leadership with whatever military support he could spare. To negotiate with Mexico, he assigned a string of diplomats who were instructed to pursue his territorial goals. As the war continued, these goals were periodically expanded. At one point, Polk became convinced that the Mexican population had lost the will to fight and he considered pursuing the conquest of all Mexico rather than settling for merely New Mexico Territory and California. Fortunately the

American negotiator in Mexico City, Nicholas Triste, recognized the potential human cost of such an endeavor and eventually settled for the land that Polk had originally sought.

The Treaty of Guadalupe de Hidalgo in May 1848 ended the war. The agreement formally established the Rio Grande as the southern border of Texas. Additionally, Mexico ceded to the United States all of the vast New Mexico Territory (which included present day New Mexico, Utah, and Arizona) and California. The victory became Polk's most notable achievement as well as the most controversial element of his legacy. On one hand, he was credited with having spearheaded the conquest and, as he claimed in his final report to Congress, enabling the nation to fulfill its manifest destiny. On other hand, the war intensified burning issues that had been smoldering for at least three decades. Most importantly, questions about the future of slavery and states' rights were elevated to a new level of debate. Likewise, fed by vast new unadministered acreage, the political relationship between northern states and their southern counterparts demanded new clarification. As some commentators recognized immediately, Polk's war with Mexico began the nation's unavoidable plunge into civil war.

Aside from managing the war, Polk's most important achievement was the creation of a permanent independent treasury. Having helped Jackson dismantle the Bank of the United States, he nevertheless recognized a need for a central banking facility that could stabilize the economy. For this reason, he had supported Van Buren's call for an independent treasury despite Jackson's complaints. Though briefly implemented, the national government's failure to maintain a treasury served as a drag upon the economy. Hoping to correct lingering economic problems, Polk again pursued creation of an independent treasury. He argued that the Constitution required federal revenues to be deposited into the national treasury and not into other facilities including state banks. In 1846, he was able to reinstitute an independent treasury.

During the last seven months of his presidency, Polk continued working to expand American influence in the hemisphere. Of particular concern was the Caribbean and the Yucatan Peninsula where political unrest invited foreign intervention. Armed with the Monroe Doctrine, Polk warned that he would consider any European assistance in either area to be a threat to the entire hemisphere. In so doing, he further defined the role that the United States intended to take throughout Central America. The policy became know as the "Polk Doctrine." Meanwhile, postwar political debates sidetracked his domestic efforts. Though some encouraged him to seek reelection in 1848, he abided by his promise made four years earlier and did not pursue a second term. Instead he chose to retire to his Tennessee home. Most agreed that the rest was much needed. Clearly the burdens of office and the exceedingly long hours he worked had taken a toll on his already frail health.

Within a month of his return home, Polk fell victim to a cholera epidemic that had swept thorough the lower Mississippi Valley. In broken health, he died two months later in mid-June 1849.

BIBLIOGRAPHY

Paul H. Bergeron, *The Presidency of James K. Polk* (Lawrence: University of Kansas Press, 1987); Samuel W. Hayes, *James K. Polk and the Expansionist Impulse* (New York: Longman, 1997); Thomas M. Leonard, *James K. Polk: A Clear and Unquestionable Destiny* (Wilmington, DE: Scholarly Resources, Inc., 2001); Charles McCoy, *Polk and the Presidency* (Austin: University of Texas Press, 1960); Charles G. Sellers, *James K. Polk: Continentalist* (Princeton, NJ: Princeton University Press, 1966); and Charles G. Sellers, *James K. Polk: Jacksonian, 1795–1843* (Princeton, NJ: Princeton University Press, 1957).

THOMAS HART BENTON
(1782–1858)

Thomas Hart Benton, Missouri's initial senator, was the fourth great orator during the Jacksonian era. Along side Henry Clay, John C. Calhoun, and Daniel Webster, he dominated Congress for thirty years. An ardent expansionist, Benton served as a powerful voice of the West. He also earned a reputation as an outspoken opponent of the Second Bank of the United States (BUS) and a hard-money advocate. Benton emerged as Jackson's chief supporter in the Senate, paying allegiance to the general both personally and politically. However, as the nation embarked on a war with Mexico, he demonstrated his political independence by challenging some of his party's policies. After the war he was identified as pro-Union and a grand promoter of a transcontinental railroad. Though somewhat less well known than his three long-time congressional colleagues, Benton's influence throughout the era was in most ways comparable to any one of them.

The Benton family came to North Carolina during the mid-eighteenth century. Among the region's earliest settlers, Samuel Benton established the family as part of the local gentry. Not long after settling in the area, Samuel entered politics. Appointed justice of the peace, he soon built a political organization that eventually carried him to the provincial assembly. Through various maneuvers, he used his growing prominence to acquire thousands of acres and build a large plantation. Ambitious, shrewd, and at times unscrupulous, Samuel dominated public life in central North Carolina through the 1760s. Of course his authority did not go unchallenged.

As new populations came to the area, often settling on land they had bought from him, local small farming neighbors came to resent his often self-serving policies.

When Samuel died in 1770, his oldest son Jesse inherited the bulk of the family possessions. Like his father, Jesse was an avaricious land speculator though he lacked his father's single-minded determination. Trained as a lawyer, the younger Benton also operated a successful plantation. Politically he remained on the periphery until late in the Revolution, when he served briefly in the state Assembly. He also avoided a full-fledged commitment to the American resistance throughout much of the war, joining the militia just three months before the fighting ended. Of all his endeavors, land speculation was his primary interest. Among his numerous speculative ventures, Jesse became one of the original stockholders in the Transylvania Company that acquired a vast tract of land in what later became Tennessee and Kentucky. Jesse eventually bought 24,000 acres of the company's land. Unfortunately his gambles did not always bring immediate profits and, as a result, the family regularly encountered debt problems.

During the late 1770s, Jesse married Ann Gooch. She was the niece of a former royal governor of Virginia, Sir William Gooch, and was reared by another uncle, Thomas Hart. Hart was a prominent North Carolina merchant, politician, and patriot leader during the Revolutionary War. An eager land speculator himself, he was friends with both Samuel and Jesse Benton. When Ann wed Jesse, who called her Nancy, she was still Hart's ward. Jesse and Ann settled on a small plantation near Hillsborough. Eventually they had eight children. Their third child and oldest son, born in 1782, was Thomas Hart Benton. The early years of Thomas's childhood were spent comfortably on his family's plantation. Though constantly plagued by debts, Jesse built his holding into the largest in the immediate area.

Thomas was eight when his father died. Burdened by family debts and financial problems, Nancy Benton struggled to maintain the family. For support she turned to Thomas, her oldest son, who willingly assumed the role of family patriarch. Fortunately Nancy's uncle provided several loans that enabled the family to retain their farm and lifestyle. To pay the most pressing debts, Nancy also began to sell western lands that her husband had bought. With slaves to provide necessary labor on the farm, the Benton children, particularly the three boys, received the sort of education expected of local gentry. By the age of ten, Thomas was reading law, philosophy, and history. In his early teens he was sent to a private school in nearby Hillsborough, and at sixteen he enrolled in the University of North Carolina.

Founded only four years earlier, the university already had a reputation for excellence and Benton was happy to be among the school's forty students. Popular and gregarious, he was soon invited to join a prestigious school literary club. As a capable debater, he earned a reputation for being both high spirited and feisty. Unfortunately, several months into his stay at the university his fiery temper got him into trouble. He became embroiled in a quarrel that ended when he drew a loaded pistol and threatened to shoot his detractor. A while later, Benton's comparative penury was the source of another serious offense. Provided with little spending money by his family, he resorted to stealing money from three students. Upon discovering his thievery, the school expelled him. It was a humiliation that Benton bore the rest of his life.

Two years later, in 1801, Nancy decided to move her family to 2,450 acres in middle Tennessee that Jesse had purchased. The land was located twenty-five miles south of Nashville along the Natchez Trace in a region inhabited by powerful Native American tribes. To raise needed money and provide a defense against Indian attack, the Bentons leased land to settlers and created the village of Benton Town (later renamed Hillsboro). As Samuel Benton had done fifty years earlier in North Carolina, the family immediately established itself as the community's commercial and political focal point. Aided by half a dozen slaves, Thomas, who assumed much of the responsibility for the family's well-being, cleared land and planted cotton and corn. However, after two difficult years he turned over the day-to-day operation of the farm to his brothers. Instead he took a position teaching school in an isolated settlement along the Duck River forty miles to the west. There, in addition to teaching, he embarked on a self-directed study of the law.

In the early nineteenth century, the land west of the Appalachians and east of the Mississippi River offered abundant opportunity for ambitious and bold entrepreneurs. People flooded across the mountains in search of new beginnings, prosperity, and the land that would make it all possible. Cotton was especially important in luring avaricious farmers into the new state. The nation was quickly becoming the world's primary cotton producer, and Tennessee was at the forefront of the new industry. Adequate administration in the burgeoning region generated a demand for backwoods lawyers. Deeds needed to be registered properly, surveys processed, and laws enforced. Consequently few credentials, aside from a rudimentary knowledge of the legal system and a pledge to maintain professional behavior, were required to practice. By these standards, Benton was well qualified and in July 1806, with virtually no formal training, he was licensed by the state. He was well read in law, history, and philosophy and had a broad, if incomplete, knowledge of legal procedures. He was also imposing physically, smart, aggressive, and very confident in his own abilities. These were all qualities that in the Tennessee backwoods compensated for gaps in a formal understanding of the law.

Benton spent the next two years litigating cases throughout the region. His activities put him in contact with the full range of Tennessee's population including some of the state's most important figures. Among them was Judge Andrew Jackson. An acquaintance of Jesse Benton, Jackson had, two decades earlier, visited the family plantation in North Carolina. Upon learning about Benton's parentage, Jackson invited him to visit his home in Nashville. Soon Jackson was treating the young lawyer as a protégé. The influence of Jackson, who was among the most powerful men in the state, played a major role in shaping Benton's future. The friendship provided contact with prominent figures that might have otherwise been inaccessible. It also brought Benton a growing list of clients.

Jackson's influence also helped propel Benton into politics. A committed Jeffersonian, Benton eagerly embraced many of the stands, including the pursuit of expanded democracy, taken by Jackson. In his quest, Benton became an outspoken advocate of judicial reform. Echoing the complaints of his small-farmer clients, he criticized the state judiciary as inefficient and, ultimately, unjust. Boldly challenging the powerful forces that administered the law in Tennessee, he wrote a series of weekly commentary during the first half of 1808. Building his arguments upon a foundation of British and American legal traditions, he skillfully demonstrated the flaws in the state system. The campaign earned him instant celebrity, which he quickly parleyed into election to the state Senate. Immediately upon assuming his seat, he formed a Senate committee to pursue judicial reforms. Ambitious as always, Benton was able to get most of his recommendations enacted within two months.

An avowed nationalist and advocate of westward expansion, Benton became an unabashed critic of the British policies toward the United States. As tensions between the two nations built, his discontent grew. Like the new generation of leaders in Washington, led by Henry Clay and John C. Calhoun, Benton concluded that armed conflict was the only solution left to the problems with the British. In early 1812, with hostilities imminent, he sent a letter to Jackson who had recently been appointed major general of the Tennessee Militia. Benton offered to raise and command a volunteer unit should Jackson need men. Three months later, in April, Benton was commissioned a captain of a volunteer infantry company that he had raised and was assigned to defend settlements in the southwestern part of the state.

By the time war against the British was declared in June 1812, Benton had been promoted to major. Though he hoped to fight the British in Canada, he was instead instructed to join Jackson in defending the lower Mississippi Valley. Reunited with the general, Benton became his aide-de-camp and was promoted to colonel. Shortly after Jackson's army began its march south, the general was instructed to return to Nashville. Angry about the change, Benton, with Jackson's blessing, set off for Washington in pursuit of a command of his own. Granted his request, he was instructed to raise an army of Tennesseans. However, when he returned home to begin recruiting, he became involved in a nasty dispute between his brother and Jackson. While he was away, the general had allowed Benton's brother, Jesse, to be shot by one of Jackson's officers in what Benton claimed was an unfair duel. Torn by his loyalty to the general, Benton nevertheless staunchly defended his brother, charging that Jackson had assisted the officer. The general was livid at Benton's apparent betrayal.

A month later, the two Benton brothers traveled to Nashville. News of their arrival brought Jackson to the tavern where they were staying. After exchanging a few bitter words, pistols were drawn and shots fired. The melee ended when a shot by Benton struck Jackson in the shoulder. Fearing the wound was mortal, the general's companions rushed him off to get immediate medical attention. Though Jackson recovered, he carried Benton's musket ball for more than twenty years. Six months after the showdown, the two former friends were again defending the lower Mississippi. Although he avoided contact with the general, Benton did provide him with important tactical information. However, Jackson eventually had Benton sent back to Tennessee while he and his men won everlasting fame battling the British in New Orleans.

By the end of the war, Benton recognized his future prospects in Tennessee were limited. Though he had risen to the rank of lieutenant colonel, he had seen limited action during the war and, more importantly, had incurred the full vengeance of one of the state's most powerful figures. Rather than remain in Tennessee he, like many Americans searching for a fresh start, was drawn to the West. Across the Mississippi lay Missouri Territory, a wide-open region that had begun to attract population. With the British threat gone and the local Native Americans at least temporarily subdued, the opportunities in Missouri for a determined, self-assured young man seemed abundant.

Benton arrived in St. Louis in the early fall of 1815. At the time, the town was little more than a frontier settlement. The Lewis and Clark expedition a decade earlier had established it as the edge of western civilization and commerce. Characterized by an unusually diverse assortment of national backgrounds and interests, the town's 2,000 residents included French, Spanish, Germans, Scots-Irish, and several displaced Native Americans. Rough and tumble river men, trappers selling skins, farmers looking for land, as well as a couple of French aristocrats coexisted within the town. The setting was ideally suited for Benton, and in a short time he became a prominent member of the growing community.

Wasting little time, Benton registered to practice law and set up an office. The demand for lawyers in Missouri Territory was even greater than it had been when Benton started practicing in Tennessee ten years earlier. Hundreds of deeds needed to be surveyed and registered. There were an equal number of recent American settlers who sought to challenge old French and Spanish claims. The region's swelling commercial activity created another broad area of opportunity. Likewise, the unsettled and at times rowdy local population regularly required legal representation. And then there were the circuit courts that served an ever-expanding number of backwoods settlements. Clearly the potential for an ambitious, young lawyer was tremendous. The only significant obstacle for Benton was learning to speak French, which was still the primary language in St. Louis. However, with the help of a Catholic bishop, he quickly mastered the language well enough to function in his new hometown.

Benton's practice flourished immediately. He was in such great demand that there were days when he took as many as fifteen cases to court. Though he focused on land claims, he regularly accepted civil and criminal cases as well. Additionally, as he had in Tennessee, he traveled to circuit courts throughout the territory. There, while pleading cases, he initiated friendships with evolving local leaders and learned the concerns and interests of the region's new inhabitants. Always with an eye on a political future, he understood the importance of his backwoods acquaintances. His steadily growing income soon enabled him to begin speculating on land that became almost as much of an adventure for him as it had been for his father. His income also enabled him to bring his mother and sister west to live with him. Within a year of his arrival in St. Louis, he had established himself as one of the region's most prominent and capable lawyers.

Of course, life in Missouri Territory included some dangerous encounters. On numerous occasions, Benton's legal battles ended with the threat of a duel. Overly sensitive, easily offended, and often uncompromising, he was not one to back down from a confrontation. Consequently he became involved in several duels, from at least one of which he came away wounded. In another duel, he was challenged by the son of a prominent St. Louis judge. After badly hurting the young man, Benton demanded that the two continue their duel after his victim had healed. A month later they faced off again. This time Benton mortally shot his counterpart. For years afterward, the man's father bitterly denounced Benton as a murderer.

In Missouri Benton began his political career as a critic rather than a candidate. In addition to his other endeavors, he took on the responsibilities as editor of the *St. Louis Enquirer*. Having recently reorganized the weekly, the new owner intended to provide competition for the city's more established paper, the *Missouri Gazette*. Benton accepted the editorship because it provided him with an intellectual forum as well as a political sounding board. Always opinionated, he wasted little time in addressing the major issues of the day. An ardent nationalist, he strongly advocated expansion into the Northwest and the acquisition of Texas. Likewise, he left no doubt that he embraced a Jeffersonian philosophy and was a states' rights champion. He also took on two issues of special local interest: banking policy and statehood. Benton was suspicious of bank notes and credit. Instead he advocated tight credit policies and the use of gold and silver, or "hard

money," to back currency. As proof for his position, he convincingly argued that unstable credit policies had created a national economic panic
during the late 1810s. Statehood was an issue with which most Missourians
agreed. The question was whether the new state should be slave or free.
Benton backed pro-slavery proponents not because he was anxious to expand slavery but because he felt strongly that the state should have the
right to decide for itself.

With Benton at its helm, the paper's circulation grew steadily as did its
opinionated editor's reputation. Through his commentary he built alliances
with powerful figures in St. Louis and throughout the territory. Additionally, his law practice attracted an ever more prosperous and influential
clientele. Soon Benton emerged as an important power broker able to sway
elections and mold political decisions. In 1820, as Missouri prepared for
statehood, Benton cagily entered the political arena. He used his growing
prominence to maneuver an appointment as one of the new state's U.S.
senators.

Unable to participate fully until the statehood issue was settled, Benton
nevertheless made an important decision while Congress wrestled over the
Missouri Compromise. Five years earlier, while he was chasing a new military assignment, he had visited James McDowell, a family friend in Virginia. Benton took a particular interest in McDowell's twenty-year-old
daughter, Elizabeth. On his return trip to Washington in 1820, he again
visited the McDowell plantation but this time to propose to Elizabeth. The
union added a vital dimension to his life. Intelligent, gracious, and attractive, she had a calming and stable influence on her husband. Although he
could be imposing, combative, and even belligerent outside his home, Benton was always kind and supportive to his family. He obviously enjoyed
his domestic life and, despite the pressures of his position, was devoted to
Elizabeth and their six children.

Once a full-fledged member of the Senate, Benton wasted little time in
becoming an active participant. He was especially concerned about land
reform policies and expansion. His first notable order of business was, on
behalf of his small farming Missouri constituents, to resolve overlapping
French, Spanish, and American land claims in the lower Mississippi Valley.
In true Jeffersonian fashion, he also fought to keep public land prices below
market value so that the typical American family could afford to buy acreage of its own. Expansion was another important matter for Benton. While
he questioned whether the United States would ever get clear title to the
Oregon Territory, he encouraged American occupation of the region. His
concern was that without an American presence, the British might dominate the flourishing northwestern fur trade that had become important to
Missouri. In addition to Oregon, Benton joined a growing coalition who
sought to acquire Texas. He was particularly angry at Secretary of State

John Quincy Adams for apparently dealing away Texas when he acquired Florida.

During his early years in the Senate, Benton came under the spell of Henry Clay. He had admired the Kentuckian since before the War of 1812. Additionally, Elizabeth Benton's cousin Lucretia was Clay's wife, providing a loose family connection. Politically Benton agreed with most of Clay's positions. Like the speaker, he proposed that the national government should encourage internal improvements and road building. Although he had some reservations about Clay's call for a protective tariff, he cautiously voted for it. The two men both claimed to be expansionists with a sense of manifest destiny that they actively pursued. Clay's defense of the Second Bank of the United States (BUS) was the one area where the two obviously disagreed. Nevertheless, Benton considered Clay to be the best successor to President Monroe and campaigned for him during the 1824 presidential election.

The maneuvering and deal making that characterized the 1824 election created a permanent breach between Benton and Clay. Though Benton did not believe the rumors that Clay and Adams had made a corrupt bargain, he was suspicious of an evolving ruling elite dominated by the New England commercial interests that backed John Quincy Adams. Likewise, Benton was dismayed by Clay's apparent disregard for his constituents when he cast the Kentucky vote for Adams. A critic of the electoral college, Benton argued that the popular vote should determine the president. Since Jackson had received more votes than any other candidate, he should be considered the winner. The break from Clay alienated some important supporters back in Missouri, but Benton proved to be an adept political power broker aligning diverse interest groups behind his leadership. As it would throughout the rest of his political career, this tactic enabled him to remain somewhat independent but still maintain the support he needed to retain his position in the Senate.

During the next four years, Benton became an unrelenting critic of the Adams administration. He disagreed with the new president on virtually every important issue. Most offensive was Adams's approach to public land. The new president intended to use public lands to pay the nation's debts. The key to the plan was selling land at a market price. Benton complained that such a policy would eliminate most average Americans and ultimately benefit only wealthy speculators. The Missouri senator was further upset by Adams's steadfast defense of the BUS and his call to raise the tariff. Both policies, in Benton's opinion, encouraged the flow of capital into the Northeast and away from the rest of the nation. In general, Benton grumbled that Adams misused his executive power, especially in regard to patronage, and that his misguided policies undermined the nation's future.

By 1828 Benton was a solid supporter of Andrew Jackson. Both had put their personal dispute behind them, and they had renewed their friendship several years earlier. Politically the two men shared similar views on most important issues, especially expansion and the BUS. In campaigning for Jackson, Benton continued to criticize effectively the Adams land policy, a stand that appealed to many Missourians. He was also able to continue the political realignment within his state that he had begun four years earlier. In the end, Jackson's victory demonstrated Benton's power in his home state and established him as a voice for westerners as influential as any, including Clay.

Jackson's presidency was a productive time for Benton. Jackson renewed interest in acquiring Texas, which encouraged Benton. Jackson also supported the land reforms that Benton had fought for since coming to the Senate. It was while negotiating land policy that Benton helped to set off the explosive Hayne-Webster debate about the tariff and states' rights, one of the most important congressional debates during the Jacksonian era. Though Benton opposed the tariff, he did not challenge the administration's reluctance to repeal it. Nor did he question the administration's stand that South Carolina enforce the tariff. He did, however, quietly work for a compromise and was happy when one was achieved (though not happy that Henry Clay was given credit for the bargain). On another notable controversy, the Maysville Road bill, Benton defended Jackson's veto. He claimed the bill was part of a secret campaign to use western and southern taxes for the benefit of northeastern commerce.

The other issue that tied Benton closely to Jackson was the controversy about the BUS. If there was anyone as outspoken in opposition to the bank as Jackson, it was Benton. In several blustery speeches, he complained that the BUS had acquired almost dictatorial power over the nation's economy. He portrayed the institution as a breeding place for special interests and special privileges. He claimed that the specie, or credit notes, it issued undermined the financial independence of most Americans and infringed upon state powers. When it became clear that Congress would pass a rechartering bill, Benton devised various amendments that defused the bank's power. He eventually resorted to obstructionist tactics to prevent the recharter vote. Upset that he had lost his battle in the Senate, he was delighted when Jackson vetoed the bill.

As he became Jackson's chief defender in the Senate, his power and influence grew steadily. His ability to fend off regular challenges in Missouri further added to his political stature. By Jackson's second term, Benton emerged as one of the most powerful leaders in Congress, generally acknowledged as the western counterpart to the Clay, Webster, and Calhoun triumvirate. Like Clay, Webster, and Calhoun, Benton was one of the more effective speakers in Congress because of his aggressive, unrelenting style. However, whereas each of the "great triumvirate" was also known for his eloquence and ability to dismember almost surgically an adversary's argument, Benton's method was to verbally pummel and smother those who disagreed with him. Some in Congress dubbed him "the great sledgehammer." Blessed with an extraordinary memory and extensive knowledge about history and literature, he was able to inundate fellow debaters with facts, figures, and opinion. The end result was an often long, sometimes blustery, but usually thought-provoking speech.

Suggested as a possible successor to Jackson, Benton, unlike many of his ambitious contemporaries, discouraged such talk. Instead he remained focused on banking reform. Happy that the nation's revenues were no longer going to the BUS, he was alarmed at the speculative frenzy that accompanied the change. Gambling on future federal deposits, recently created "wildcat" banks issued credit notes that encouraged speculation. Armed with notes that quickly became overvalued, speculators were able to monopolize land purchases that pushed land prices higher and generated more need for credit. Although Benton agreed that each state, rather than the national government, should have the power to administer their banks, he was concerned that spiraling credit would soon push the nation into another economic panic. His solution was to establish the value of money on the value of gold and silver. Nicknamed "Old Bullion" for his stand, he became the leader of hard-money advocates in Congress.

The panic that Benton feared descended upon the nation just weeks after Jackson left office. Eventually President Van Buren proposed the creation of an independent treasury as a solution. Benton, who suspected that the panic was the product of a plot by the BUS to get a new charter, agreed with the plan and defended it in the Senate. He also pressed the administration to lower the price on public lands, arguing that lower prices would reduce the demand for credit and enable average Americans to purchase land. The revenues could be used to pay government debts, which would help to alleviate further the economic problems. Benton fought fiercely to get approval for his proposals in the Senate only to see them fail in the House of Representatives.

As the economy slowly recovered, Benton's attention shifted to two equally explosive issues: expansion and slavery. Tension with Great Britain in the Oregon Territory grew as population migrated into the region. Since 1820 Benton had contended that the region should be American. However, alarmed by the rhetoric during James Polk's 1844 presidential campaign, he was not ready to go to war for the land. Instead, he maintained that the United States should negotiate a border somewhere between the 49th parallel and the 54°40" line. In 1846 the Polk administration, despite threatening to seize the region forcibly, acted upon Benton's calls and evenly split the Pacific Northwest with the British.

Benton considered the situation in the Southwest even more dangerous. For two decades, he had eagerly sought annexation of Texas. However, by the 1840s he worried that annexation might produce some dire consequences including a war with Mexico. With relations between the two nations deteriorating, he devised legislation that called for the gradual annexation of Texas. He hoped that a compromise, much like the one with the British in the Northwest, could avert hostilities. Even after American forces battled Mexican troops along the Rio Grande, Benton strongly urged negotiations rather than an armed conflict. During the congressional debate about a formal declaration of war, Benton joined the Whig opposition. Nevertheless, in a show of solidarity, he voted with the Democratic majority despite maintaining grave reservations about the eventual outcome.

An important reason that Benton tempered his long-time support for annexing Texas was the slavery dilemma. He was certain that any expansion into the Southwest would entail a risky debate about the institution. It was a problem that had significantly intensified during the previous decade. Initially Benton blamed anti-slavery forces for attempting to polarize the nation over the issue. However, in time he concluded that southern slave proponents were equally responsible. He feared that they were using Texas as a way to force the issue and possibly dissolve the Union. With a crisis looming ever larger, Benton increasingly challenged Calhoun, who he accused of maneuvering the South into an irreversible stance. Morally Benton was not opposed to slavery but for political reasons he disapproved of its expansion. While agreeing that slavery should be permitted in states where it already existed, he argued that Congress was responsible for determining the status of slavery within new territories. Straddling the rapidly shrinking middle ground between two uncompromising factions, he worried that a war with Mexico, which he was certain the Untied States would win, could push the slavery debate to a new, potentially dangerous level.

Throughout the war Benton supported the administration, but his drift away from the Democratic mainstream continued. Though he and Polk had worked closely together on numerous occasions, Benton was concerned that the new president had become too aggressive about expansion and too supportive of slavery. The breach became complete when Polk accepted the court-martial of John C. Fremont, Benton's son-in-law. Married to Benton's oldest daughter, Fremont had already established himself as one of the premier adventurers in the Rocky Mountains and far West. At the outset of the war, he was commissioned into the army but soon collided with another officer in the West. The confrontation ended in Fremont's court-martial, a trial that Benton followed closely. Entirely supportive of his son-in-law, Benton was angry at the verdict and livid when Polk agreed with the decision.

As he had feared, the conclusion of the war significantly heightened tensions between North and South. Rejecting Calhoun's claim that Congress had no authority in deciding the slave issue, Benton argued that the Wilmot Proviso, which would have prohibited slavery in new territories, was consistent with the Northwest Ordinance in 1789. Additionally, since slavery did not exist in New Mexico, California, or the Oregon Territory, he concluded that the Proviso was already in operation. As Clay's Omnibus Bill took shape, Benton criticized it for trying to do too much in a single piece of legislation. Instead he advised that the bill should be offered as five separate pieces, a suggestion that Clay and Stephen Douglas successfully pursued. Benton's support for the Compromise of 1850 further separated Benton from the southern Democratic leadership.

Benton's stand on slavery became a target of mounting criticism from many in Missouri. After he voted against the Fugitive Slave bill that had been endorsed by the South, some Democratic leaders openly derided him as pro-northern. Meanwhile, his traditional Whig opponents continued to oppose his economic and land policies. Still a powerful force, both politically and physically, Benton aggressively fought back, attempting to forge once again the kind of coalition that he put together so many times throughout his political career. However, this time the opposition was too strong. In 1851, unable to maneuver around his detractors, he lost the seat he had held for thirty years. Instead, a pro-slavery Democrat was selected to replace him in the Senate.

After his defeat Benton remained active politically. Reorganizing his support, he won election to the House of Representatives in 1852, where he served one term. While in the House, he became an outspoken advocate of a transcontinental railroad. In promoting the venture, he took the lead in organizing the Nebraska Territory. Unfortunately questions about slavery stymied his efforts. When it was decided that Nebraska Territory should be split in half with popular sovereignty employed to decide the status of slavery in the southern half, Kansas, Benton balked. In his last significant congressional speech, he warned that popular sovereignty was a recipe for disaster. Despite his efforts the Kansas-Nebraska Act was approved, and within months vicious fighting and bloodshed characterized Kansas.

After his term in the House, Benton made an unsuccessful run for governor of Missouri in 1856. He also spent much of the last four years of his life pursuing scholarly projects. He had, after leaving the Senate, written a two-volume account of his thirty years in Congress. Encouraged by the work, he began a massive sixteen-volume record of the debates in Congress from 1789 through 1850. Battling cancer, he completed the final volume just hours before his death in April 1858.

BIBLIOGRAPHY

Benton Collection (St. Louis: Missouri Historical Society); Benton Papers, Personal Miscellany (Washington, D.C.: Library of Congress); William Nisbet Chambers, *Old Bullion Benton, Senator from the New West: Thomas Hart Benton, 1782–1858* (New York: Russell and Russell, 1956); L. T. Collier, "Recollections of Thomas H. Benton," *Missouri Historical Review* 8 (April 1914): 136–141; Thomas J. C. Fagg, "Thomas Hart Benton," *Missouri Historical Review* 1 (October 1906):

22–37; Robert W. Johannsen, *Manifest Destiny and Empire: American Antebellum Expansionism* (Arlington: Texas A&M University Press, 1997); Perry G. McCandless, "Thomas H. Benton: His Source of Political Strength in Missouri from 1815 to 1837," Ph.D. diss., University of Missouri, Columbia, 1953; Theodore Roosevelt, *Thomas Hart Benton* (Boston: M.S.G. Haskell House, 1899); and Elbert B. Smith, *Magnificent Missourian: The Life and Times of Thomas Hart Benton* (New York: J. B. Lippincott Company, 1958).

SAM HOUSTON
(1793–1863)

The saga of Sam Houston is one of the more fascinating during the Jacksonian era. President of the Republic of Texas, governor of Tennessee and Texas, war hero, adventurer, and avaricious land speculator, Houston was a unique personality. With Andrew Jackson as his role model, he shared much of his mentor's political philosophy and emulated the path to prominence that Jackson had taken. Quixotic, egotistical, and at times ill-disciplined, he could also be a shrewd and compelling leader. He was the consummate opportunist whose quest for wealth and power had few limits. Among the most outspoken expansionists of the period, he backed up his words with deeds. At the same time he was one of the few to defend Indian rights, in part because he periodically lived among the Cherokee and developed an unusual appreciation of Native American civilization. A man of deep loyalties and strong convictions, he nevertheless compromised his support of slavery to spare the nation civil war. Without question, Houston was one of the more complex characters during the Jacksonian era.

Sam Houston was born in 1793. He spent his first twelve years on his family's moderate plantation just east of Lexington, Virginia. The fifth of nine children, he never had a particularly close relationship with his immediate family. Though he was his father's namesake, young Sam had little regard for his father. Even his father's service as a captain under George Washington during the Revolutionary War had little influence on young Sam. His mother, Elizabeth, burdened by children and necessary household chores, never developed a close relationship with her son. Estranged from parents and siblings, Sam did become close to several in his extended family. One of them, the Reverend Samuel Houston, introduced the boy to classical literature, which remained a passion throughout his life. Sam was also drawn to a few cousins, aunts, and uncles as surrogate parents.

When the elder Houston died in 1806, he left his family deeply in debt as a result of several risky investments. Selling the family farm, Sam's mother moved her children to land near Maryville in central Tennessee. The family soon established a successful plantation and, within two years, Elizabeth became part owner of a local general store. Sam, who had little interest in farming, was expected to assist in the store but proved no more attracted to commerce than he was to agriculture. Instead, he preferred literature and exploring in the woods. At sixteen, with tensions growing between him and the rest of his family, he simply ran away. Except for an occasional brief visit home, for the next three years he lived with a village of Cherokee. Named "Raven" by the village that took him in, he easily adapted to life with the Cherokee, learning their language and customs. Had it not been for the growing hostilities that accompanied the War of 1812, he might have stayed with them longer.

Division among the Cherokee as well as pressure on them from both the British and Americans forced Houston out of his village and back to Maryville. In need of money and still reluctant to assist in family enterprises, he opened a school. Though he had rarely ever attended school himself, he had a reputation as well read and intelligent. Twenty local children with few alternatives available in the backwoods settlement enrolled in the school. After a successful 1812 summer term, Houston paid his debts, closed his school, and began pursuit of a military career. His first step was to enroll briefly in a nearby academy to better learn mathematics. Six months later, a day short of his twentieth birthday, he enlisted in the United States Army. His strapping six-foot-five frame and intelligence soon attracted the attention of his commanding officer, Thomas Hart Benton. Within a month the young private was made a drill sergeant and, three months later, commissioned an ensign.

In early 1814 Houston's regiment joined Andrew Jackson's army as it began a campaign against Indians in the lower Mississippi River Valley. At the bloody Battle of Horseshoe Bend, Houston, who had recently been promoted to lieutenant, was shot in the thigh with an arrow almost as soon as the battle began. Later, after wrenching out the arrow, he led his men back into battle at Jackson's command. Limping into the enemy's volleys he was struck by two musket balls, one in the right shoulder and one a few inches lower that shattered his arm. Given up as dying, he was carried from the battlefield to await the inevitable. Despite the prognosis, Houston survived and along with other badly wounded troops was hauled back north for medical attention. After a long recuperation, much of which was spent back in Maryville, he eventually recovered most of the use of his right arm, but his thigh never completely healed.

Certain that his future lay in the military, Houston in late 1814 accepted reassignment to Jackson's army. After briefly joining the general in New Orleans, he was sent to New York to have the musket ball removed from his shoulder. By the time he was able to return, Jackson was back in Nashville laying the foundations for future political endeavors. The general remembered Houston's bravery at Horseshoe Bend and included him in his activities. It was Houston's first brush with politics and helped pave the way for his appointment as Indian subagent to the Eastern Cherokee. Aware of his unique relationship with the Cherokee, Jackson recommended him for the position. However, Houston resigned in less than five months after being smeared by unsubstantiated charges that he had provided Indians with whiskey and because of personal differences with his new boss, Secretary of War John C. Calhoun.

In mid-1818, with almost a year's back pay in his pocket, Houston returned to Nashville to study law. Freed from having to seek employment and blessed with a capable intellect, he mastered his lessons quickly. At the same time, he joined several local organizations and spent many hours sampling the wares of local taverns. He also made regular visits to Andrew Jackson's plantation, the Hermitage. The general considered Houston to be a budding protégé, and Rachel Jackson treated him as a surrogate son. Passing the state bar examination just six months after beginning his studies, he accepted an offer to practice in a small town thirty miles south of Nashville. Because he was the only lawyer in the area, his business flourished, but he was increasingly drawn to politics, Jackson, and life in Nashville.

Along with his legal activities, Houston rapidly climbed the state's political ladder. With Jackson's assistance he was appointed adjutant general of the Tennessee militia shortly after beginning his law practice. Carrying the rank of colonel, the position entailed few actual responsibilities but brought much new prominence. Building upon his growing status and connections, he was elected attorney general of Davidson County the following October. A year later, in 1821, he was elected major general of the state militia. Confident, popular, and ambitious, in just two years he had become an integral part in Jackson's Tennessee organization. The next stop was election to Congress in 1823, the same year that the Tennessee legislature selected Jackson for the Senate.

From his seat in the House, Houston mirrored most of his mentor's positions in the Senate. Advocating expansion and internal improvements in the West, he spent much of his time promoting Jackson's 1824 presidential candidacy. After John Quincy Adams's disputed election, Houston immediately became part of the opposition to the new administration. Within months he was writing pro-Jackson pamphlets and helping to build momentum for another presidential run by the general. Meanwhile he was also maneuvering for his own gubernatorial run. With few detractors in Tennessee, and, as always, Jackson's support, Houston won a convincing victory in the 1827 gubernatorial election. Jackson's election a year later further enhanced his ever growing political status.

Soon after Jackson's victory, Houston's political career came to an abrupt halt. In January 1829 he married Elizabeth Allen. Seventeen years younger than he, Eliza was the daughter of a prominent planter and horse breeder who Houston had first met four years earlier. Eliza was intelligent, attractive, and an excellent equestrian. She was also strong willed and accustomed to being the center of attention. Watching her mature from a girl to a young woman, Houston became captivated. After a brief formal courtship, the two were wed. Unfortunately the marriage came apart immediately. The young bride expected a dutiful husband but Houston, who throughout his life had rebelled against any constraints placed on him, regularly abandoned Eliza in favor of his favorite taverns. He was also in the midst of planning a reelection campaign and had little interest in domestic activities. His jealousy and temper added to his wife's growing contempt. Just three months after their wedding, Eliza moved back home to her parents. Houston pleaded with her to return to Nashville, but she would not. Disgraced by the events, he recognized that he would not win reelection the following fall. In mid-April, overwhelmed by his marital problems, he resigned as governor, sneaked out of Nashville, and exiled himself to the West.

Houston spent three weeks traveling from one Mississippi riverboat to another, gambling, drinking, and considering where and how to begin a new life in the West. Thoughts of Oregon Territory were appealing, but the lure of Texas was undeniable. For almost a decade, Houston had been interested in the region. In 1822 he bought into a speculative Texas land company. As a congressman he had advocated acquisition of the Texas and criticized the Adams-Onis Treaty, which apparently made such an acquisition impossible.

Amid rumors that he was on his way to start a revolution in Texas, Houston returned to the Cherokee in Arkansas. Many questioned his motives. On one hand, Jackson's Indian removal policy was creating ever growing inter- and intratribal tensions. Likewise, hostilities with settlers on the frontier seemed unavoidable. Houston was one of the few who could calm the potential troubles. At the same time, there were concerns that he intended to organize tribes and invade Texas. Among those quietly encouraging him was his former regimental commander, Thomas Hart Benton, who from his seat in the Senate coveted Texas. Regardless of Houston's ultimate intentions, few doubted that his adventure included a quest for wealth and power.

Soon after rejoining the tribe, Houston was accepted as a citizen of the

Cherokee Nation. The designation enabled him to function as an official Cherokee representative. Armed with his new status, he and three Native American compatriots traveled to Washington to negotiate on behalf of the tribe. It was the first of two journeys Houston made to the Capitol between the fall of 1829 and early 1830. Ostensibly his purpose was to pursue tribal business, and dressed in Indian attire he presented a list of Indian grievances to President Jackson. Aside from tribal matters, he concocted a number of his own schemes. After lambasting the government's Indian agents, he unsuccessfully maneuvered for a contract to deliver to the Cherokee various staple supplies that their treaties with the United States called for. In essence he hoped to become a government Indian agent while also serving as a Cherokee representative. In another escapade he tried to round up investors in speculative land ventures in eastern Tennessee and Texas. When not promoting his various money-making plans, he could be found at a local tavern boldly proposing an armed expedition against Mexico. It was a call that worried even Jackson.

Unsuccessful in his various promotional activities, Houston made a stop in Nashville on his trip back to Arkansas. Once again in search of investors, he instead discovered that he was not welcomed in his home state, and with few alternatives he completed his journey back to Indian Territory. Using $6,000 he made by selling the last of his Tennessee land and a loan from a Cherokee chief, he opened a trading post, bought some livestock, and tried to settle into life as a merchant. Meanwhile, acting as a self-appointed spokesman for the tribe, he initiated a series of published commentaries lamenting Indian conditions. He also married Tiana Rogers, the widowed daughter of a Scots trader and a Cherokee woman. Though not yet divorced from Eliza, his Cherokee citizenship apparently put him beyond the reach of American law. Likewise, as a member of an Indian nation, he was able to circumvent regulations that prohibited him from selling alcohol to his native neighbors. However, his devious business ethics and heavy drinking soon disillusioned Cherokee leaders.

Restless as ever and thoroughly unsuited for life as a merchant, Houston launched another effort to acquire a chunk of Texas. Proposing to operate as a land agent, he secured tentative backing from several New York speculators. He also requested and was issued a government passport from President Jackson. His instructions were to negotiate with border Indians. Jackson wanted to keep border relations peaceful. Houston, on the other hand, hoped to enlist the natives in the Texas revolution that he planned to lead. Though his investors' funding fell through, Houston would not be deterred any longer. Bidding farewell forever to Tiana, he transferred possession of the trading post to her and in December 1832 at last plunged south of the American border.

Texas in 1832 was a bubbling caldron of avaricious speculators, unscrupulous adventurers, unsavory officials, as well as families in search of farmland. In less than a decade the American population had grown to outnumber Mexican nationals by more than 5 to 1 (Long, 48 and Almonte). From the beginning, relations between settlers and Mexican authorities had been troubled. In 1824, the year that Stephen Austin brought the first 300 migrant families south of the border, Texas lost its status as an independent Mexican state, thus removing the potential for political autonomy. Mexico also required the new, predominately Protestant settlers to support the Catholic Church. Likewise, Americans who intended to use slave labor on their farms discovered that Mexico prohibited the institution. Unstable Mexican governments and ever changing policies further alienated the newcomers. Finally, the Americans considered Mexican officials inherently inferior to those of northern European heritage. These political and cultural differences as well as the increasingly seamy character of the new population made Texas ripe for rebellion by the time that Houston arrived.

Houston's first year in Texas was filled with opportunities. His initial stop was in central Texas where, during a visit with Stephen Austin, he was given, at no cost, a tract of land in Nacogdoches, one of Austin's settlements. Though a newcomer, his military, political, and legal experiences instantly established him as a prominent member of the community. Soon after, he was elected to represent the town in discussions with the Mexican government. Meanwhile he joined two others in acquiring more than 150,000 acres and applied for thousands of additional acres of free land. Recognizing another opening, he began practicing law again. He also pursued his self-defined duties as an American Indian agent by negotiating with the Comanche Indians along the Red River border region. When reporting the discussions to Jackson, he warned that Texas was bound to revolt against Mexico and if the United States did not actively support the rebellion, Great Britain would. At the same time he was advocating rebellion, he converted to Catholicism to strengthen his relationship with Mexican authorities.

By the autumn of 1835, Texas was on the verge of a revolution. Thousands of eager, land-hungry immigrants and adventurers who were flooding into the region added to the instability. Whereas some leaders, including Austin, advocated peace, Houston and others encouraged rebellion. During the previous year, Houston had made trips to Washington and three other cities in search of investors and support for Texas independence. Upon his return he, like a half-dozen compatriots, organized his own band of "defenders" who pledged to resist Mexican authority. His military background and aggressive stance earned him appointment by the insurrectionists' provisional administration, the General Council, as commander of all Texas forces. Concerned about the problems involved in defending the northern border against Indians and launching an attack against Mexican forces at the same time, Houston cautiously directed his armies. However, with the General Council lacking authority and badly divided, various rival rebel commanders, acting as virtual warlords, pursued their own interests. By early 1836, chaos reigned throughout Texas.

Independence was finally declared in March 1836. At the time there were at least four different rebel armies scattered throughout Texas. Officially appointed commander and chief of the Republic of Texas, Houston technically commanded all rebel forces but in reality still had little control. As he continued to focus on the threat of an Indian attack in the north, several independent armies disregarded his directives and prepared to battle Mexican forces throughout central and southern Texas. In late February, after he had successfully negotiated a border agreement with Cherokee, Houston turned his full attention to the Mexican army and geared up to assist the southern troops. However, by that time Mexican General Santa Anna, a skilled military leader who was known as "Napoleon of the West," was about to engage the divided Texas forces. His initial attack would soon come against a band of Texans barricaded at a San Antonio mission.

Houston first heard about the battle at the Alamo while attending independence activities 150 miles to the northeast. Two weeks later, as he cautiously organized his own forces, he learned about another massacre at Goliad. The two defeats effectively ended the Texas resistance in the south. Shocked by the losses and aware of Santa Anna's approaching armies, Houston began a month-long retreat to the east. The exodus was joined by hundreds of fearful migrant families. Criticized by troops who wanted to stand and fight and accused of being thoroughly inebriated much of the time, Houston kept his army away from the enemy. Finally in mid-April at the San Jacinto River, he turned and confronted Santa Anna. In the battle that followed, Houston, disregarding a severe ankle wound, fearlessly led the charge. In only eighteen minutes his men routed the larger Mexican force and the next day captured Santa Anna. Houston emerged from San Jacinto a hero though not above criticism that he was completely intoxicated throughout the entire confrontation.

Weakened by infection from his shattered ankle, Houston, after negotiating a tentative armistice with Santa Anna, was taken to New Orleans for medical treatment. He spent the next three months recuperating in the Crescent City. By July, when he returned, a new internal struggle for control had begun. The provisional president, David Burnet, one of Houston's most severe critics, proved incapable of leading the new Republic. He stood by as the military degenerated to near anarchy. Quasi-warlords continued to prowl throughout Texas and were encouraged by hundreds of recently arrived mercenaries. Additionally, land-hungry newcomers threatened the cautious peace with the Cherokee and Comanche along the northern border. Burnet had also allowed the Republic's coffers to be drained dry while debts mounted. The new nation's approaching presidential election appeared to offer little chance for immediate improvement. The two candidates, Stephen Austin and former Governor Henry Smith, represented extremes on the political spectrum with almost no acceptable middle ground. Houston's return added a new dimension. The popular hero had vast support among the general population as well as in the military. With a little encouragement he joined the presidential campaign and in September was elected, garnering an overwhelming 80 percent of the votes.

As the Republic's first president, Houston focused on a variety of priorities. In an effort to generate new unity, he chose cabinet members who represented a broad range of political positions. He also aggressively sought annexation or, at a minimum, official recognition from the United States. However, despite regular pleas to his former mentor and friend, Andrew Jackson, the American administration steadfastly resisted recognition until Jackson's very last day in office. Economic stability was another concern. Houston pursued loans and trade agreements with the United States and various European nations. Unfortunately, Europeans, troubled by the use of slavery and uncomfortable about the Republic's general instability, provided little assistance. The real economic salvation for Texas, as always, remained land. Despite all the problems, speculators and anxious farmers continued to flood into the new Republic. They bought land and created numerous new settlements, one of which was named for the Texas president and temporarily served as the capital city.

Though Houston was able to begin solving some of his new nation's troubles, one problem that remained divisive was the Indian issue. Still concerned about an alliance between Indians and the Mexican government, he labored feverishly to head off hostilities but was unable to pacify either side. To appease the Comanche and Cherokee he offered gifts, made promises, pursued new treaties, and attempted to initiate a formal survey of Indian lands. When diplomacy and gratuities failed, he cajoled and threatened. Meanwhile he implored fellow Texans to abide by previous agreements and implied that he would use the military to defend Indian lands if necessary. His efforts were no more effective at assuaging Texans than they were with Indians. Instead his support on both sides ebbed and, much to his chagrin, by the end of his one-year term in office both sides had begun resorting to violence.

Once out of office, Houston intended to refill his empty pockets. Traveling throughout the Gulf States, he sold land in the proposed town of Galveston. One prospective buyer was Nancy Lea, a resolute Alabama widow of a Baptist minister. While making his sales pitch, he was introduced to Lea's twenty-year-old daughter, Margaret. He was instantly smitten. She was equally taken by the tall Texas hero. Even before concluding his business with her mother several days later, Houston and Margaret began discussing marriage. Resuming his travels, he promised to return for her and, after a brief stay in Nashville, he did. The reunion, however, was not as comfortable as he had hoped. The Lea family was well aware of

Houston's reputation as a hard drinker, a controversial general, and a way-ward husband. Unwilling to hand over young Margaret, the family care-fully scrutinized her suitor. Reluctantly, Nancy agreed to the marriage only after an appropriate engagement period. In May 1840, a year after they had met, Houston and Margaret were wed.

The union had an immediate effect on Houston. At Margaret's insistence he curtailed his consumption of alcohol, eventually joining several temper-ance organizations. Additionally, for the first time family became important to him and during the next twenty years he and Margaret had eight chil-dren. A woman of strong religious convictions, his wife encouraged him to share her beliefs, which over time he did. Margaret was prone to health problems, some real and some imagined, which kept Houston, who was often away pursuing various political activities, constantly involved with his wife's travails. She had also lived a very sheltered life before meeting her husband, and he attentively worked to maintain her patriarchal pro-tection throughout their marriage. In so doing he became, aside from chil-dren and church, the focus of her existence.

Land rich but cash poor, Houston set out to provide his bride with a suitable new Texas home. Building just north of Houston in Huntsville, he considered farming but the endeavor he knew best was politics. Within months of his return, he was enmeshed once again in a pursuit of power and, more specifically, the approaching presidential election. Conditions in Texas had deteriorated during his absence. His successor, Mirabeau Buon-aparte Lamar, took a far more aggressive approach toward both Native Americans and Mexico. Though eventually successful, wars against the Co-manche and Cherokee had ravaged a portion of Texas. Meanwhile, Santa Anna was back in power and appeared anxious to challenge the Republic's independence. A concern about an alliance between Mexico and various Indians nations loomed over the Lamar administration. In response the Texas president, without approval from his legislature, launched an ill-conceived military campaign to Santa Fe. The effort was a dismal and ex-pensive failure that significantly added to the Republic's debts. Likewise, foreign nations, including the United States, remained wary and unwilling to provide much-needed financial aid. Fortunately, newcomers were still eagerly buying land, but most other commercial activity was almost para-lyzed by the various problems.

Once Houston committed to the 1841 presidential campaign, there was little doubt about the outcome. Garnering three times more votes than his opposition, he easily won a second term as president. Back in office, this time for a three-year term, he immediately prepared to restart an accom-modating Indian policy. Though opposed by most Texans, Houston argued that his efforts would provide some new options for the Republic. Obvi-ously an end to the warfare would free up money and men that could be used against Mexico. Likewise, peace with the Indians would undermine

Santa Anna's attempt at a military alliance. With peace the Indian trade could be resumed, thus aiding the floundering economy. Despite sharp complaints from the Texas Congress, Houston began to implement his plans. The new president also took a far more cautious approach toward Mexico. He sought to withdraw Texas troops from the Santa Fe region and called for an end to the Republic's alliance with rebellious states in the Yucatan. His goal, as it had been four years earlier, was to fortify a defense before initiating an offensive. Again the Texas Congress balked. Instead legislators passed a bill calling for the annexation of a huge portion of northern Mexico including both Upper and Lower California as well as what later became the New Mexico Territory.

Saddled with an aggressive Mexican policy and a weak Texas military, Houston sought alternatives. Tensions in the disputed region between the Rio Grande and the Nueces River added some immediacy to the problems. In 1842, amidst sporadic hostilities, the Texas Congress voted to declare war against Mexico. Houston, however, vetoed the bill and instead pursued diplomatic options. Requesting military assistance from the United States, he again encouraged annexation. At the same time he sought European alliances. Though falling short of a defensive partnership, he was able to win formal recognition from Great Britain despite the ongoing British concern about slavery in Texas. Skillfully playing British interests against American anxieties, Houston presented yet another possibility to both nations. He openly contemplated the creation of a new western nation that would include Texas, the northern states of Mexico, and the Oregon Territory. His efforts paid off in early 1845. Despite stiff opposition from antislavery advocates in the United States, the Tyler administration narrowly approved annexation.

Statehood immediately followed annexation and, as expected, led to war between the United States and Mexico. As one of the new state's first senators, Houston was a grand supporter of the war and one of the first to advocate an all-Mexico strategy. Throughout the rest of his life, he called for the conquest of Mexico, if not by the United States then by Texas. An outspoken proponent of America's manifest destiny, he considered the acquisition of Mexico as simply a step along that path. Additionally, the downfall of Mexico would provide an opportunity for his home state to expand its borders both to the south and especially to the west. Striding through the Senate chambers attired in traditional Texas garb, he consciously used his reputation as a living western hero to promote his war goals. He also used his image to encourage suggestions that he might someday soon become a formidable presidential candidate.

Even before the war began, Houston understood how ominous the slavery issue was to the nation's future. Representing a slave state and a slaveholder himself, he supported the institution. He also agreed that only the states had the right to legislate slavery within their borders. However, more important to him than the status of slavery was national unity. Although he denounced invective northern abolitionist rhetoric, he considered southern "fire eaters" even more threatening. Their goal appeared to be disunion. Unlike idealistic young abolitionist leaders whose influence was limited to pockets of supporters, "fire eaters" were usually from prominent southern families that had held powerful positions at all levels of government for generations. At the top of Houston's list of dangerous slave defenders was John C. Calhoun. Houston and Calhoun had had a nasty run-in in 1818 while the South Carolinian was secretary of war. Calhoun had accused Indian agent Houston of misappropriating government funds. During Jackson's presidency, personal relations between the two festered. Now, as the war with Mexico concluded and the slavery issue polarized the nation, a new chapter in their feud began.

In opposing Calhoun's apparent push toward secession, Houston found himself in an increasingly vulnerable position. After the Mexican War, many in Texas and the South considered any limits on slavery a threat. By abstaining from the vote on the proposed Guadalupe de Hidalgo Treaty to end the Mexican War, Houston stood out as the only southern senator who did not officially oppose the agreement. He also supported admitting California to the union as a free state and prohibiting slavery in the Oregon Territory, though not in New Mexico. In 1850 he was one of the few southern leaders who refused to attend the Nashville Convention because the creation of a southern confederacy was to be discussed. Later that year Houston supported the Compromise of 1850, which included limits on slavery. On several occasions he did verbal battle in the Senate with Calhoun and others. He impassionedly argued that the nation could only achieve its manifest destiny through unity. Secession, he claimed, would be a folly for the South as well as the nation, and he implied that those who promoted separation might be committing treason. Although his moderate stand established him as a nationalist rather than a sectionalist and brought him a growing following in the North, it badly eroded his support in Texas.

Houston attempted to use territorial expansion to fortify himself in his home state. He continued to encourage the acquisition of large portions of Mexico, particularly the Yucatan peninsula. Additionally, with a growing insurrection in Cuba, he believed that the island was ripe for American occupation. Though he supported the Compromise of 1850 as a whole, he complained about limits that the Compromise put on Texas expansion into New Mexico. He also joined Jefferson Davis in enthusiastically supporting a southern route for a transcontinental railroad, understanding that the railroad would cross Texas and, therefore, bring many commercial opportunities to his state. For this reason, as well as the consequences he feared for Great Plains Indians, he voted against the controversial Kansas-Nebraska Bill. However, despite his efforts to placate Texans, the state legislature became so disillusioned by his stand on slavery that fully two years before his term in the Senate ended, his successor was chosen.

Houston's political career did not end when he left the Senate. In 1857 he ran for governor but with no party support and, as always, short on funds, he lost. Three years later he again ran for the same office. This time he was able to build a coalition of support from various interest groups and fragments of the state's disintegrating Democratic Party. Charismatic as ever, he was elected governor on the eve of the Civil War. Still an outspoken opponent of secession, he resisted separation but by early 1861 recognized that Texas could not stand alone against the rest of the South. In mid-February, with grave reservations about the future, he accepted the call for a referendum vote on secession. Overwhelmingly, Texas voters chose secession. The same day that Lincoln was inaugurated, Texas officially left the union of states and prepared to join the Confederacy. Unable to pledge allegiance to the new Confederate government, Houston left the governor's office and retired to his home in Cedar Point near Galveston.

Houston spent the last three years of his life attempting to avoid financial ruin and lamenting the war. Always short on cash, in the past his land holdings had provided a way out of debt. However, the war killed the Texas real estate market and significantly limited Houston's ability to pay creditors. Even more upsetting than his family finances was the course of the war. On a personal level, his oldest son, Sam, Jr., was shot and nearly killed near Vicksburg. The war also posed a threat to his own well-being. Despite his abiding support for his state, he was periodically denounced by overly passionate confederates for not being a true patriot of the South. Occasionally the criticism included threats against his life. On a broader level, the carnage and suffering that shrouded Texas, the South, and the nation was almost more than he could endure.

In mid-July 1863, two weeks after Lee's devastating defeat at Gettysburg, Houston contracted pneumonia. He died on July 26. Controversial in life, he remained so after his death. During the remaining years of the war, his detractors continued to portray him as a traitor to the South. However, soon after the war his reputation was restored. Texans again considered him to be the founder of their state, emphasizing his courage and leadership during both the Republic era and the initial years of statehood.

BIBLIOGRAPHY

Juan N. Almonte, "Statistical Report on Texas," *Southwestern Historical Quarterly* 28, no. 3 (January 1925); William C. Davis, *Three Roads to the Alamo* (New York: HarperCollins, 1998); Donald Day and Harry H. Ullum, eds., *The Autobiography of Sam Houston* (Norman: University of Oklahoma Press, 1954); Llerena Friend, *Sam Houston, the Great Designer* (Austin: University of Texas Press, 1954); Jack Gregory and Rennard Strickland, *Sam Houston with the Cherokee, 1829–*

1833 (Austin: University of Texas Press, 1967); Marquis James, *The Raven: A Biography of Sam Houston* (New York: Macmillan, 1990); Jeff Long, *Duel of Eagles* (New York: William Morrow, 1990), 48; and John Hoyt Williams, *Sam Houston: A Biography of the Father of Texas* (New York: Simon and Schuster 1993).

THE WHIGS

HENRY CLAY
(1777–1851)

There was no more adept nor ambitious politician in Jacksonian America than Henry Clay. A brilliant lawyer, an indomitable statesman, a magnificent public speaker, and a charismatic personality, he was one of the era's preeminent leaders. He was also one of the era's more controversial figures. Although he could win friends easily, his fiery temper and razor-sharp verbal attacks occasionally produced bitter enemies. Likewise, his constant quest for power alienated colleagues and cast suspicion upon even his most magnanimous actions.

Henry Clay was a child of the American Revolution. He was born in Hanover County near Richmond, Virginia, in 1777. As a youngster he was dubbed "the mill boy of the slashes," a nickname that referred to a low, swampy area around his childhood home and implied that he was of meager means. In reality, Clay was reared in relative comfort. His father was a Baptist minister who operated a tobacco plantation that included twenty-one slaves. Henry was four years old when his father died, but even then the family fortunes remained relatively stable. Henry inherited two slaves and stayed with his mother, who quickly remarried, on the family's land. Although the death of his father certainly required an adjustment, it did not cast young Clay into poverty as he would later claim.

Clay's childhood was filled with stories about the exploits and ideas of local American patriots including Patrick Henry, Thomas Jefferson, and George Washington. His formal education was limited to three years under the tutelage of an itinerant teacher, something that Henry lamented throughout much of his life. Ready to make his own way in the world, he became an assistant court's clerk at the age of fifteen. Soon after, he attracted the interest of George Wythe, a signer of the Declaration of Independence and a distinguished professor of law. Wythe recognized Clay's innate intellect and informally took charge of the young man's studies. Over the next few years, with Wythe's help, Clay read law with several of the tidewater's better lawyers and in 1797 earned a license to practice law.

The same year he was admitted to the Virginia bar, Clay crossed over the Appalachians and came into Kentucky. At the time, Kentucky was a year away from statehood and the western extension of American society. For a young man ready to make his mark in the world, the Bluegrass region offered opportunities for fame and fortune not matched east of the mountains. Armed with his law license, a gregarious personality, and a burning ambition, Clay set up shop in Lexington. Over the next decade, the young lawyer established himself as one of the outstanding barristers west of the mountains.

Clay's fortunes in some ways mirrored those of his adopted home. Lexington in the early nineteenth century was a town characterized by growth. It was already recognized as a western center of commerce, banking, and land speculation. Laid out only two decades earlier, the town had nearly 2,000 residents when Clay arrived. Over the next ten years, the population doubled as a diverse collection of western farmers, eastern entrepreneurs and speculators, and eager adventurers became part of the community. Along with the population came institutions that established Lexington as something more than simply a western population center. The first college west of the Appalachians, Transylvania University, was formally established the year after Clay arrived. A public library, a dancing school, two weekly newspapers, and numerous churches and "societies" that offered cultural activities further identified the town, in some circles, as the "Athens of the West."

Henry Clay flourished in Lexington. Six months after arriving, he opened a law practice. His success was immediate. Though he handled whatever cases came his way, his special talents lay in criminal law. Within two years, he was recognized as one of Kentucky's more capable defense attorneys. His ability to move juries, his rhetorical adeptness, and his skill at cutting through an opponent's legal arguments earned him an ever expanding list of clients. Outside the courtroom Clay's reputation also grew. He was active in numerous local civic organizations as well as Lexington's taverns and gambling facilities. An accomplished fiddler, a natural actor, and generous with his money, Clay was a popular patron wherever he went. He was also a fastidious dresser who cut a dashing figure and became one of the town's more conspicuous personalities. His marriage in 1799 to Lucretia Hart, the daughter of a prominent local merchant, further enhanced Clay's standing in the community.

Family and home provided a welcomed diversion in Clay's life. During the first twenty years of their marriage, the Clays had eleven children. Sadly, two children died in infancy and only four survived their father. Though absent from home for long periods, Clay was an indulgent father who cherished time with his children. He also cherished his home, Ashland. In 1806 he had the house built amidst a grove of ash trees one and a half miles south of Lexington. During the next five years, he acquired almost 400 surrounding acres. Considered modest by the standards of the day, the house resembled the Virginia farmhouses Clay had known as a boy. The central section was two and a half stories with single-story wings on either end. Clay operated the property as a farm. Employing an overseerer to handle most of the daily business, he eventually bought between four and five dozen slaves who raised livestock and grew various crops on his land.

Although Clay's profession during his first decade in Lexington was the law, his passion was politics. His first significant political foray occurred in 1798 during a fierce campaign to rewrite the state constitution. Taking a decidedly Jeffersonian stance, Clay emerged as a spokesman for democratic reform. At the core of his arguments was the belief that sovereignty rested with the enfranchised citizen. He argued that in a democratic republic, the will of a free and enlightened people should only be checked by the people themselves. At both the state and the federal levels, government ought to provide the individual with maximum freedoms and protection. Though over the years he significantly revised his understanding of how government could best accomplish its responsibilities, the heart of Clay's political philosophy in 1798 remained constant throughout the rest of his life.

With one exception, Clay, at the beginning of his political career, enthusiastically supported Jeffersonian Republican positions. He agreed with Jefferson that the federal Constitution ought to be interpreted strictly and that the states and the federal government should share power relatively equally. As did Jefferson, Clay was reluctant to acknowledge that the federal government had significant implied powers because of the potential threat to citizen rights and liberties. In 1798 the best examples of this concern were the Alien and Sedition Acts. Passed by congressional Federalists to limit criticism of the Adams administration's French policy, the acts threatened Americans' freedom of speech. Clay vehemently denounced the Acts as did most Democratic-Republicans. He argued that the acts were devices through which the Federalist Party could permanently subdue its opposition. Agreeing with Jefferson that the state ought to have a primary role in determining the constitutionality of federal legislation, Clay endorsed the Kentucky and Virginia resolutions, which were designed to nullify the Alien and Sedition Acts. Clay was also wary about allowing the federal government to maintain a large permanent military. Such a force might be used against those who disagreed with the government.

In 1798 Clay agreed with Jefferson's vision for the future of the nation. He expected the United States to remain essentially agrarian. Manufacturing ought to be for domestic consumption and a step toward self-sufficiency. Competition for world markets did not become a goal of Clay's until later. For him the future lay in the West, and when he did depart from strict Jeffersonian philosophy, as he did in supporting a protective tariff, it was to promote expansion and economic development in the West. He also embraced Jefferson's opposition to the Bank of the United States (BUS) and, fifteen years later, voted against rechartering the bank. He was concerned that the bank was a potential tool through which a wealthy American elite or, worse, foreign investors might gain control of the government. Banks, in Clay's opinion at the time, should be administered privately or by the state. However, by the end of the War of 1812 Clay had reversed his position and staunchly defended the federal legislation to create of a second BUS.

His ardent support of Jefferson in the 1800 presidential election further established Clay as a committed Democratic-Republican and potential officeholder. Three years later, he was elected to the Kentucky legislature. As a member of the state Assembly, Clay advanced commercial interests within the state and defended the state's charter of the Kentucky Insurance Company. The charter, which small farmers generally opposed, enabled the company to act as a banking institution. In defending the company Clay, in essence, advocated the power of the state to charter banks.

Clay's attitude about banking practices began to change shortly after Jefferson's election as president. The change reveals much about Clay as a politician and serves as the first significant example of the economic nationalism philosophy that would characterize his political career. In 1802 the Kentucky legislature chartered the Kentucky Insurance Company. The charter established the company as a monopoly and allowed it to issue an unlimited amount of credit notes. Opponents argued that the legislature had stepped beyond its legal bounds by creating a banking monopoly. Clay defended the company, arguing that the state had the power to charter a bank. Apparently contradicting his own Jeffersonian ideology, he proposed that a bank supported by the government was essential to the establishment of a sound economy. It was an argument that Alexander Hamilton had made while secretary of the treasury and one that Jeffersonians vehemently denounced as aristocratic. Clay countered that his stand was democratic and consistent with Jeffersonian republicanism because a sound banking system would ultimately help small farmers as much as the entrepreneurial classes. The argument, however, did not convince all Kentuckians.

Led by Felix Grundy, Clay's opponents waged an effective campaign against the company. Grundy, acting on behalf of the state's "common folk," argued that the company was merely a trick to cheat honest Kentuckians out of their money and benefit only the "monied classes." He also questioned Clay's motives, pointing out that Clay held stock in the company, his father-in-law was on the company's board of directors, and several of Clay's wealthy supporters stood to make considerable profits if the company was allowed to operate as a bank. Referring to the company as "the monster" just as Andrew Jackson would later label the Second Bank of the United States, Grundy was able to persuade fellow legislators to repeal the company's charter. However, Clay was not willing to concede defeat. Instead he adroitly outmaneuvered his opponents by convincing the governor to veto the repeal and then threatening the bank's opponents with immediate debt collection if the veto was overturned.

The episode provided an immediate boost to Clay's political career. At the most basic level, his chief rival, Felix Grundy, scarred and disillusioned, left the state legislature and became a judge. Two years later, he left Kentucky altogether. The campaign also cemented Clay's ties to powerful entrepreneurial forces in the state and beyond. He emerged as the acknowledged spokesman for the state's commercial and industrial interests. At the same time, because he had strategically sought to allay concerns about his motives, Clay maintained significant support among the state's small farmer population. Afterwards some observers predicted that he was destined for high political office.

Over the next five years, Clay became one of the more powerful men in the nation. In 1806, less than a year after his legislative duel with Grundy, the young Kentuckian was on his way to Washington. He was chosen by the state's legislature to serve out the remaining months of John Adair's term in the U.S. Senate. The journey to Washington was delayed, however, so that Clay could help defend Aaron Burr from charges of treason. Burr was accused of concocting a scheme while serving as Jefferson's vice president to wrestle a portion of the Louisiana Territory away from the United States. The trial was a high-profile event followed throughout the nation. In winning Burr's acquittal, Clay again demonstrated exceptionable skills as a trail lawyer and added to his growing reputation. Only twenty-nine when he entered the Senate, the youngest senator in the nation's history, he spent an uneventful few months in the capital. Upon his return home, he resumed his position in the legislature and in 1808 was chosen as speaker of the lower house of the Kentucky Assembly. Two years later, Clay parleyed his post in the Kentucky legislature into a seat in the U.S. House of Representatives.

Clay's climb to power culminated in 1811 when he was chosen as speaker of the House of Representatives. At the age of thirty-four, Clay had climbed to a place of significant responsibility within the national government. However, at the time few recognized the power that the position possessed. Since the founding of the national government, the speaker's principal role had been to maintain order and facilitate the flow of legislative activity. Clay changed that. He envisioned the position as an American equivalent of the British prime minister. Despite being merely a first-term congressman, Clay understood that from his new post as speaker he could directly influence the policies of the nation.

Clay's rapid ascent was aided by good timing. The nation in 1811 was embroiled in a debate about our relationship with Great Britain. Since the 1790s the British navy had been impeding American shipping in the Atlantic. The British in Canada were also accused of assisting Native American resistance to American settlement in the Ohio valley. These tensions existed before Jefferson came to the presidency but grew significantly throughout his two terms in office. Despite efforts by his successor, James Madison, relations continued to deteriorate into the 1810s. By the time that Clay was elected to Congress some Americans, particularly westerners, had begun to demand action. Others, however, feared that an aggressive policy might lead to a disastrous second war with the British. Henry Clay was an outspoken advocate of an aggressive policy. Also working to his benefit, the debate about the American relationship with England occurred at a time when many of the founding fathers' generation, including Jefferson and Madison, were retiring from public life. This created an opportunity for a new generation to begin directing the course of the nation. Henry Clay relished the opportunity.

From his post as speaker of the House, Clay was able to influence the debate about the nation's British policy. The guiding light of a young, aggressive, and quite capable group of congressmen dubbed the "War Hawks," he invited war. He claimed that a second war with the British would complete the work begun thirty-five years earlier at Lexington and Concord. A war would serve as a final statement of American independence. More pragmatically, he proposed that a war would provide the United States with an opportunity to acquire Canada. He boasted that, despite having no military experience, if provided with several hundred Kentucky riflemen he could clear the British out of Canada within six months. Likewise, a war would enable the United States to at last operate autonomously in the Atlantic thus enhancing American maritime commerce. Clay was among those congressmen most satisfied with Madison's declaration of war in June 1812.

The war provided several opportunities for Clay to demonstrate his leadership among Democratic-Republicans. As speaker of the House and an outspoken advocate of war, he dutifully defended the Madison administration against bitter Federalist attacks despite privately questioning whether Madison was capable of directing the war efforts. On numerous occasions Clay became embroiled in debates with antiwar Federalist congressmen. Skillfully maneuvering through those encounters, he solidified his reputation as a compelling speaker. Although the war was much more difficult than anticipated, he remained committed to an aggressive policy even though it meant sacrificing some of his power as speaker of the House. On the other hand, the demise of the Federalist Party at the end of the war provided potential new support for ambitious and solicitous politicians such as Clay.

With the war at a standstill, in early 1814 Clay was appointed to the five-man delegation that was sent to Europe to negotiate a peace with the British. The experience had a profound effect on him. During his fifteen-month stay, he learned a great deal about the European economy and society and, in so doing, confirmed his own confidence in the potential of the American nation. Through his travels he came to admire European industry and envy the European infrastructure, particularly Holland's canal system. In Ghent, where the negotiations took place, the frustration of diplomacy and the friction within his own delegation were eased by a steady array of festivities. He conferred with European intellectuals, was feted by heads of state, and the French affectionately dubbed him "Prince Hal," an appellation that Clay's future political opponents would often use against him. Though on the surface the Treaty of Ghent achieved few of Clay's original goals, by the time he arrived back in the United States he realized that, in fact, the treaty opened a new chapter in the nation's history.

His experience in Europe brought Clay new status as a statesman and negotiator. In the years that followed, he was offered several prestigious diplomatic posts. Madison offered to appoint him to the American mission in Russia, but Clay refused. A year later Monroe invited Clay to serve as secretary of war, but Clay again refused. Instead he had sought to become secretary of state and would accept no other cabinet post. There were also rumors that Monroe wanted Clay to become the American representative to Great Britain serving at the Court of St. James. The various offers were gratifying and confirmed to Clay that he was among the nation's most capable leaders.

Clay's travels in Europe also reinforced his belief in the greatness and destiny of the United States. In several speeches upon his return to Congress, he lauded the prowess of the American military and the nation's ability to defend itself. He praised American institutions and democratic government and proposed that the United States possessed the potential to dominate the western world. Blessed with abundant natural resources and an industrious population, the nation was ready to begin an aggressive campaign to develop fully its capabilities. Clay proposed that the national government had a responsibility to initiate and direct this campaign. He concluded that national prosperity and dominance would be achieved by developing all facets of the American economy through a policy that became known as economic nationalism.

During the decade following the war, a time often referred to as the Era of Good Feelings, Clay reshaped his political attitudes to accommodate his vision for the American future. On the surface the changes appeared to have carried him away from Jeffersonian Republicanism. In fact, he steadfastly sought to uphold the goals of republican government by promoting nationalistic economic growth. To do this and to keep the American people secure, he believed that the interpretation of the Constitution must be allowed to evolve. He understood that ever changing circumstances would generate an ever changing range of issues and debates. This, in turn, would pit one group of Americans against another. To prevent potential civil conflict, the national government must have powers not specifically written into the Constitution. Only then could the democratic principles of government espoused by Jefferson be maintained. Clay's increasingly nationalistic philosophy was one that many Jeffersonian Republicans as well as some former Federalists readily embraced.

An example of Clay's evolving nationalism was his stand on the BUS. Prior to the war, he had opposed rechartering the first Bank of the United States. Like other Jeffersonian Republicans, he contended that the Constitution did not provide the national government with specific powers to create a bank and that a central bank would encourage aristocracy. Instead, state governments ought to be responsible for overseeing banking operations throughout the nation. By 1816, Clay had reversed his views. As the economy unraveled after the first BUS went out of existence, Clay came to realize that in order to maintain a sound currency and a stable economy, the national government must have the power to operate a central bank. He concluded that if left to the states, the banking system would eventually come under the control of wealthy speculators, thus encouraging aristocracy. Therefore, to encourage both economic growth and democracy, the creation of the Second Bank of the United States was essential.

Clay's budding nationalism was further reflected by his stand on a protective tariff. Traditionally Jeffersonians had opposed such a tariff. They claimed that such legislation benefited a small segment of the economy, industry and commerce, at the expense of all other Americans. Still embracing Jeffersonian principles, Clay advocated passage of a moderate protective tariff on a few selected items. This would provide important emerging industries such as cotton, woolen, and iron manufacturers with some insulation from European competition. It would also strengthen the interdependent relationship that linked farmers with manufacturers and merchants. After the War of 1812, Clay was particularly concerned that European manufacturers were flooding American markets with superior goods at competitive prices. Without protection, American manufacturers would not mature, and without a vibrant commercial/industrial sector, the United States would remain subservient to European economies. Therefore, the judicious use of a protective tariff was in the best interest of all Americans.

After the war, Clay also supported legislation designed to provide federal money for the construction of roads and canals. Since the 1790s, Jeffersonian Republicans had argued that the national government did not have the constitutional authority to implement internal improvements. Clay, however, maintained that an improved infrastructure was essential for both defensive as well as commercial reasons. He recognized that during the War of 1812 the nation's infrastructure had been a major obstacle for American armies. Likewise, an improved infrastructure would facilitate commerce throughout the nation. Although many, including Presidents Madison and Monroe, preferred that internal improvements be left to the states, Clay understood that only the national government had the resources to implement such extensive projects.

Over the next few years Clay merged his support for these issues—the Second Bank of the United States, a protective tariff, and federally implemented internal improvements—into a program he called the "American System." He proposed that his American System was a way to strengthen the economic bonds that tied states and regions together into a nation. Additionally, because it was designed to promote all facets of the economy, the American System was consistent with the goals of Jeffersonian government. According to Clay, the American System would enable the nation to adjust to a modern market economy while at the same time maintaining the Democratic-Republican government created by the Constitution.

An unstated element of Clay's American System was territorial expansion. As were virtually all Americans during the period, Clay was an expansionist, and initially he, like most Americans, advocated expansion through conquest. As leader of the War Hawks prior to the War of 1812, he justified going to war as an opportunity for the United States to acquire Canada. He had also taken an aggressive stance concerning the Louisiana Purchase, claiming that the agreement included Texas. However, Clay's approach to territorial expansion changed dramatically after the War of 1812. The conflict demonstrated the human and financial costs of warfare. After the war, Clay concluded that the United States could more effectively control new lands through negotiation and commerce rather than through conquest. Additionally, Clay's postwar position was more consistent with the American principles of democracy and self-government, as was his strong support of emerging independence movements in South America.

Throughout the last half of his life, Clay sought to avoid military confrontation. In 1818 he strongly opposed Andrew Jackson's aggressive campaign into Florida. Clay reasoned that the adventure committed the United States to an inflexible, dangerous policy. Further, the contested land would eventually come under American control without warfare. As secretary of state during John Quincy Adams's presidency, Clay sought to strengthen the American role in the world by negotiating nine commercial agreements. Later, amidst growing tensions with Great Britain over the borders in Maine and in the Oregon Territory, Clay again advocated negotiations. He argued that because of commercial and demographic factors, the United States was destined to dominate in both, but particularly in the Oregon territory.

The annexation of Texas became the most significant challenge to Clay's brand of expansion. By the mid 1830s, some Americans supported a war with Mexico. At stake were Texas, the Southwest, and California. Throughout the crisis, Clay endorsed negotiations rather than warfare. He had no doubt that the United States military would defeat the Mexican army but argued that a war was not necessary. The burgeoning American economy and growing population would eventually control the disputed lands without warfare. Clay was particularly worried about the likely human cost of a war as well as inevitable postwar political tensions. Governing the new lands would certainly involve a debate about slavery, and such a debate would have the potential to rip the nation apart.

Preserving harmony within the nation was especially important to Clay. Perhaps better than anyone else in his generation, he understood the potential for division. Nurtured by ever changing circumstances, by tensions between economic interests, and by debates between the states and the nation, national unity was constantly being challenged. Clay believed that statesmen like himself were responsible for finding solutions to these differences. For him that meant compromise. Numerous times throughout his career, Clay was instrumental in crafting compromises that resolved potentially explosive episodes.

The first episode to test Clay's abilities as a statesman was the Missouri statehood controversy in 1820. At issue was the question of slavery in Missouri, but more important in the long term was the status of slavery in all future states coming from the Louisiana Territory. As speaker of the House of Representatives, Clay accepted much of the responsibility for guiding Congress through the increasingly hostile controversy. Rekindling passions that had been dormant since the Constitutional Convention in 1787, the debate pitted fervid defenders of slavery and states' rights on one side against equally strident congressional opponents of slavery on the other. Faced with the twin specters of slavery and states' rights, Clay adeptly maneuvered Congress past the increasingly fiery rhetoric of sectionalism. The result was the Missouri Compromise of 1820, which helped preserve the Union for more than three decades and established rules by which the nation could continue to expand.

Upon Clay's return from Europe, the presidency was never far from his mind. In 1824 with memories of the Missouri Compromise still fresh and his potential as a national leader growing, Clay was often mentioned as a possible successor to James Monroe. Clay's emerging economic nationalism appealed to eastern commerce. Many in the West saw him as one of their own, and because he was a slaveholder, he was acceptable to southern planters. In the November election four candidates, including Clay, shared most of the votes cast. None, however, won the necessary number of electoral votes. As a result, for the second time in the nation's history, the presidential election was decided by the House of Representatives. It was a decision that haunted Clay for the rest of his life.

In addition to Clay, John Quincy Adams, William Crawford, and Andrew Jackson received electoral votes. However, because he had finished fourth, Clay was not constitutionally eligible when the election went to the House. In the runoff Congress quickly passed over Crawford because of ill health. Considering his options, Clay recognized that as speaker his influence with fellow representatives could determine the winner. Heavily courted by both sides, his decision was a relatively easy one. He considered Jackson little more than a military chieftain who had minimal experience in the national government and ill-defined policies. On a personal level, Jackson had emerged as Clay's chief rival among western voters. Adams, on the other hand, had extensive experience in government. He shared Clay's vision for the nation's future and supported all elements of Clay's American System. Additionally, Adams did not challenge Clay's base of western support. Amid charges that Clay and Adams had made a "corrupt bargain," Clay threw his full support behind Adams, virtually guaranteeing Adams the presidency. Immediately after Adams won the election, he offered Clay the secretary of state post, thus apparently confirming the corrupt bargain about which Jackson supporters had warned. Although there was no secret deal between Clay and Adams, Clay never satisfactorily explained the "corrupt bargain" episode and his political opponents never let him forget it.

Reacting to Adams's victory, Jackson supporters began a four-year attack on the new president and his administration. Clay was a primary target. He was derided as a political opportunist who had delivered the reigns of government to a wealthy, eastern elite. Even in Kentucky there were charges that Clay had arrogantly abused the power of his office. Adding to Clay's distress, Adams's presidency, pushed by the emerging Democratic Party, quickly began to self-destruct. Making matters worse, Clay did not enjoy the duties of his new post, nor was he a particularly notable secretary of state. However, rather than satisfy his enemies he perservered for four years.

The 1828 election was a bitter contest that in some ways marked the beginning of the modern two-party political system. On one side was the Democratic Party, which had coalesced around Andrew Jackson. On the other was a lesser defined group whose supporters, in 1828, identified themselves as National Republicans but five years later would become the Whig Party. Though Adams was their candidate, the nascent party's emerging leader was Henry Clay. Jackson's overwhelming victory in 1828 solidified Clay in the role of party organizer.

After the election of 1828, Clay returned to Kentucky. Deeply concerned about Jackson's election, he spent the next three years organizing the opposition. Within months of his return home, he began traveling throughout the West, particularly up and down the Mississippi River, denouncing Jackson. The president's veto of the Maysville Road Bill became the first of many policies Clay challenged. The National Road was the nation's first federally funded highway. Beginning in Baltimore and extending across central Ohio and Indiana then terminating in the Illinois Territory, it was constructed to facilitate east-west travel. Supporters of the Maysville Road intended to use federal money to link central Kentucky and the lower Ohio River valley with the National Road. Clay denounced the veto as an example of Jackson's effort to limit economic development in the West. He labeled Jackson's Indian removal policy, which led to the infamous "Trail of Tears," as inhumane; and he criticized Jackson's use of patronage as merely an attempt to expand the power of the presidency. By 1831 Clay had established himself as the most outspoken opponent of the Jackson administration.

At the same time, Clay lay the foundations for a more formal challenge. In December 1831 he was elected to the Senate. The same month, the National Republicans nominated him for the presidency. In designing a platform, Clay combined his opposition to Jackson's policies with his American System. His hope was to appeal particularly to commercial interests in the Northeast and West. Although Clay called for a revised tariff, planned expansion, and federally financed internal improvements, it was his support for the rechartering of the Second Bank of the United States that became the cornerstone in his campaign. The strategy, however, proved to be a major miscalculation. Portraying the bank as part of a plot to impoverish average Americans, Jackson rallied popular support and easily won reelection.

Though defeated, Clay remained a powerful political leader. Just a month after the election, he completed negotiations on another important compromise. For four years, South Carolina had refused to implement a federal tariff passed during the final days of the Adams presidency. Led by John C. Calhoun, opponents of the tariff argued that within a state's borders the state had the right to nullify federal legislation. By late 1832 South Carolina warned that it would secede from the Union if required to carry out the tariff. President Jackson, who inherited the tariff, reacted to the threat as a personal affront. In December 1832, amid rancorous bickering, the president prepared to lead the army into South Carolina and compel compliance. With the nation on the brink of division, Clay skillfully devised a compromise tariff acceptable to both sides. The compromise tariff averted potential civil war and added to Clay's reputation as a statesman.

Clay remained in the Senate for another ten years. During that time he continued to advocate economic nationalism while aggressively opposing Jackson and his successor, Martin Van Buren. No one disliked Jackson more nor was anyone more critical of the president than Henry Clay. Clay repeatedly referred to Jackson as a mere military chieftain whose populist policies were dangerously shortsighted. He warned that by destroying the Second Bank of the United States, Jackson threatened the American economy. Later, Clay blamed the Panic of 1837 on Jackson's banking policies. He was able to get Congress to formally censure Jackson for defying Congress and depositing federal revenues into state banks. Throughout Van Buren's presidency, Clay continued to hammer away at the administration's economic policies. Though he respected Van Buren more than Jackson, Clay remained the most outspoken critic of Democratic policies.

Clay also remained as a guiding force of the Whig Party that, by 1834, challenged the Democrats throughout the nation He was well suited for his unofficial role as the new party's organizer and leader. Likewise, the Whig platform was in many ways a restatement of Clay's own political philosophy and, therefore, provided him with a vehicle through which he might attain the presidency. Considered as a possible nominee in 1836, he lacked his party's confidence because of his defeat four years earlier. In 1840, however, he aggressively pursued the nomination but was passed over in favor of Indian fighter William Henry Harrison. Harrison had done surprisingly well in 1836, and some saw him as a Whig version of Andrew Jackson. Though very disappointed, Clay endorsed the candidate with a typical flair and campaigned for Harrison.

Though Harrison won the 1840 election, Clay expected to play a major role in choosing the new administration. He became so demanding that once in office Harrison refused to see him. After Harrison's death just four weeks into his presidency, Clay turned his attention to John Tyler. Aside from an obvious quest for power, Clay's goal was to undo the independent Treasury Bill that the Van Buren administration had passed as an alternative to a new Bank of the United States. Clay intended to create a third BUS and expected Tyler to support him on the issue. A long time defender of states' rights and opponent of the BUS, Tyler refused to defer to Clay's wishes. In reaction, Clay arrogantly tried to use Congress to bully the new president. Unfortunately for Tyler, many Whigs in Congress, although annoyed by Clay's haughty, often intolerant behavior, were even more angered by Harrison's successor. Within two years of ascending to the presidency, Tyler was virtually without support. The growing tensions worked to Clay's benefit. Despite alienating some, he emerged solidly in control of the Whig Party. When he resigned from the Senate in March 1842, it was to prepare for the approaching presidential election two years in the future.

In 1844 Clay made another attempt at the presidency. So confident was he of winning the Whig nomination that he quietly set in motion his campaign strategy even before knowing against whom he would be running. He reasoned that because there were no other notable candidates, former president Martin Van Buren would be his opponent. In several pleasant visits with Van Buren, Clay determined that on the most controversial issues—annexation of Texas and slavery—the two men generally shared a similar opinion. Thus, his platform could avoid significant statements about either. However, the strategy backfired when the Democrats nominated James K. Polk instead of Van Buren. An astute political strategist who outmaneuvered Clay at almost every opportunity, Polk made the annexation of Texas a primary campaign promise.

During the early months of the campaign, Clay's position on Texas was constantly questioned. Pushed to clarify, he issued three statements: the Raleigh Paper and two Alabama Papers. In them he argued that any attempt to acquire Texas without Mexico's approval would constitute an act of war. Further, even with Mexico's approval annexation should be avoided because it would disturb the delicate balance of power between slaveholding states and nonslaveholding states. Annexation would also jeopardize the American market revolution and encourage international tensions. Although not opposed to eventually adding Texas to the union of states, Clay contended that it should be the product of intelligent, judicious negotiations and planning rather than impetuous campaign promises. Many southern planters who had long advocated annexation were alienated by Clay's statements and, in the end, the letters had a devastating effect on his campaign.

Slavery was another perplexing issue for Clay. A slaveholder himself, he generally took the middle ground between abolitionists, such as William Lloyd Garrison, and southern "fire eaters" who fiercely defended the institution. To Clay, slavery was a necessary evil that should be benevolently administered and gradually eliminated. As did most southerners, he contended that the Constitution gave the responsibility for administering slavery to the states. Immediate emancipation would undermine the entire southern economy and threaten democratic government. If freed, few slaves would have the training and skills necessary to sustain themselves. Additionally, immediate emancipation would create fierce competition and possible conflict between freed slaves and the poor white population. Instead, Clay advocated gradual emancipation and his preferred method was colonization. He proposed that government and civic organizations purchase slaves and relocate them in Africa. Although Clay's stand had been acceptable prior to the Nat Turner insurrection in 1832, by 1844 Americans on both sides of the debate viewed Clay's stand suspiciously.

Plagued by Texas and slavery, Clay experienced his most bitter defeat in the 1844 election. He was so upset by the results that initially he considered the election to be the end of his political career. However, buoyed by public adulation, he soon began preparing for the future once again. Among his immediate concerns was his financial condition. Deeply in debt, he considered selling his beloved Ashland. When a group of his friends learned about his financial problems, they anonymously paid all his debts. Family and health problems also plagued Clay. One son, John, had to be institutionalized and another, Thomas, needed financial help. Most unsettling was the death of his son Henry, Jr., during the Mexican War. Clay's own health also became a growing concern. He had suffered a minor heart attack prior to the 1844 election, and after the election was plagued by recurring fevers and persistent coughs. Despite his travails, Clay remained in regular communications with Whig leaders and subtly began to prepare for yet another run at the presidency.

In the spring of 1848, Clay formerly announced his intention to seek the Whig presidential nomination once again. He had spent the previous year lining up support from northeastern commercial interests and various Whig leaders. Although his stance on most issues had not changed since 1844, he was convinced that the postwar mood of the country had swung toward his positions. Increasingly divided by the unsettled ramifications of the Mexican War, the nation needed a statesman president. Likewise, the new intensity of the slavery debate required an acknowledged leader who could speak to both sides of the issue. What the nation did not need, according to Clay, was another warrior president. Zachary Taylor, who had emerged from the Mexican War as a national hero, appeared to be Clay's chief rival for the nomination. However, because Taylor had virtually no political experience and would accept no compromise on the slavery issue, his election as president would be a mistake according to Clay.

The Whig convention in 1848 was a contentious gathering. Growing tensions about slavery made cooperation between northern and southern Whigs ever more difficult. Likewise, Taylor's popularity and doubts that Clay could win the presidency further split Whigs. When the Kentucky delegation, led by Clay's longtime friend John J. Crittenden, joined the Taylor supporters, Clay recognized defeat was once again inevitable. After four ballots, Taylor won the nomination.

Disheartened by yet another painful defeat, Clay once again redirected his political career. In early 1849, the Kentucky legislature elected him to the Senate. Back in Washington, despite steadily failing health, Clay immediately resumed his leadership within the Senate. However, conditions in Congress proved even more trying than he had anticipated. Polemical arguments heightened by the war with Mexico divided both the House and the Senate. Concern about disunion hung on every issue and every debate. Some southern members were calling for an organizational convention of slave states. As one of the nation's most revered statesmen and foremost nationalists, Clay focused all his remaining strength on finding a way past the troubles that threatened the union of states.

The tensions became a crisis in early 1850. Southern states appeared ready to leave the Union as a result of five apparently unsolvable issues, each of which engendered questions about slavery and states' rights. Cautiously Clay devised an all-encompassing compromise, the Omnibus Bill, which he hoped would save the union of states. Addressing growing tensions about slavery in the land acquired after the Mexican War, he proposed that California should immediately be admitted to the Union as a free state. In New Mexico, however, he suggested delaying a decision about slavery until enough people had migrated there to establish formal territories. Then the decision should be left up to territorial residents. On a third issue, slavery in the District of Columbia, he recommended that slavery should be permitted but that the slave trade should not. According to Clay's plan, slave owners could bring their slaves to Washington but would not be permitted to buy or sell slaves in the nation's capital. On another issue, responding to pro-slave demands, Clay called for a new, more encompassing fugitive slave law with harsh penalties for those caught aiding runaway slaves. Finally, his compromise proposed that the western border of Texas should be permanently set where it had been when Texas was admitted to the Union in 1845, thus ending expansion of the state's authority and slavery into the New Mexico territory. Suffering from tuberculosis and barely strong enough to address his fellow legislators, Clay eloquently presented his series of proposals to a hushed Senate. Though the bill was initially defeated, Clay's plea had so moved one young senator, Stephen Douglas, that a second effort at passage was made. With Douglas's help, the bill was repackaged into five separate proposals. Responding to Clay's wisdom and Douglas's indomitable energy, Congress passed all five bills. Known as the Compromise of 1850, the agreement postponed the inevitable secession by southern states.

The Compromise of 1850 was the last great achievement of Clay's career. He resigned from the Senate ten months after the Compromise. Six months later, on June 29, 1851, he died. In the many eulogies that followed, Clay's friends and adversaries alike agreed that he been among the most effective leaders in the nation's history. William Seward, a former Senate colleague, called him "the greatest, the most faithful, and most reliable . . . statesman" of his time and proposed that his ability to control Congress had been almost magical (Colton, 3: 250–51).

Henry Clay was one of the Jacksonian era's most effective leaders. In a public career that spanned more than four decades he, perhaps more than anyone else, determined the nation's course through the first half of the nineteenth century. Guided by the founding fathers' idealism, Clay redefined and implemented those ideals to meet the needs of a rapidly expanding nation. His economic nationalism helped to transform the United States into one of the world's foremost industrialized powers. Though he never achieved his ultimate political goal, the presidency, he held many positions of power and responsibility including secretary of state, speaker of the House of Representatives, ambassador, and member of both the House of Representatives and the Senate. Three times he crafted compromises that carried the union of states through potentially divisive crises. He provided the philosophical foundation of the Whig Party and was instrumental in institutionalizing the permanent two-party political system that has become characteristic of American democracy. A brilliant lawyer, a powerful speaker, and a visionary political leader, Henry Clay had a profound influence on the course of American history during the Jacksonian era.

BIBLIOGRAPHY

Calvin Colton, ed., *Works of Henry Clay, Comprising His Life, Correspondence, and Speeches*, vol. 3 (New York: Henry Clay Publishing Company, 1897); Clement Eaton, *Henry Clay and the Art of American Politics* (Boston: Little, Brown and Co., 1957); Michael Holt, *The Rise and Fall of the American Whig Party: Jacksonian Politics and the Onset of the Civil War* (New York: Oxford University Press, 1999); Daniel Walker Howe, *The Political Culture of the American Whigs* (Chicago: University of Chicago, 1979); Merrill Peterson, *The Great Triumvirate: Webster, Clay and Calhoun* (New York: Oxford University Press, 1987); Robert Remini, *Henry Clay: Statesman for the Union* (New York: W.W. Norton, 1991); and Glyndon G. Van Deusen, *The Life of Henry Clay* (Boston: Little, Brown and Co., 1937).

DANIEL WEBSTER
(1782–1852)

Daniel Webster was as complex and contradictory a personality as any Jacksonian leader. John Quincy Adams described him as "the gigantic intellect, the envious temper, the ravenous ambition, the rotten heart" of his generation. He became one of the nation's most powerful political leaders though was never a serious presidential candidate. He evolved from being a regional advocate to a staunch nationalist, but his popular support never reached beyond New England. He was one of the highest priced, most successful constitutional lawyers of his day but was constantly plagued by debt. He was honored and respected for his public service yet considered manipulative, untrustworthy, and an opportunist with few bounds. He was an outspoken Hamiltonian Federalist who is generally considered to have been America's first true conservative. An elitist by nature, he generally rejected the evolving populist posture that characterized Jacksonian America. Likewise, he was vainglorious and haughty, and he demanded deference. In an age of great orators he was arguably the greatest, but his single-minded quest for power tainted all his public endeavors. Dubbed "Defender of the Constitution," "Godlike Daniel," "Defender of Peace," and "Dark Dan," he earned all of his sobriquets.

Born in 1782, the same year as Martin Van Buren, John C. Calhoun, and Thomas Hart Benton, Daniel Webster grew up in the isolated interior of central New Hampshire. During his childhood Webster's world consisted of the woods between his father's farmstead near the Merrimack River and

Salisbury, a hamlet three miles to the west. Surrounded by rugged mountains and a dense forest, the family eked out an existence farming. Because Daniel, the sixth of seven surviving children, was prone to illness, his daily farm chores were limited and often shared by his three older brothers. Instead, encouraged by both parents, he spent much of his youth reading.

The most important influence in Daniel's early years was his father Ebenezer. A tall, powerful man well suited for the rigors of life in the New Hampshire backwoods, Ebenezer participated in Sir Jeffrey Amherst's Canadian campaign during the Seven Years' War, rising to the rank of captain. Soon after American independence was declared, he helped organize a local militia and was elected its captain. Over the next few years he fought in several important engagements alongside George Washington, who he revered. By the time that Daniel was born, Ebenezer had returned to his New Hampshire farmstead. During the years that followed, he was elected to several local posts. A staunch Federalist, he passed on his political attitudes to his children. He also encouraged his sons to pursue educational opportunities. Though self-taught, he expected his children to attain at least a rudimentary formal education. However, because of Daniel's obvious intellectual potential, his father was adamant that the youngster receive as much academic training as was available in his rural community. For Daniel, his father stood as a towering role model whose influence would be felt throughout the younger Webster's life.

Ebenezer was not the only one who recognized young Daniel's intellectual potential. His mother, about whom little is known, devised various methods to encourage her son's education. Two older brothers, mediocre students themselves, deferred to Daniel in school matters, even doing his chores so that he could study. Early teachers were also impressed, particularly with Webster's powerful memory. A voracious reader even as a child, by the time he was ten years old he had already memorized long poems and speeches. Years later he regularly sprinkled many of his famous speeches with passages he had memorized as a young boy. Constantly looking for new academic challenges, he began to learn Latin by reading law books. His father, aware that Daniel had surpassed the knowledge of his instructors, enrolled his fourteen-year-old son in the prestigious Phillips Academy in Exeter. A year later, family finances and homesickness prematurely ended Daniel's stay at Philips but not his education. After Daniel had briefly studied with a local minister, his father mortgaged the family farm and enrolled him in Dartmouth College.

Webster thrived at Dartmouth. Guided by well-trained faculty, he matured intellectually. Though struggling with mathematics and science, he excelled in courses that required verbal skills. His powerful memory and ability to reason clearly immediately established him as one of the school's very best orators. By the end of his sophomore year, he was being called upon to deliver various college addresses including a Fourth of July speech delivered to the entire town. It was an oration that he remembered warmly throughout his life. At the same time, he worked to develop his writing style. Composition did not come as easily to Webster as did public speaking but with careful attention he became a compelling essayist. To further develop his skills during his last two years at Dartmouth, he became a regular contributor to the local weekly newspaper.

Both when speaking and when writing, his favorite topics were political ones. Like his father, he embraced the Federalist philosophy of government, opposing change in favor of tradition. He advocated maintaining the ideals of the Revolution and the western traditions upon which those ideals had been established. He regularly defended the John Adams administration as well as the implementation of a strong central government. In 1800 he enthusiastically endorsed Adams's campaign for reelection. Webster also advocated several nationalistic themes. He proposed that territorial expansion was necessary for the nation to maintain its autonomy. He viewed Florida as especially important to the American future. In assessing European affairs, he challenged the motives of the French Revolution, complaining that radical ideals undermined Napoleon's regime. Other Federalist stands—encouraging industry, internal improvements, and the Bank of the United States (BUS)—were also endorsed in his essays. Throughout the rest of his life, Webster altered only slightly his position on many of these issues.

Popular outside the classroom, Webster developed a number of lifelong friendships while at Dartmouth. His ability to enthrall fellow students with spellbinding stories and dramatic readings established him as an immediate favorite. Possessing a thin but solid physique, a pale complexion, and dark, piercing eyes, he had both a commanding and often a brooding presence even as an adolescent. His classmates dubbed him "Black Dan." As a child he had enjoyed sporting endeavors. At Dartmouth he participated in various student gaming activities and was a member of several prominent college social organizations. When he entered the college, he was generally oblivious to his appearance, probably because of his penury. However, by the time he graduated he had acquired a keen fashion sense. To afford an appropriate wardrobe and the other fineries he felt incumbent upon a Dartmouth student, he resorted to borrowing, a proclivity that plagued him throughout his life. Though he was not asked to give the graduation address, an administrative decision he never forgave, Webster considered his college years among the happiest of his life.

A concern about his financial well-being was a specter that constantly haunted Webster. During the years following his graduation, money problems periodically interrupted his plans to pursue a legal career. After leaving Dartmouth, Webster hoped to study law but feared that he would not be able to afford life as a law student. Returning home to Salisbury, he began apprenticing in a local law office. However, just six months into his training he was forced to suspend his studies. His family could no longer afford to provide for him. Additionally, an older brother had enrolled in Dartmouth, further limiting the family income. Though distressed, Webster found employment as a schoolteacher at a small school, Fryeburg Academy, in Maine. To supplement his meager income, he also worked at the local magistrate's office copying deeds. By living frugally and earning extra money, he was able to save enough during his year in Fryeburg to afford to resume his legal studies.

Back in Salisbury, Webster was disillusioned. Bored and again impoverished, he contemplated abandoning his law studies. As a diversion, he became involved in local Federalist activities. It was his first significant foray into politics. A steadfast opponent of Jeffersonian democracy like his father, Webster lamented the inroads that Democratic-Republicans had made throughout New Hampshire as well as the nation. His particular concern was that because the Constitution allowed slaves to be counted when determining congressional representation, southern planters gained an unfair advantage in the national government. Aided by that advantage, Jefferson and his supporters had been able to take over the government and were undoing Federalist principles. Through regular newspaper commentary, Webster gained a degree of notoriety and was invited to become part of his state's Federalist organization.

Amidst his political activities, Webster accepted his brother's offer to move to Boston with him and finish his legal studies there. For the next two years he studied and apprenticed in the office of a well-respected Federalist lawyer, Christopher Gore. The intellectual stimulation and the swirl of life in the city were invigorating. Likewise, the numerous notable Federalist leaders who visited and consulted with Gore inspired him. Deeply influenced by his mentor, Webster completed his studies and was admitted to the bar in March 1805.

After the excitement of Boston, the New Hampshire backwoods had little appeal, but as he had promised his father, Webster returned home upon completion of his studies. He established a practice in a village not far from Salisbury, close enough that he could help his father. Honing his speaking abilities, he soon earned a reputation as an effective lawyer. His ever-growing political involvement also established him as a local Federalist spokesman. Invited to speak at local gatherings, he regularly criticized the Jefferson administration and Democratic-Republican policies in general. The deteriorating relationship with Great Britain was a particular concern. Webster argued that the New England economy would suffer grievously if trade with Great Britain were halted. The culprit, he proposed, was Jefferson who encouraged the problems, in part, as a way for the president to punish his Federalist opposition.

The death of his father in 1806 released Webster from his family commitment in Salisbury. Anxious to seek his fortune in a setting that offered more opportunity, he chose to move to Portsmouth, New Hampshire's busy port city. Portsmouth was also the home of a young schoolteacher, Grace Fletcher, who he had met in Salisbury. Upon relocating, Webster soon established himself as an outstanding young lawyer. At the same time, he courted and married Fletcher. During the next nine years, he became one of the town's most notable lawyers. However, despite an ever-expanding clientele and more generous fees, he was continually plagued by financial problems, periodically relying upon friends and relatives to bail him out of potentially embarrassing obligations. The source of the problem was simply his injudicious management of his earnings.

Although Webster's vocation was the law, his passion remained politics. With relations between the United States and Great Britain deteriorating, he left little doubt about his concerns. His primary target was the Jefferson administration. He warned that Jefferson had allowed the nation to become entangled in the Napoleonic War between Great Britain and France. The president's increasingly restrictive policies toward the British threatened American maritime commerce. Webster questioned the constitutionality of the controversial Embargo of 1807. Enacted in retaliation for the British attack upon the U.S.S. *Chesapeake*, the embargo immediately stifled international trade throughout New England. Webster complained that a primary reason the Constitution had been adopted was to protect commerce and, therefore, the embargo contradicted the framers' intent. In 1808 Webster vigorously campaigned for Federalist Charles Pickney against James Madison. He wrote pamphlets and editorials and gave speeches throughout the state. His efforts helped Pickney win in New Hampshire, though Madison easily won the election. After the election, Webster emerged as one of the chief Federalist spokesmen in the state.

As the nation drifted closer to a second war with England, Webster stepped up his opposition. In various pamphlets he grumbled that New England interests would not be served by a war. Despite his unswerving opposition, once war was declared in June 1812, he took a nationalistic stance by supporting the nation's military efforts. When some New Englanders began contemplating secession, Webster, alarmed by the possibility, lobbied against disunion. At the same time he maintained his criticism of the administration. He blamed the war on Madison, complaining that the president had been tricked by Napoleon and coerced by congressional "War Hawks." Campaigning against Madison again in 1812, he vigorously supported Federalist Dewitt Clinton of New York.

During the presidential campaign, Webster authored the Rockingham Memorial, which was considered by many as a definitive statement about the political interests of New England Federalism. In appreciation, New Hampshire Federalists in October 1812 nominated him as one of their six congressional candidates. All six were elected with Webster finishing second. His election to the House of Representatives began his career in national politics. Over the next thirty-five years, by effectively defending conservative policy in general and New England interests in particular, he established himself as one of the most powerful leaders in the nation.

Webster first came to Congress in May 1813 to attend a special session called by the president. At the time, the war was not going well. The American invasion into Canada had stalled dismally and a British blockade sealed off the Atlantic coast south of New York. In response Madison requested that Congress consider several emergency actions. Like his fellow Federalists, Webster greeted the proposals with much trepidation. Quietly condemning them, he voted against the loans, tariffs, and taxes that Madison maintained were necessary. Likewise, Webster opposed legislation designed to conscript men into the military. Upon his return to Congress the following year, he renewed his opposition but this time became a more vocal participant. His efforts immediately earned him a reputation as one of the best orators in either house. On several occasions he became embroiled in debates with another young, powerful speaker, John C. Calhoun. These would be the first of many notable encounters.

While actively opposing Madison's war efforts, Webster also opposed attempts to divide the nation. During the summer of 1814, Federalists held a convention in Hartford, Connecticut. At the meeting, several Federalist leaders proposed that the New England states formally leave the union of states. As he had done since talk of secession began a few years earlier, Webster vehemently opposed the effort. So committed was he that he convinced New Hampshire's governor not to appoint state representatives to the convention. Webster's efforts ultimately spared him from the embarrassment dumped upon many other Federalists a few months later when the war ended.

After the war, in addition to the decline of his party, the ebullient outlook of many Americans troubled Webster. A new generation with its own vision for the nation's future came to power during the war. The new leaders, who included Henry Clay and John C. Calhoun, seemed convinced that the nation lay at the threshold of profound economic growth and expansion. They proposed that aggressive policies directed at internal improvements would create a market revolution and immediately transform the nation into a world power. Though part of the new generation, Webster did not share its enthusiasm about a market revolution. Instead, he worried that such change would pervert the ideals upon which the nation had been founded. The changes that Clay, Calhoun, and others sought would enable a wealthy, entrepreneurial class guided by market considerations to steer the course of the nation with little concern about the principles of democratic government.

Attempting to temper change, Webster challenged the increasingly nationalistic policies promoted by Clay and Calhoun. At the heart of his opposition was a concern that the powers of the national government were being expanded in ways that threatened individual liberties. Among the issues that most concerned him was the creation of a second Bank of the United States. Although generally in favor of a central bank, Webster warned that the one proposed by the nation's new leaders did not provide enough governmental supervision. Rather, the proposed bank was over-capitalized and gave investors too much autonomy. The tariff was another concern. Claiming to be neither a friend nor a foe of manufactures, he feared that a high protective tariff brought too much prominence to in-dustry. He predicted that this would tie the nation's economy to the well-being of the industrial sector. At the local level, he envisioned the evolution of factory towns composed of an impoverished, dependent laboring class. Opposing Clay and the emerging industrial sector, Webster advocated a low tariff that would subject manufacturers to international competition, thus slowing growth and enabling the nation to remain independent from the specific interests of the industrial sector.

Always concerned about his personal finances, Webster, to supplement his congressional income, began what became a prolific career of pleading cases before the U.S. Supreme Court. Between 1814 and 1852, he argued 223 cases, winning approximately half and appearing before the Court at almost every session during that time. His most important cases included twenty-five constitutional challenges. When arguing before the Court, he often focused upon defining the separation of powers and encouraging the Court to draw sharp distinctions between state and federal authority. Using his legal arguments to fortify his political stances, Webster quickly became a spokesman for conservative government. Coupled with his efforts to maintain traditional political values and ideals, he earned the sobriquet among his colleagues in Congress as "Defender of the Constitution." His work before the Court also earned for him a substantial additional income, though never enough to satisfy completely his debts.

During the next decade Webster argued a series of cases that became benchmarks in American constitutional law. In 1819 he was hired by his alma mater to defend the school against state intervention. He argued that states were bound by the charters they issued and could not alter or impair those charters. This case in particular provided a legal foundation upon which hundreds of turnpike and canal companies were established over the next two decades. The same year as the Dartmouth case (*Dartmouth College v. Woodward*, 17 U.S., 518, 1819), he successfully defended the Second Bank of the United States from taxation by the state in *McCulloch v. Maryland* (17 U.S., 316, 1819). In proposing that if a state had the power to tax the federal government, then the state also had the power to destroy the nation, Webster further defined federal authority. Five years later, in 1824, he again defended the national government's authority in *Gibbons v. Ogden* (22 U.S. 1) by successfully arguing that the state could not in-terfere with the power of Congress to regulate interstate commerce. In each case, Webster proposed that the Constitution limited state powers in favor of federal authority.

After the Dartmouth case, Webster's reputation began to soar. Former President John Adams called him the consummate orator of modern times. On several occasions, even the Supreme Court justices were visibly moved by his arguments. Justice Joseph Story, who at the time was the best legal mind on the Court, considered him the most skillful lawyer in the nation. Chief Justice John Marshall admired Webster's distinction between common law and constitutional law and the clear, reasoned manner that he presented his arguments. He left no doubt that he considered Webster to be as capable as any lawyer he had ever encountered. Further reflecting the chief justice's esteem were court opinions he wrote concerning Webster's cases. Many were heavily sprinkled with Webster's own arguments.

With his law practice booming, Webster became a bit less active in fulfilling his congressional duties. In 1816, shortly after being reelected to Congress from New Hampshire, he moved to Boston. Since his days as a legal apprentice for Christopher Gore, he had considered Boston to be at the center of American civilization. The theaters, libraries, and other cultural endeavors within the city were alluring. Likewise, he relished the chance to become part of the city's elite. And of course, Boston's burgeoning merchant population provided his own practice almost unlimited opportunities.

Life in Boston proved to be all Webster had hoped it would. A full schedule of cultural activities satisfied his intellectual and aesthetic interests. At the same time, his growing law practice provided him with a substantial income and an ever-expanding reputation. Serving a prosperous merchant clientele, he became involved in numerous cases of national importance, many requiring him to travel to Washington. Though he had temporarily retired from Congress after his term expired in 1817, he continued to influence the government through the cases he tried. As he had while in Congress, Webster acted upon a philosophical conviction that at the heart of laws, government, and even civilization lies the right of the individual to pursue property. By asserting the authority of the federal judiciary, as he commonly did, he believed that he was also defending individual rights from abuse by the state. His approach proved very effective, thus providing the Marshall court with many opportunities to further define the federal court's authority. By 1822 he had established himself as the preeminent lawyer among those pleading cases before the federal courts.

Though his law practice continued to be the focus of his endeavors between 1817 and 1823, Webster remained active politically. With the Federalist Party still functioning in Massachusetts, he became involved in the party's leadership but did not pursue office. However, in 1822 a fractious dispute over the mayoral election in Boston splintered the party and again brought him to prominence. Suggested as a compromise candidate or as a possible U.S. Senate appointee, Webster rejected both proposals. Instead he was elected to a less demanding post in the Lower House of the Massachusetts General Court. Later that year, the Federalist congressman from Boston announced he would not seek reelection. Webster was encouraged to run but initially declined because service in Washington would severely limit his law practice thus entailing a substantial reduction in his annual income. Undeterred, some of his wealthy supporters raised subscriptions for him, initially in the form of preferred stocks, which were intended to supplement his congressional income. This began thirty years of similar enhancements including loans and gifts, which enabled Webster to remain in government while still receiving enough income to satisfy his increasingly opulent lifestyle.

Upon his return to Washington, Webster immediately established himself as one of the most compelling speakers and a future leader in Congress. His maiden speech was much anticipated, well attended, and enthusiastically received. Speaker of the House Henry Clay, who admired Webster's legal skills as well as his leadership potential, assigned him to chair the Judiciary Committee. Soon after, the two became entangled in a polite debate concerning the tariff. It was the first of many debates, which, during the next thirty years, involved the era's three great congressional orators, Clay, Webster, and Calhoun.

Avoiding the evolving coalitions associated with the factious presidential election in 1824, Webster continued to advocate traditional Federalist ideals. Not until after the general election and shortly before the election in the House did Webster finally align himself with the eventual winner, John Quincy Adams. However, once committed to Adams he played a significant role in maneuvering congressional support for Adams.

With his reputation both as a congressman and as a constitutional lawyer growing, Webster began to shed the parochialism that had characterized his early political career. The shift was best reflected by his stand on three key issues: internal improvements, the tariff, and the Second BUS. Once concerned that internal improvements sponsored by the federal government would benefit one part of the nation at the expense of the rest of the nation, by 1824 he understood that such improvements would both strengthen and unite the entire nation. Likewise, though still generally advocating free trade, he acknowledged that the federal government had the constitutional authority and periodically had the responsibility to legislate protective tariffs. Within a few more years, his transition to tariff defender was complete. Regarding the BUS, Webster had initially been a wary supporter. However, he admired and trusted Nicholas Biddle, who became the bank's president in 1823. Any lingering doubts he had about the bank were erased when Biddle hired him to do legal work for the bank and later arranged to have him elected to the bank's board of directors.

Political ambition also played a role in Webster's transformation. For the first time, he supported those in power and, therefore, anticipated some tangible benefits. Recognizing that the old Democratic-Republican Party of Jefferson and Madison was disintegrating, he saw an opportunity to assume leadership in one of the dominant emerging coalitions. His alliance with Henry Clay in particular broadened his potential base of support. After Clay became secretary of state in 1825, the Adams administration looked to Webster as its chief spokesman in Congress. Never lacking ambition, Webster reasoned that with careful planning his evolving political status might carry him to the presidency.

In 1827 Webster was appointed to the Senate. Though somewhat reluctant to leave the House where he had become a powerful leader, he acquiesced to pressure from his Massachusetts supporters. Taking his place among the most influential leaders in the nation, he was troubled by the political polarization within the federal government. Most upsetting were efforts by Jackson Democrats, led by Martin Van Buren, to undermine the John Quincy Adams presidency. Sharing similar views with Adams and his National Republicans, Webster prepared to defend the administration.

Unfortunately his move to the Senate was dampened by personal tragedy. In January 1828 his wife Grace died. Grief stricken, he took solace in his three surviving children. The following year his beloved brother and only surviving sibling, Ezekiel, also died, plunging him more deeply into depression. A year later, still emotionally adrift, Webster met and married Carolyn Le Roy, the daughter of a wealthy New York merchant. The union provided Webster's children with a stepmother and Webster with a partner who could help promote his career. A popular hostess, Carolyn was at ease amid the social swirl of both Washington and Boston and accepted the demands of her ambitious husband. On the other hand, she had extravagant tastes that her husband obligingly satisfied despite his constant concern about finances.

During his initial years in the Senate, Webster spent as much time pleading cases before the Supreme Court as he did in Congress. Nevertheless, he participated in several important policy debates, including one particularly notable controversy involving the Tariff of 1828. Referred to as "the Tariff of Abominations" by its opponents, the legislation was part of a maneuver by Jackson Democrats to shear away President Adams's support. Democrats expected that if Adams endorsed the proposal, he would alienate much of the West and Mid-Atlantic region. If he opposed the tariff, he would antagonize commercial interests in New England, his primary base of support. Webster immediately recognized the real intent of the tariff but voted for it because he felt it was in his New England constituents' best interest. As he had anticipated, the bill's passage further weakened Adams politically and helped to assure Jackson's election. Most expected that once in office, Jackson would quickly initiate tariff reduction. However, as president, Jackson took no action because the tariff generated revenues that enabled him to pay down the national debt. The president's decision began a debate that soon threatened to split the nation and brought Webster new acclaim.

At issue was the right of a state to nullify federal legislation, such as the tariff, within the state's borders. South Carolina Senator Robert Hayne, armed with a compelling essay, the *South Carolina Exposition*, which had been published anonymously by Vice President John C. Calhoun, proposed that nullification provided the ultimate check upon the national government's authority. Without it, a state would be unable to protect itself against tyranny from the federal government. Webster quickly accepted the challenge, defending the authority of the national government. He maintained that without the power to enforce legislation, the federal government could not endure. Hayne responded persuasively several days later, warning that Webster's arguments threatened the very foundation of southern civilization.

Webster's response the following day was much anticipated. Before a crowded Senate chamber, he masterfully shredded Hayne's arguments. In an eloquent defense of federal authority, he charged that Hayne was placing the interests of the state above the interests of the people. The Union is more than merely a compact between state legislatures. If each state had the power to decide which laws to obey and which to disregard, the rights and liberties of the individual would be imperiled and the nation would come undone. Webster warned that nullification would create struggles between states and the nation and would inevitably lead to civil war. He concluded his four-hour speech by promising "Liberty and Union now and forever, one and inseparable," a statement that remains a part of his legacy. So powerful and compelling were his arguments that even Hayne, while refusing to admit defeat, acknowledged Webster's rhetorical triumph.

Three years later the nullification debate reemerged, and again Webster became one of its most vocal participants. With the passage of a new tariff in 1832, South Carolina enacted an ordinance of nullification. Encouraged by Hayne who had recently been elected governor and Calhoun who had been appointed to fill Hayne's seat in the Senate, the South Carolina legislature announced that the tariff legislation was null and void within the state. In a rare example of support, Webster aligned himself with Jackson in defending the tariff. Systematically countering Calhoun's arguments, Webster lived up to his "Defender of the Constitution" reputation. He again asserted the authority of the national government, arguing that the state could not dissolve the relationship between the national government and the people who had created it. He concluded that nullification is, therefore, unconstitutional. Though his defense was compelling, the debate ended with both sides claiming victory. In the end, it was Henry Clay who achieved a practical solution. He convinced Congress to enact a compromise tariff that was acceptable to both sides.

Amidst the nullification debate, Webster also played an instrumental role in defending the Second BUS, this time against President Jackson. Anticipating Jackson's opposition, Webster, along with Henry Clay, encouraged the bank's president Nicholas Biddle to apply for rechartering four years early in an effort to make the BUS an issue in the 1832 presidential campaign. Though initially wary of the BUS, Webster had become a great proponent of the bank because it provided a stable foundation for the national economy. In May 1832, after almost six months of maneuvering, he was able to win Senate approval for the recharter. A month later, the House also approved rechartering. The efforts were dashed, however, when President Jackson vetoed the legislation, claiming that the bank was unconstitutional. Webster immediately launched a vigorous rebuttal, demonstrating beyond question that the BUS was constitutional and that by refusing to acknowledge it as such Jackson was disregarding both the Supreme Court and Congress. His endeavors nevertheless failed to win enough support to override the veto.

Always ambitious, Webster recognized that the 1836 election offered an opportunity to attain his ultimate political goal—the presidency. Along with Clay and Calhoun, he was one of the three most powerful members of Congress. However, Clay had lost to Jackson in 1832 and after the nullification battles Calhoun was increasingly identified as a sectionalist. During the summer of 1833, Webster was further encouraged by warm receptions throughout the Midwest. Upon his return to Washington, he began maneuvering for support, cautiously positioning himself whenever possible between Democrats and the various coalitions that comprised the nascent Whig Party. Buoyed by his apparent popularity, influential supporters also began quietly to organize a campaign for him. In 1834 the Massachusetts legislature formally nominated him as the state's favorite-son candidate. However, with the election year approaching, Webster's potential candidacy faded as various others emerged. The biggest challenge came from William Henry Harrison. Webster had considered him as a potential running mate, but by 1835, Harrison had solid support in the West and growing appeal in the Middle Atlantic states. Additionally, the South generally opposed Webster. The mortal blow came when Pennsylvania Whigs formally committed to Harrison. Soon after, Maryland Whigs also agreed on Harrison. By 1836 Webster contemplated withdrawing from the campaign altogether but was asked to continue by his Massachusetts supporters. Fully aware that he had no chance of winning, Webster became increasingly depressed as the election approached. Winning only Massachusetts, his home state, he was humiliated by the results. Most dispiriting, he recognized that he had minimal appeal nationally. With his ultimate prize apparently unattainable, he considered retiring from politics.

The years following his presidential defeat were difficult ones for Webster. In addition to the presidency, Democrats controlled both houses of

Congress, and five Jackson appointees dominated the Supreme Court. The changes on the Court proved especially irritating. In 1835 Roger B. Taney, Jackson's controversial secretary of the treasury, replaced John Marshall as chief justice. Webster had a basic philosophical disagreement with Taney, a states' rights proponent, about the responsibilities and authority of the national government. On numerous occasions, these differences were reflected in the court's decisions about cases pleaded by Webster. In the Senate, Webster remained a powerful voice but was unable to defeat the administration's legislation. His most notable stand was against the creation of a subtreasury as an alternative to the BUS. Adding to his woes was a growing list of debts. A string of risky investments and unwise speculative land purchases forced him to borrow large sums from friends. The economic panic that gripped the nation shortly after Van Buren took office intensified Webster's financial troubles.

The election of 1840 noticeably improved Webster's outlook. Though he still longed for the presidency, he was happy that his rival in the Senate, Henry Clay, had not gotten the Whig nomination and, as a result, saw an opportunity to challenge Clay's party leadership. Webster became an active and influential campaigner for the Whig candidate, William Henry Harrison. In return, he was invited by a gracious president-elect to serve as secretary of state. Accepting the offer, Webster's Cabinet post provided him new power and prominence. The post also enabled him to satisfy some of his outstanding debts by appointing several of his more generous contributors to coveted ambassadorial positions.

Harrison's death just four weeks into his presidency created a crisis for Webster and the nation. Never before had a president died in office and some, most notably Henry Clay, questioned the extent of the ascending president's constitutional authority. At Clay's direction, Cabinet members were strongly encouraged to resign rather than serve John Tyler. Comfortable in his new position, Webster, who had already begun negotiating several delicate issues with the British, was the only Harrison appointee to disregard Clay's call. Instead, he skillfully steered the nation past several troublesome maritime confrontations and a potential border conflict with British Canadians. The end result was the Webster-Ashburton Agreement, signed in 1842, which established a permanent border between Maine and Canada.

While secretary of state, Webster pursued several other noteworthy diplomatic ventures. As it had been in Maine, a formal border between the United States and British Canada in the Northwest was becoming a pressing issue. For twenty years, the two countries had shared the Oregon Territory but as the migration into the region swelled, relations deteriorated. Though his efforts were not successful, Webster did initiate negotiations that a few years later led to a mutually acceptable permanent border. He was also responsible for establishing the Tyler Doctrine that outlined an American policy toward the Hawaiian Islands and China. Fashioned after the Monroe Doctrine, Webster's statement was not as encompassing but did enable the United States for the first time to pursue actively commercial relations while discouraging European colonization in both Hawaii and China.

Webster's tenure in the Tyler administration cast a shadow over the future of his political career. His success as secretary of state in an otherwise unsuccessful administration and his repeated refusal to resign even after the Webster-Ashburton agreement alienated party leaders. When he finally did resign in 1843, Tyler supporters criticized him for abandoning the president. Depressed, tired, and as always fending off creditors, Webster returned to Marshfield, his Massachusetts farm. Aside from pleading cases before the Supreme Court and accepting a couple of speaking invitations, he remained away from public service for almost a year.

The 1844 election provided Webster with an opportunity to recapture his prominence. Upon receiving the Whig nomination, Henry Clay sought his support. Even though the two had been bitter rivals for more than a decade, Webster responded by vigorously campaigning for Clay throughout the Northeast. As powerful a speaker as ever, he again asserted himself as the champion of industry and Whig economic policy in general. His efforts helped Clay carry four New England states. Though the Whigs lost the election, Webster regained many supporters in Massachusetts and was rewarded with an invitation to return to the Senate. In fact, so adamant were his new sponsors that, aware of Webster's constant money problems, they collected $100,000 in subscriptions as an incentive to insure his return (Remini, 600–601). In January 1845, the upper house of the Massachusetts legislature unanimously agreed to send Webster back to Congress.

Webster returned to Congress amidst increasingly strident discussion about territorial expansion. Three days before James K. Polk's inauguration, President Tyler formally annexed Texas. Oregon was another dilemma that potentially threatened the nation. Polk, during his campaign, announced that he was ready to go to war to defend the nation's claim to the entire Oregon Territory. Upon becoming president, he also set in motion efforts to wrestle New Mexico Territory and California away from Mexico. Fortunately, the new administration was able to negotiate a compromise that split the Oregon Territory with Great Britain. However, the agreement heightened chances of a war with Mexico over the southwestern lands.

Webster had opposed annexation of Texas while he was secretary of state and continued to oppose it upon his return to the Senate. Most importantly, he recognized that the acquisition would require an ugly, potentially divisive debate about slavery. Although not an abolitionist, he did consider the indefinite continuation of slavery to be morally, socially, and politically unacceptable. He also agreed with abolitionists that the primary motive for annexing Texas as well as acquiring New Mexico and California was to extend slavery into the southwestern frontier. Therefore, should a war be fought with Mexico it would be for indefensible reasons. Likewise, he worried that financing a war might imperil the nation's slow economic recovery from the Panic of 1837. The Polk administration proposed reducing the tariff to stimulate the economy through free trade. Webster countered that the tariff protected northeastern manufacturing and commerce as well as free labor and farmers throughout the nation.

While reluctantly supporting the war effort once it began, Webster also continued to challenge Polk's motives. He charged that the president had exceeded his constitutional authority when committing the nation to war. To insure that slavery would not be carried into land acquired during the war, he embraced the Wilmot Proviso. Democrats labeled his opposition traitorous. Further, they formally questioned his integrity by launching an investigation into charges that he had misappropriated funds during his tenure as secretary of state. Though the accusations were never substantiated, they undermined Webster's credibility. Adding to his difficulties, two of his three surviving children died shortly after the war. His son Edward had enlisted in the army when the war began and died near Mexico City in early 1848. Two months later, his daughter Julia succumbed to tuberculosis.

The Guadalupe de Hidalgo Treaty brought more rebukes from Webster. Again he protested that the president had misused his powers when approving the treaty and that the treaty was tainted. Unaware that two months earlier gold had been found near Sacramento, he complained that the lands acquired in New Mexico Territory and California were of little value. Only the San Francisco harbor seemed to offer any real future worth. Administering the vast new region would be extremely difficult and fraught with potentially disruptive political debates, especially the unavoidable question about slavery. These debates, Webster worried, might eventually threaten the union of states. Despite the opposition from him and a few others, Congress approved the treaty, setting in motion a course of events that Webster feared.

Webster's opposition leadership during and immediately after the war fed his presidential aspirations. In assessing the potential field of Whig candidates in 1848, he rationalized that if pursued wisely, his chances of winning the presidential nomination were good. The front-runner, General Zachary Taylor, was a political neophyte who had never even voted in a presidential election. Webster reasoned that as a plantation holder with more than 300 slaves, Taylor would have difficulty winning northern votes, and because he claimed to be uncommitted to perpetuating slavery he would have troubles in the South. Another Mexican War hero, General Winfield Scott, was also mentioned as a possible candidate but again lacked political experience as well as Taylor's quiet charisma. The other potential candidate was Henry Clay, but having lost three times already his candidacy seemed unlikely. Buoyed by great expectations, Webster attended the Whig nominating convention only to have his high hopes quickly dashed. On the first ballot, he finished a distant fourth and fell farther behind the eventual winner, Taylor, on subsequent ballots.

Depressed by his lack of national support and the scant political credentials of his party's candidate, Webster reluctantly endorsed Taylor. Though he had always been an energetic campaigner, even on behalf of his longtime rival Henry Clay, in 1848 he campaigned unenthusiastically. When he did speak out, it was to denounce the Democratic candidate, Lewis Cass. Webster feared that Cass's popular sovereignty platform would push the nation toward crisis. Convinced that many within his party no longer reflected his ideals, still gripped by depression from the death of his two children, suffering from several annoying physical ailments, and, as always, deeply in debt, Webster began to contemplate ending his political career.

Disunion hung heavily over Zachary Taylor's brief presidency. Troubled by unresolved questions after the Mexican War, Webster joined efforts to create compromise. In a much-anticipated speech, he condemned the Wilmot Proviso that he had once supported and proposed maintaining slavery where it already existed. Despite sharp criticism from his anti-slavery Massachusetts constituents, he also endorsed Henry Clay's Omnibus Bill, which included a new stringent fugitive slave law. After the bill's defeat Webster encouraged efforts, led by Stephen Douglas, to repackage the grand compromise into five separate bills, known as the Compromise of 1850. Though he had left the Senate before the final passage of the five bills, Webster, as did many others, believed that the Compromise would successfully resolve the sectional crisis that had intensified after the Mexican War.

The death of President Taylor in 1850 brought Webster an unexpected opportunity to serve again as secretary of state. Though he had reservations about leaving the Senate amid the Compromise of 1850 debate, he felt that he could serve both the nation and himself better from the State Department than from Congress. The most experienced member of Millard Fillmore's cabinet, he immediately became the president's chief advisor. He used his new power to promote passage of the Compromise of 1850 as well as implementation of the controversial new fugitive slave law. In crafting foreign policy, he skillfully extended the Tyler Doctrine, opening formal commercial relations with Japan. However, his policies in Latin America and Europe were not as productive. In Mexico he bungled negotiations to secure transportation rights necessary for building a railroad that would link the Gulf of Mexico and the Pacific Ocean. His European efforts were characterized by unnecessary diplomatic difficulties with Great Britain and an embarrassing personal affront to the Austrian charge d'affaires. On a personal level, his return to the State Department provided him with new ways to satisfy debts.

His new prominence also provided Webster with one last run at the presidency. Recognizing the growing split in the Whig Party, he attempted to organize a bipartisan coalition intent upon preserving the union. Though he was able to attract some notable supporters, including several southern Whigs, he was unable to win his party's nomination. As in his previous efforts, he came to the Whig convention with vaunted expectations that were quickly rebuked. Finishing a distant third on the first ballot, Webster was bypassed in favor of General Winfield Scott.

Bitterness at losing the nomination was merely one of several conditions that colored Webster's life after the convention. Seventy years old, he suffered from numerous maladies including allergies and digestive problems. More serious were the lingering effects of a concussion that he had experienced in a fall from a carriage several months before the convention. Chronic depression was another demon that he had battled throughout his life. Alcohol in ever-greater quantities had become his chief medication. However, a life of hard drinking had taken a toll both psychologically and physically. During the summer of 1852, his liver began to fail, hastening his decline. Still clinging to his Cabinet post, Webster battled the problems through the early fall but finally resigned in mid-October. A week later, on October 24, 1852, he died.

Webster's passing marked the end of an era. The last of "the Great Triumvirate," he along with Clay and Calhoun had for over forty years forcefully framed many of the issues that had confronted the nation. Throughout that time, Webster became the chief spokesman for nation's emerging commercial and industrial interests. He also left a permanent mark upon constitutional theory and law. Despite his controversial and at times self-aggrandizing behavior, political friends and foes alike recognized him as one of the preeminent leaders of his generation. Ralph Waldo Emerson eulogized that Webster had raised popular political debate "out of rant and declamation to history and good sense." Others acknowledged him as the finest orator of his age and a statesman who had few peers. With his death, there were those who feared that without his intellect, Clay's skill at forging compromise, and Calhoun's ability to contain southern animosities, the nation's immediate future became ever more perilous.

BIBLIOGRAPHY

Maurice Baxter, *Daniel Webster and the Supreme Court* (Amherst: University of Massachusetts Press, 1966); Maurice Baxter, *One and Inseparable: Daniel Webster and the Union* (Cambridge, MA: Harvard University Press, 1984); Norman Brown, *Daniel Webster and the Politics of Availability* (Athens: University of Georgia Press, 1969); Richard Current, *Daniel Webster and the Rise of National Conservativism* (Prospect Heights, IL: Waveland Press, 1995); Robert Dalzell, Jr., *Daniel Webster and the Trial of American Nationalism 1843–1852* (Boston: Houghton Mifflin,

1973); Sydney Nathans, *Daniel Webster and Jacksonian Democracy* (Baltimore: Johns Hopkins Press, 1973); Merrill Peterson, *The Great Triumvirate: Webster, Clay, and Calhoun* (New York: Oxford University Press, 1987); and Robert Remini, *Daniel Webster: The Man and His Time* (New York: W.W. Norton and Co., 1997).

JOHN QUINCY ADAMS
(1767–1848)

John Quincy Adams provided a bridge between his generation and his father's generation. Exceptionally well prepared for public service, he embraced the nationalistic goals of Jacksonian America but often rejected the methods employed to achieve them. He was a leader whose vision of the American future stretched beyond that of most of his contemporaries. At the same time, he lacked patience for those who did not share his convictions. A brilliant statesman but an unsuccessful president, he became, in some ways, the conscience of his age. Feisty, cantankerous, and fiercely independent, he stridently confronted issues that many others cautiously avoided. Ultimately his crusading spirit helped to push the nation closer to civil war.

Adams was born in 1767 in Weymouth, a fishing village just south of Boston. He was the second child and oldest son of John and Abigail Adams. His parents' forebears had deep roots in the Massachusetts Bay Colony. His father's family came to New England in 1632, just a few years after the colony's founding. Farming the rugged New England soil for more than a century, the Adams family included ties that connected young John to the romantic legend of John and Priscilla Alden as well as several leaders within the colony. His mother's family was also among the earliest to settle in the colony. Rather than farming, they sustained themselves primarily through commerce, shipping, and the church. His great grandfather, Colonel John Quincy, became the namesake of Quincy, Massachusetts. The town was established in part on long-held family land that was later made famous by one of Nathaniel Hawthorne's finest stories, "The Maypole of Merry Mount."

At the time of John Quincy's birth, his father was a young lawyer with a growing reputation. He had already achieved a bit of notoriety by assisting James Otis in challenging British authorities and the constitutionality of the writs of assistance. His father's cousin, John Quincy's uncle, Samuel Adams was an outspoken patriot leader who on numerous occasions called upon John to support the emerging colonial protest. Despite reservations about the consequences of the evolving tensions, the elder Adams was inexorably drawn into the debate and by the time of independence had become a patriot leader himself. Among young John's earliest memories was his father's defense of the British regulars involved in the Boston Massacre in March 1770. The younger Adams was also deeply influenced by the Revolutionary War activities that permeated Boston society during the mid-1770s. Throughout his life, he remembered vividly watching the battle at Bunker Hill and hearing firsthand accounts of the various local hostilities.

Even as a child, Adams understood that his parents had high expectations for him. Both parents established specific bounds for their son's behavior, then encouraged personal independence within that framework. His mother was a stern disciplinarian who instilled strict moral standards. She demanded obedience and constantly warned him not to do anything that would disgrace his family. Throughout his early life, her approval of virtually all personal matters was a requirement. Although John was devoted to his mother, he revered his father. Away fulfilling Revolutionary War responsibilities during much of young John's early years, the elder Adams closely guided his son's intellectual growth. He encouraged young John to make scholarship the focus of his life. In letters, young Adams was challenged with Latin declensions and translations. His father regularly instructed him to search for truth by carefully scrutinizing the past and in all matters to be guided by reason. These paternal admonitions began for Quincy Adams a lifelong quest for knowledge.

In late 1777, the Continental Congress invited John Adams to join Benjamin Franklin and Arthur Lee in Paris and serve as part of an American diplomatic mission to France. Adams accepted the invitation and decided to take along his ten-year-old son. A trans-Atlantic voyage was dangerous at any time of the year but particularly during the winter. Additionally, being at war with one of the world's strongest navies made the trip even more perilous. Nevertheless, both parents agreed, Abigail more reluctantly than John, that their oldest son should accompany his father. The journey would help to lay important foundations for John Quincy's future endeavors and success.

Quincy Adams spent much of the next seven years studying and traveling in Europe. His first journey lasted almost eighteen months and had a truly transforming effect upon him. In May 1778, shortly after arriving in Paris, his father enrolled him in a weekday boarding school. The curriculum was far more rigorous than he had experienced at home, but the studious young Adams enjoyed it and soon won praise for his academic achievements. He particularly enjoyed his language and literature courses. Weekends were spent with his father, who shared a house with Benjamin Franklin, attending concerts and theater. Though he missed his mother and siblings, young Adams relished the cultural and academic life in Paris.

After returning to Boston for a brief stay during the fall of 1779, Quincy Adams accompanied his father back to Paris. This time, his younger brother Charles also came on the journey. Though Quincy Adams periodically served as his father's secretary, the primary purpose of his second European trip was to focus upon his education. As before he was enrolled in a boarding school and again excelled, though neither he nor his father was completely satisfied with the curriculum. When diplomatic work took his father to Holland, young John was enrolled in the prestigious University of Leyden. At the university his intellectual abilities, particularly his aptitude for languages, earned him recognition.

Adams's life as a scholar was abruptly interrupted after a year at the university. Francis Dana, the American commissioner to Russia, was in need of a translator. Though only fourteen, Adams had already demonstrated a masterful knowledge of French, the language used in the Russian court, and was signed on to escort Dana as a translator and secretary. The work proved minimal, which allowed Adams time to continue his studies as well as begin learning German. He also regularly sampled the vibrant cultural life in St. Petersburg. In October 1782, with his assignment in Russia completed, he parted company with Dana and traveled alone to Sweden, where he spent much of the winter. Then he went on to Denmark and northern Germany and finally back to Holland, where he was joined by his father in July 1783. After another year studying and assisting his father in Paris, the two, in mid-summer 1784, journeyed to London and prepared to return to America. The travels had obviously matured young Adams. Upon being reunited with John Quincy after almost two years, John Adams noted his son's new self-confidence and sense of independence. The younger Adams had seen and experienced as much of contemporary European life as had any American. He had become a man of the world who his father called "the greatest traveler of his age."

John and Abigail Adams had decided that upon his return, their son would attend Harvard. Although the young Adams had some reservations about leaving the cultural life of Europe behind and beginning studies at Harvard rather than completing them at Leyden, he remained the dutiful son and prepared to attend his father's alma mater. After some negotiating by his father, John Quincy was enrolled tuition free and with some advanced placement. His two years there were happy ones in which he excelled academically, graduating second in his class of fifty-one. He also earned the reputation as a promising orator and compelling debater.

After Harvard, it was expected that Adams would pursue a legal career as had his father. Not enthused about three years of legal apprenticing, young Adams nevertheless saw few alternatives and prepared to read law. As he had anticipated, his legal studies, although at times challenging, proved confining for him. Likewise, life in Newburyport, a small town that was a twelve-hour ride north of Boston, lacked the culture and society to which he had become accustomed. Self-doubt about his own unrealized potential further clouded his years of legal training. The combined effect of these circumstances was the first of numerous depressive episodes that plagued Adams throughout the rest of his life. Despite having only completed the equivalent of one full year of legal training, he moved back to Boston and opened his own law office.

His legal practice proved no more rewarding than had his apprenticeship. With few clients and dependent upon his father for law books and an office building, John Quincy again questioned his own ability to provide for himself. However, a trip to Philadelphia in early 1791 to visit his father, who had recently become the nation's first vice president, provided a turning point. During his two-month stay, he renewed an interest in public service. Upon returning to Boston, he initiated a series of publications and editorials. Over the next two years, he became an outspoken critic of Jefferson and his political programs, focusing especially upon foreign policy issues. Though he had spent time with Jefferson in Paris and had greatly admired the Virginian, Adams believed that implementation of Jeffersonian principles would be harmful to the new nation. Adams's editorials made him a Federalist favorite in Boston.

One of those stirred by Adams's writings was George Washington. The president had met Adams several years earlier and had been impressed by the young man's intellect. In early 1794 he proposed the appointment of young Adams as the American minister to the Netherlands. Adams had mixed emotions about the position. The annual salary would enable him to at last become independent of his parents. Additionally, the appointment would allow him to escape his law practice and return to Europe. However, he questioned whether he was capable of fulfilling the position's responsibilities. He was also sensitive to the appearance of nepotism and accusations that, despite assurances to the contrary, his father, the vice president, had been instrumental in securing the assignment. Despite his reservations, young Adams accepted the post and set sail for Europe.

Adams remained in Europe for the next six years. Completing his initial assignment to the Netherlands, he spent the final three years in Berlin. Instructed to observe and report European affairs, he proved very well suited for his position. His previous European travels and command of languages were reflected in exceptionally comprehensive and insightful assessments of the evolving conditions on the continent. His most notable task involved reviewing the controversial Jay Treaty. However, beyond the Jay Treaty and corresponding with other American ministers, much of his time was spent pursuing his own literary interests and attending cultural events. It was a comfortable life that suited Adams well.

In late 1796 on a visit to England, John met Louisa Catherine Johnson, who was the daughter of an American merchant in London. Extending his stay, John began a fitful nine-month courtship that ended with his marriage to Louisa in July 1797. During their fifty-one-year marriage, despite several long absences and various difficult times including the deaths of three of their four children, John and Louisa remained confidantes, supporters, and companions. Louisa had an independent spirit and an active mind, and she shared John's passion for literature. She was a gracious hostess and loyally supported John's varied endeavors. She accompanied him on his diplomatic travels and encouraged him through most of his political battles. Though there were periods when their relationship was tested, they shared a mutually supportive marriage. It was a relationship that provided necessary stability in John's life.

The defeat of his father in the 1800 presidential election temporarily ended the younger Adams's ministerial work. Returning to the United States in late 1801, he decided to pursue a career in politics. The thought of resuming his law practice was unappealing. On the other hand, his diplomatic work had demonstrated that a career in public service would enable him to provide for his family and allow time to pursue scholarly endeavors. Setting his sights upon state government, he was elected in April 1802 to the Massachusetts Senate. A year later, after some adept partisan maneuvering, he was selected by the state legislature to represent Massachusetts in the U.S. Senate.

Even during his initial days in elective office, Adams demonstrated the independence and idealism that came to characterize his political career. While a member of the Massachusetts legislature, he challenged the state's partisan leaders by attempting to provide the state judiciary with additional autonomy. Immediately upon becoming a U.S. senator, he took a stand on the Louisiana Purchase that collided with both sides of the debate. In supporting the purchase, Adams alienated the Massachusetts Federalists who had sent him to Washington. At the same time, he criticized the Jefferson administration for not pursuing a constitutional amendment that would formally establish a method for future land acquisitions. Further angering Federalists, Adams demanded that the British honor the border with Canada that had been negotiated after the Revolutionary War. Federalists proposed moving the border well south in an effort to ease tensions and generate new trade with Great Britain.

Adams's support of the Louisiana Purchase and his stand on the border issue reflected his growing nationalism. Keenly aware of the circumstances that limited European nations, he was inspired by the young American nation's potential. Like many of his generation, he anticipated a time when the United States would dominate the entire continent and perhaps the hemisphere. Territorial expansion was a prerequisite for that destiny. However, unlike many Jacksonians, Adams advocated a planned, negotiated, and carefully administered method of territorial expansion. He believed that expansion through compromise and treaty, as had been accomplished by the Louisiana Purchase, was far more productive and less threatening than expansion through conflict.

Life as a senator proved arduous for Adams. Although he generally enjoyed debating issues, he quickly became disillusioned by other aspects intrinsic to his position. He regularly complained that many of his colleagues disregarded the nation's interests in favor of petty personal gain. On several occasions, he lambasted congressmen for abusing their Post Office privileges. He also found that serving in the Senate was expensive. Only by accepting an endowed chair at Harvard was he able to maintain the lifestyle that he felt was expected of a senator. Most troubling was the partisan criticism that he experienced. As tensions with the British mounted during Jefferson's second term in office, Adams increasingly supported the president's policies. Despite vehement Federalist opposition, Adams came to agree with Jefferson that by withholding trade, the Untied States could coerce the British into easing their confrontational policies in the Atlantic.

In 1808, disagreements with Massachusetts Federalists ended Adams's career in the Senate. At issue was Adams's support of Jefferson's very controversial embargo. Maritime merchants complained that the embargo had the potential to suspend all international commerce done by the United States. In New England, some Federalists labeled Adams a traitor. Rumors of a secret deal between Adams and the Democratic-Republicans swirled throughout Boston. While attending the 1808 Democratic-Republican caucus, there were reports that Adams would become part of a Madison administration. Though he maintained that his interests were neither partisan nor personal, Adams was unable to convince his opponents. Rather than reappoint Adams to a second term in the Senate, Federalist leaders in the Massachusetts Assembly selected a Harvard classmate and staunch Federalist, James Lloyd, to replace Adams. Deeply disappointed, Adams returned to Boston and immersed himself into his teaching and scholarship, and he briefly resumed his law practice.

His defeat in the 1808 senatorial election brought Adams an unexpected opportunity to return to Europe. Soon after becoming president, James Madison requested that Adams serve as the American minister to Russia. Though he regretted leaving Harvard, Adams was anxious to return to Russia and happy to be away from the ever more intense political struggles in the United States. In St. Petersburg, the Russian capital, he and Louisa found life a bit expensive, but very satisfying. He became close friends with the czar, Alexander I, with whom he shared many intellectual interests. He also enjoyed observing, gathering, and reporting to Madison information about evolving conditions in Europe. Further, the post provided time for him to personally direct his youngest son Charles's early education, much as his father had done for him. So satisfied was he in Russia that in 1810 he turned down a presidential nomination to the U.S. Supreme Court.

The War of 1812 ended Adams's stay in Russia. A year after the war began, Madison assigned him to head the five-man American delegation negotiating peace terms with the British at Ghent, Belgium. The task proved quite frustrating, though ultimately rewarding. Most aggravating was the slow pace of the talks. Entangled in negotiations with France, Parliament had sent England's primary negotiators to deal with the French. Consequently, a less capable team met with the Americans. Perhaps as a delaying tactic or perhaps because they lacked authority, the British diplomats required parliamentary approval of even minor decisions before committing to them. Adams found the process tedious. Meanwhile, during the long delays, tensions developed between Adams and his fellow Americans, particularly Henry Clay. Adams disapproved of what he considered the excessive social life Clay and the others enjoyed. There were times when he complained that his fellow Americans were conspiring against him. At other times, he moaned that they were not concerned enough about the details of the peace treaty. His temper also alienated delegates on both sides of the negotiating table. Nevertheless, despite the difficulties, Adams persisted and after almost eighteen months a treaty acceptable to both sides was crafted. In the end, he considered the Treaty of Ghent a significant personal achievement.

Madison was also pleased with the agreement. In recognition, the president reassigned Adams to London, the most important American ministerial post. Adams accepted the assignment and for almost two years enjoyed performing his official responsibilities as well as the intellectual and cultural life in London. His stay ended in 1817 when recently elected President James Monroe requested that Adams serve as his secretary of state. It was a position that Adams considered second only to the presidency and, though a bit reluctant to reenter the political world, he eagerly accepted the offer. In August, 1817, after eight years in Europe, Adams returned to the United States.

The nation had changed significantly during Adams's absence. The successful conclusion of the War of 1812 inspired the American people. For the first time since independence, they were confident about the future. The war had demonstrated convincingly that the United States could defend itself against any European power. With a veil of doubt and concern lifted, Americans eagerly began to pursue the nation's potential. It was an attitude embodied by a new generation of leadership. By 1817 the Federalist Party that had been so critical of Adams was dead. In its place, a collection of regional coalitions had evolved. On the surface they appeared willing to cooperatively carry out Jeffersonian democracy. However, embedded within these various groups were the seeds of division. Regional leaders reflected a buoyant, self-confident attitude and, unlike the previous generation, aggressively sought power. They were obviously ambitious and committed to their personal vision of the nation's future. It was a generation that in most ways included Adams but one with which he refused to identify.

Although Adams often criticized the nation's emerging leaders, he generally embraced their methods. He regularly denounced those who allowed their personal ambition to dictate a political position. Instead he portrayed himself as the kind of selfless leader who he believed characterized his father's generation. However, when his leadership was challenged, Adams was not above self-promotion. Likewise, his ambition to lead and, consequently, his quest for power included the kind of adept political maneuvering that he condemned. Although he claimed to be free from regional bias, he consistently supported policies promoted by northeastern commercial interests. Adams also lamented the social requirements expected of powerful political leaders, but he and Louisa plotted a path to the height of Washington society. Philosophically Adams in many ways maintained the ideals of an earlier generation but practically he was as much a Jacksonian as any of his contemporaries.

Adams became secretary of state at a pivotal time for American foreign policy. The successful conclusion of the War of 1812 offered the nation an opportunity to begin asserting its world interests more forcefully than ever before. The American relationship with Great Britain obviously had changed significantly. Both nations enthusiastically reestablished commercial activity after the war and immediately Great Britain again became the primary American trading partner. However, the economic and political consequences of that relationship were still uncertain. Likewise, the final defeat of Napoleon and the end of hostilities between Great Britain and France engendered a revision in the American policy toward France. The growing prominence of Russia and Prussia had also become ever more important to the United States. Finally, the collapse of the Spanish empire and emergence of independent states in Latin America further complicated foreign policy considerations. These new realities would be crucial to the future of the nation. There was no one better suited to devise and administer solutions to these circumstances than was John Quincy Adams.

As secretary of state, Adams sought to further secure the nation from foreign threats and to expand the American domain. Potential border problems were particularly important to him. Among his notable achievements was negotiating a border east of the Rocky Mountains between the United States and the British in Canada. Set at the 49th parallel, the line resolved debates between the two nations that dated back to the American Revolution. At the same time, the agreement allowed unlimited American set-tlement into the region west of the mountains, an area that Adams believed was destined to be inhabited by Americans. Additionally, the British affirmed American fishing rights in bountiful north Atlantic waters east of Newfoundland and Labrador.

Even more notable was the Adams-Onis agreement with Spain. In one of the more brilliant diplomatic maneuvers in American history, Adams transformed a potentially threatening confrontation with two European powers into a significant American land acquisition. Like the border with Canada, the American border with Spain in the southeast and along the Louisiana Purchase region was a source of tension. In 1817 a military campaign by Andrew Jackson into west Florida added to the concerns. Chasing hostile Native Americans into west Florida, Jackson defiantly violated Spanish authority. He compounded the difficulties by executing two British trappers who he claimed were aiding the natives. Jackson's actions created an international incident that had potentially grave consequences for the United States.

Opposing Monroe and the rest of his Cabinet, Adams defended Jackson, setting the stage for the treaty. Better than anyone else in the administration, he understood the problems Spain was having holding onto its Latin American possessions including Mexico. Although important to the United States, Florida was of only limited value to Spain and therefore, Adams reasoned, expendable. Blaming the Indian problems on Spain's inability to adequately administer Florida, Adams pressed Spain for compensation. In the end, Spain agreed to transfer possession of Florida to the United States and in exchange the United States assumed $5 million in damages that Spain owed to individual Americans. Additionally, Spain surrendered its claim to the Oregon Territory to the United States, and the United States agreed not to assist the evolving independence movement in Texas, which was then the northern state of Spanish Mexico. Finally, a border was established between the United States and Spain from the Mississippi River to the Pacific Ocean. The agreement brought to the United States all of Florida and lay the foundation for future expansion into the Southwest. In return, the United States simply promised not to pursue immediately the acquisition of Texas.

Though it carried the president's name, the Monroe Doctrine was one of Adams's most important achievements as secretary of state. Throughout his years on Monroe's Cabinet, Adams paid close attention to the independence movements taking place in much of Latin America. He considered them to be continuations of the quest for democratic self-government that had begun with the American Revolution. Likewise, he recognized that the United States had a unique interest in the fate of Latin America. Concerned that expansionistic European nations might attempt to colonize the nascent Latin states, he pushed Monroe to establish a forceful policy toward Latin

America. Such a policy would establish the United States as the dominant power in the Western Hemisphere and provide a step toward establishing U.S. commercial ties in Latin America. Although Monroe was not enthusiastic about Adams's recommendation, he finally agreed and, during his last year in office, issued the Monroe Doctrine that Adams had prepared for him. It announced to the rest of the world that the Western Hemisphere was closed to future colonization and that any attempt by European nations to expand into the hemisphere would be deemed a threat to U.S. security. The doctrine immediately became the foundation for U.S. policy in Latin America and would remain so for more than a century.

During his last four years as secretary of state, Adams increasingly focused upon the presidency. Comparing himself with the others most often mentioned as Monroe's successor—Henry Clay, William Crawford, John C. Calhoun, and General Jackson—Adams was convinced that he was the most qualified candidate. Therefore, he felt justified in suspending his philosophical opposition to active campaigning. Though he tried to remain above the fray, by 1824 he was thoroughly involved in the contest. Directing supporters, maneuvering the media, and actively seeking voters, there was no doubt that he was running for the presidency.

Adams was disappointed by the election results. He finished second to Jackson in both the popular and electoral votes. However, because none of the candidates had received the required number of electoral votes, the House of Representatives would determine the winner. Anticipating the February election, Adams immediately began wooing representatives. He recognized that some Crawford backers would switch to Jackson, and therefore he aggressively pursued Clay supporters. Because Clay had finished fourth, he was not eligible in the House election but as speaker of the House and as a spokesman for western voters, the Kentuckian potentially held the election in his hands. Though there was little doubt that Clay favored Adams, rumors of a secret bargain between Clay and Adams began to swirl through Washington. Jackson supporters alleged that in return for his support, Clay had been promised a prominent position in the Adams cabinet. When, in the House election, three crucial Clay states guaranteed an Adams victory, the rant of "corrupt bargain" immediately echoed throughout the Capitol and became a Jackson mantra during the entire Adams presidency.

The four years Adams served as president were the most frustrating in his life. Coming into office, he understood that the bitter feelings leftover from the election would not be forgotten quickly. He was also distressed that considerably more than half of the constituency had voted against him. In addressing these concerns, he took a very idealistic approach. He sought to promote growth within the nation while maintaining the general harmony that had characterized Monroe's eight years in office. Unfortunately, in pursuing his goals Adams generally disregarded political realities and instead alienated supporters while providing fodder for his opponents. Even his cabinet, three of whom had served with him on Monroe's cabinet, became active critics of his policies. Vice President John C. Calhoun was another who regularly challenged his decisions.

Though his support in Congress was tenuous, Adams nevertheless embarked upon a broadly defined and ambitious program of internal improvements. In many ways, his efforts were a continuation of Monroe initiatives to improve the nation's roads, canals, and waterways. However, southerners who had been somewhat reluctant to oppose Monroe felt no such constraints in challenging Adams. In other ways, he created his own problems. Calling for sweeping improvements in the nation's cultural and intellectual life, Adams rankled Americans throughout the country. He contended that without a national university, a program of geographic exploration, and a national astronomical observatory, the United States would forever remain intellectually behind Europe. Many Americans considered the call a haughty presidential rebuke.

Management of the public debt was another element integral to the Adams domestic policy. The goal was to retire the national debt. Crucial to Adams's plan was the Second Bank of the United States (BUS). The BUS had been controversial since its chartering in 1816. So divisive were bank policies that its supporters and opponents in some Kentucky and Tennessee communities nearly resorted to armed conflict to resolve their differences. At issue were tight credit policies that generally encouraged eastern commercial and industrial interests while limiting small farmers. Adams supported BUS policies and proposed allowing the BUS more authority in regulating state banks. The proposal renewed factious debate about the bank that did not end until 1832 when Andrew Jackson, a fierce BUS opponent, vetoed the bank's recharter application.

The Adams Indian policy also alienated many Americans. As a nationalist and advocate of expansion, Adams generally agreed with the concept of Indian removal. However, when Georgia requested that the national government assist in moving Indians out of the state, Adams demanded restraint. Acting upon government instructions, the Creek and later the Cherokee tribes had written their own constitution in which they asserted sovereignty. Recognizing the legal validity of the claims, Adams refused to aid Georgia. He announced that the state did not have the authority to enter Indian territory as long as the Indians presented no threat to the people of Georgia, at least not until the national government had time to redefine Indian rights. Further, he warned that if necessary, the U.S. military would defend Indian lands. Although legally correct, the Adams policy angered many expansion-minded Americans, especially those in the lower Mississippi River Valley.

Even in its foreign policy, the Adams administration floundered because President Adams was not able to maintain the nation's hemispheric leadership that he had begun to establish while secretary of state. The source of his problem was Cuba. With the Latin American independence movement spreading into the Caribbean, the United States became concerned that Mexico and Colombia might invade Cuba. In an abortive effort to prevent hostilities, the Adams administration was outmaneuvered by the British who used trade agreements to entice Latin American cooperation. Trying to recapture the initiative, the Adams administration arranged a hemispheric conference in Panama. Though well conceived, the conference was a diplomatic disaster for the United States. As a result, Great Britain further reduced the United States' role within the hemisphere and gained a more secure negotiating position in the Northwest. The United States, on the other hand, lost significant trade opportunities in the West Indies.

The Tariff of 1828, or "Tariff of Abominations" as many in the South called it, became the final assault upon the Adams presidency. Since the 1790s the nation had debated the merits of a protective tariff. Like most from the Northeast, Adams supported a tariff on specific items to stimulate American industry. Jackson supporters in Congress, anticipating the 1828 election, used the tariff debate to once again undermine Adams's presidency. They proposed an exceedingly high tariff, calculating that if signed into law, the tariff would further alienate Adams from the South. If vetoed, it would alienate northern industrialists. Additionally, because the tariff failed to protect woolen manufactures, it would anger at least some northern industrialists even if not vetoed. Passed by Congress, the legislation came to the president's desk. Armed with the power to veto the bill, Adams, like his five predecessors, nevertheless believed that a presidential veto should only be used on constitutionally questionable legislation. Since he saw no constitutional problems with the bill, he signed it into law. By approving the tariff, Adams sealed his own political fate and, at the same time, opened an explosive debate that over the next four years threatened civil war.

In some ways, the Adams presidency was a failure. However, such an evaluation reflects more about the politics of the times than the success of his administration. To his credit, Adams brought about significant internal improvements that, in turn, expanded the economy. Likewise, he nearly paid off the national debt, an achievement that his successor later claimed. Adams's policies also paved the way for a new surge of westward expansion and domestic nationalism. When he failed to accomplish his goals, it was for two basic reasons. One reason was the unprecedented political maneuvering by his opposition. Spawned by the contentious 1824 election and encouraged by the growing popularity of Andrew Jackson, Adams's opponents skillfully and aggressively used the legitimate policy debates to mold diverse regional factions into a united political party. The other problem that doomed Adams's presidency was his own idealism. Although his goals were often visionary, he ignored existing political realities. Instead he expected the nation to embrace his nonpartisan approach to governing. Adams simply was not willing to participate in the evolving political world that surrounded him. Consequently, many of his well-intended initiatives went unfulfilled and his reputation as president suffered.

The election of 1828 was over long before the votes were counted. By mid-September Adams realized that, like his father, he would serve as president for only one term. Nevertheless, the defeat was painful. The campaign was particularly nasty, characterized by vicious personal attacks, and he considered his opponent, Andrew Jackson, completely unfit for the presidency. Through it all, Adams usually remained true to his personal code of ethics, relying upon supporters to solicit votes on his behalf. The size of Jackson's victory only added to Adams's pain. He interpreted his overwhelming defeat as a victory for personalized partisan politics and a repudiation of the virtuous campaigning methods his father's generation had employed.

For someone who usually dwelled upon adversity, Adams put the 1828 election behind him quickly. Within months, he was contemplating a run for the House of Representatives. Both Louisa and son Charles opposed the idea, protesting that such an endeavor was beneath a former president. Adams disagreed. He contended that he could best defend his administration's achievements from a seat in Congress. Additionally, because he had no future political ambitions, he could be an unrestrained foe of the Jackson administration whenever necessary. He also needed the approbation that he believed could come only by winning an election. Finally, and probably most importantly, at sixty-four he was not ready to end a career of almost fifty years in public service. He still possessed an insatiable passion for public life and was willing to endure whatever barbs and aggravations came with it. For Adams, life away from public service was simply unacceptable.

Winning a particularly gratifying election in 1830, Adams began a seventeen-year stint in the House of Representatives that he referred to as his "second career." An idealist as president, he became a pragmatic critic as a congressman. During his tenure, he sharpened many of the qualities that had characterized his earlier political life. Most importantly, he sought independence, reveling in the role of political maverick. Though he refused to identify completely with any political party, in most ways he embraced the policies of the emerging Whig Party. Likewise, he usually promoted the interests and attitudes of New England. Always fierce when defending a position, he was capable of eloquence but just as often resorted to invective attacks. Friends and foes alike considered him tough, irascible, often abrasive, and usually combative. He became so reviled by some southern Congressmen that they dubbed him "the madman from Massachusetts."

As it had been during his presidency, internal improvements remained a priority for Adams. Beyond further developing the infrastructure, he focused upon building new industrial capabilities. Embracing and updating Hamiltonian economic policies, Adams advocated the creation of a national economy administered by the federal government. He contended that modern industrial and manufacturing capabilities must be developed within the United States if the nation was to avoid future European domination. Crucial to such capabilities was a protective tariff. Adams argued that a tariff would insulate budding American manufacturing from European competition and encourage industrial growth. Likewise, the BUS was an essential ingredient to Adams's economic nationalism. The BUS was needed to maintain stable monetary and credit policies throughout the country. Though he shared with most Americans a basic distrust of banks, Adams staunchly supported the BUS during its divisive debates with the Jackson administration. He believed that the BUS provided an opportunity to stitch together all parts of the American economy.

Expansion was another important element in Adams's campaign for internal improvements. An advocate of demographic growth, he was nevertheless concerned that unregulated expansion would squander a potentially valuable national asset. Unsettled public lands could provide the nation with significant revenues if sold at market value. Adams proposed that these revenues could then be used to fund new roads, canals, and railroads that, in turn, would enhance the value of the land. Additionally, this method of internal expansion would be orderly and controlled, providing further benefits to purchasers. Adams sharply differed with Jackson's plan to sell off public lands at the lowest possible price and recognize squatter's rights. The Jackson method wasted a valuable national asset and invited tensions between land-hungry settlers.

The issue with which Congressman Adams became most closely identified was slavery. Until the early 1830s he had done little to oppose slavery. Although he denounced the institution as a stain upon the nation, on numerous occasions he agreed that slaves were the property of their masters. During his term in the Senate, he had voted against limitations on slavery several times. As both a diplomat and secretary of state, he had resisted efforts to eliminate the Atlantic slave trade. During the debate about Missouri statehood and slavery in the Louisiana Territory, he had cautiously remained silent. As president, he had done nothing to limit the institution and agreed with some southerners that the abolitionist movement encouraged slave insurrections. When he did agree with abolitionists, it was to oppose other anti-slavery activists who sought to create African colonies using former slaves.

Two considerations transformed Adams into an anti-slavery spokesman. One was his election defeat in 1828. Never one to forgive and forget, he attributed his loss, in part, to the three-fifths clause that he contended gave southern slaveholders unfair power and undermined democratic government. He complained that regardless of the will of eligible voters, slave states could control the national government simply by expanding nonvoting slave populations. The other transforming factor was a "gag rule" implemented by southern congressmen to prohibit debate about slavery. Adams denounced the rule as demagoguery. Challenging it whenever possible, he cleverly devised seemingly endless ways which included reading anti-slavery petitions and letters, to circumvent the rule. Abolitionists eagerly responded by providing ample ammunition, in the form of petitions, for his assaults. Finding ingenious ways to present the petitions, Adams emerged as the most effective anti-slavery voice in Congress.

His role in defending thirty-nine African captives who were seized from the Spanish slave ship *Amistad* further established Adams as an opponent of slavery. In July 1839, the captives successfully rebelled against the ship's crew. Lacking navigational skills, the Africans were led into American waters, where they were captured and then jailed. In the trial that followed, they were deemed to be free but the Van Buren administration immediately appealed the decision to the Supreme Court. At that point, the defense sought to fortify itself and persuaded a somewhat reluctant Adams to join them. Initially, he simply hoped to expose Van Buren's efforts at pandering to southern slave interests. However, as the case continued he became ever more upset about the administration's blatant disregard for the captives' basic human rights. In a powerful yet eloquent closing statement, he raised the controversy above merely political concerns to one of basic humanity. The address established him from that time on as an anti-slavery spokesman (*U.S. v. Amistad*, 40 U.S., 518, 1841).

Texas was another issue that linked Adams to the anti-slavery movement. From the beginning of the Jackson presidency, Adams believed that the Texas issue was a scheme engineered to promote southern interests. He accused both Jackson and his successor, Martin Van Buren, of violating neutrality agreements and of covertly assisting the insurgence in Texas. He called the Texas revolution a criminal act designed to steal land from Mexico in order to guarantee domination of the American government by slave interests. Adams's fierce opposition helped to prevent annexation until the last moments of the Tyler presidency. Afterward, with a war looming, Adams remained outspoken in his resistance and was one of only fourteen representatives to vote against the war.

His vigorous battles against annexation and slavery, as well as age, sapped Adams's strength. During the Mexican War, his participation in congressional debates waned though he left no doubt about his position on important issues. In late 1846, shortly after winning election to the House for an eighth term, he suffered a mild stroke while walking on the Harvard campus. Though he recovered enough to resume his legislative duties, his health never completely returned. Fourteen months after his first stroke, in February 1848, Adams suffered a second seizure while sitting at his desk in Congress. Two days later, he died.

During more than sixty years of public service, Adams brought a unique perspective to Jacksonian America. Throughout his life, he had attempted to integrate the values of his father's generation with the nationalistic goals of his own generation. An idealist who steadfastly promoted his vision of the American future, he was willing to attack controversial issues, including slavery, which many others avoided. Ultimately the passions that he aroused helped to open a breach within the nation that would only be resolved through civil war.

BIBLIOGRAPHY

Mary W. M. Hargreaves, *The Presidency of John Quincy Adams* (Lawrence: University of Kansas Press, 1985); Marie B. Hecht, *John Quincy Adams: A Personal History of an Independent Man* (New York: American Political Biography, 1972); Paul Nagel, *Descent from Glory: Four Generations of the John Adams Family* (New York: Oxford University Press, 1983); Paul C. Nagel, *John Quincy Adams: A Public Life* (New York: Alfred A. Knopf, 1997); Greg Russell, *John Quincy Adams and the Public Virtues of Democracy* (Columbia: University of Missouri Press, 1995); and William Earl Weeks, *John Quincy Adams and American Global Empire* (Lexington: University of Kentucky Press, 1992).

WILLIAM HENRY HARRISON
(1773–1841)

In a era when westward expansion and personal ambition galvanized American society, William Henry Harrison was well suited for national leadership. Although he was from the tidewater gentry that had led Virginia for more than a century, he built his political career upon the image of a simple backwoods statesman and a brave Indian fighter, much like Andrew Jackson. Popular with Whig leaders more because of his image than his political stands, he brought to the party the grassroots appeal that it needed to challenge the Democrats. His election in 1840 ended a twelve-year hold on the presidency by the Democrats. Serving for only four weeks, he became the first president to die while in office.

Portrayed as a simple backwoods statesman and a "log cabin" presidential candidate, William Henry Harrison was, in fact, born into the upper crust of Virginia society. His forebears came to the colony shortly after its founding and established a prosperous plantation along the James River. From that beginning, the family's patriarchs played a significant role within the colony. They were regularly elected to the House of Burgess and served in a variety of important colonial offices including attorney general and treasurer of the colony. Harrison women brought additional stature to the family. Most notably, William Henry's grandmother was the daughter of "King" Robert Carter, one of the wealthiest planters in Virginia. It was from him that the family acquired Berkley Plantation, where William Henry was born in 1773. At the time, his father was concluding over twenty years of service in the House of Burgess. Deeply involved in the growing colonial protest, he joined Patrick Henry, Thomas Jefferson, and George Washington in staunchly supporting independence. During the war, he served on numerous revolutionary committees and was a member of the Virginia delegation to the First and Second Continental Congresses. A signer of the Declaration of Independence, he became friends with many American revolutionary leaders including Benjamin Franklin, John Dickinson, and John Adams. In 1781, during the final days of the war, he was elected to the first of his three terms as governor of Virginia.

William Henry was eight when his father became governor. Growing up amidst the turmoil and tumult of the war, young Harrison no doubt knew well the heroic stories of his father's famous patriot friends and colleagues. On several occasions, the youngster was himself directly touched by the war. One of his two older brothers as well as numerous cousins fought in the war, and in early 1781 a British army under Benedict Arnold made its headquarters on a neighboring plantation. Soon after the war Harrison was enrolled in Hampden-Sidney College, a Presbyterian school that had been established in 1775. The choice was a curious one because his family had been involved in founding William and Mary College, which the Harrison boys had traditionally attended. From Hampden-Sidney, he briefly attended an academy in Southampton and then at age seventeen began studying medicine with a doctor in Richmond. A year later he was sent to Philadelphia, where he briefly studied under one of America's preeminent physicians and scientists, Dr. Benjamin Rush, at the College of Physicians at the University of Pennsylvania. Harrison's stay, however, was a short one. After only a few months in Philadelphia, he left the school and with the help of Virginia Governor Richard Henry Lee secured a commission as an ensign in the United States infantry.

At the time that Harrison joined the military, the United States was unsuccessfully waging a war against Native Americans in the Ohio frontier. Two disastrous campaigns, the first led by Josiah Harmer and a second by Arthur St. Clair, reflected the sad state of the western defenses. Aging Revolutionary War officers and ill-disciplined, poorly equipped recruits characterized the military. Political debates in the new national government concerning the role of a permanent military also limited the defenses. Assigned to protect the region's growing American population, Harmer and St. Clair instead sharpened already hostile relations in the region. Throughout 1791, bloody attacks on settlers were reported almost weekly in eastern papers. A potential union between the Indians and the British army, which had not yet vacated their western fortifications as promised after the Revolutionary War, further troubled Washington's administration.

After recruiting in Philadelphia for several months, Harrison marched with his company to Pittsburgh and then traveled down the Ohio to Fort Washington (Cincinnati). He arrived in the late fall of 1791 just as St. Clair and his beaten forces were returning from their unsuccessful foray. The months that followed tested Harrison's resolve. At a low point, the western army had barely enough men to maintain its position. An unusually cold winter compounded the problems. On a personal level, Harrison was not popular with his comrades. The troops disliked his aristocratic demeanor, and fellow officers resented that he had received his commission through influence rather than cadet training. Fortunately, the following spring Congress approved of the army's reorganization and President Washington assigned command of the troops to Anthony Wayne. Bringing an army of more than 5,000 men with him, Wayne reassembled the western forces, instilling new discipline and order.

Joining Wayne's army in Pittsburgh, Harrison benefited from his new commander's leadership. Shortly after arriving, he was promoted to captain and became an aide-de-camp to Wayne. The new responsibilities provided him with constant contact to Wayne and an opportunity to learn military principles from the army's most capable officer. For more than a year, Harrison studied Wayne's methods while assisting in training and preparing the revamped forces. The army's ultimate objective was to subdue Indians in central Ohio and open new land for American settlement. When the campaign began, Harrison volunteered to accompany Wayne in leading attacks against Indian strongholds throughout the region. The efforts culminated in a decisive victory at the Battle of Fallen Timbers that shattered the opposition. For his dauntless support, Harrison earned official recognition from Wayne. He was also invited to assist his commander in negotiating the Treaty of Greenville that followed. Harrison emerged from the three-year sojourn under Wayne's command as an acknowledged champion of the West.

Harrison returned to Fort Washington soon after the Treaty of Greenville and was assigned to a settlement fifteen miles south of Cincinnati. There he met Anna Symmes, the daughter of a local judge and major land speculator. After a brief courtship, he and Anna were married in November 1795 despite temporary disagreement with Judge Symmes. Over the next nineteen years, he and Anna had ten children. Two-and-a-half years after his marriage, having served almost seven years in the military, Harrison resigned his commission in favor of a political career. It was a path that the ambitious young man had plotted for more than a year. Aided by a recommendation from Wayne and by Judge Symmes's support, Harrison was appointed secretary of the Northwest Territory. His stay in the post was brief, however. With the Indians subdued, enough population had relocated into the region to require a more formal territorial government. Again, assisted by his father-in-law and several transplanted Virginians, Harrison in 1799 was narrowly chosen by the territorial legislative council as its first representative to Congress. Advocating land reforms that included further administration, delegate Harrison convinced Congress to carve out a new jurisdiction, Indiana Territory, in the western part of the Northwest Territory. Soon after it was created, President Adams appointed him the new territory's first governor.

Harrison had reservations about his appointment. The new territory was immense, including land that later became Indiana, Illinois, Wisconsin, the western half of Michigan including the Upper Peninsula, and a small part of Minnesota. The infrastructure was little more than a collection of foot-paths, making communication and transportation extremely difficult. The sparse population that inhabited the region was a combination of rough and tumble backwoods trappers, many of French descent, and subsistence farm families. An uneasy truce with the Native Americans further compli-cated circumstances. The territory was also well removed from the centers of power where Harrison had hoped to make his reputation and fortune. On the other hand, the new governor had almost absolute authority. Ini-tially he had total legislative power and presided over the three federally appointed justices who comprised the territorial courts. All territorial ad-ministrative appointments were his to make. Additionally, the opportuni-ties for both land and commodities speculation were enormous. He also received a comfortable salary. Weighing the advantages and disadvantages, Harrison established himself at Vincennes and began twelve years as ter-ritorial governor.

The duties of Harrison's office fell into two general categories. His pri-mary responsibilities involved establishing law and order. At the same time, he was expected to administer the nation's Indian policies throughout the vast region. In bringing order to the territory, he worked with the three federal judges to adopt laws that provided a foundation for a formal ter-ritorial government. To implement an administration, he appointed virtu-ally all of the territory's first officers including the attorney general, treasurer, sheriffs, and county justices. In addition to establishing govern-ment, he spent much time dealing with various land controversies. The most pressing issue involved determining the validity of a complex array of land claims. These included grants made by French, British, and Virginia governments prior to passage of the Northwest Ordinance in 1787 as well as more recent squatter claims. Once he had established land offices, Har-rison was also empowered to supervise the sales of public lands.

Indian affairs also required much attention. Harrison's primary duty was to carry out the Jefferson administration's Indian policy. This meant se-curing as much Indian land as possible. To that end, he steadfastly carried out several controversial treaties through which he acquired millions of acres from the region's tribes. At the same time, he hoped to maintain harmony by fairly administering territorial laws. This included punishing those who preyed upon the indigenous population. It also required enforc-ing limits on certain goods, especially alcohol, traded to native population. Although several Indian chiefs applauded the efforts, most did not, thus heightening tensions between Native Americans and settlers. By 1806 confrontations became common. The rise of Shawnee Chief Tecumseh and his brother, the Prophet, added to the growing unrest. The brothers denounced Harrison's treaties and his interference in tribal activities. They soon began organizing an Indian confederation capable of resisting further white settlement. The tensions culminated at the Battle of Tippecanoe in 1811. Of little strategic importance, the encounter nevertheless ended the united Indian front. For Harrison, who led 1,000 Indiana militiamen into the skirmish, the battle had great significance. Throughout the rest of his life, he was identified as the hero of Tippecanoe.

As the population in Indiana grew, so too did criticism of Harrison. By 1805 when the first territorial government was elected, an opposition party had begun to form. At the heart of the discord were questions about the governor's extensive use of patronage and his land policies. Detractors accused him of using his appointive authority to create a loyal coterie of supporters and an omnipotent political base. His land policies served to reward his friends and discourage competition. A speculator himself, the governor was chided for approving projects, including the construction of roads, river facilities, and mills, for his own purposes. He was also accused of participating in several fraudulent transactions. Likewise, many of his decisions about land claims were condemned as blatant favoritism. Additionally, antagonists complained that his Indian policy was designed to promote his own interests rather than peace.

Harrison's policy regarding slavery further fed his opposition. Even though the Ordinance of 1787 forbid slavery throughout the region, the governor devised legislation that permitted slaves to be brought into the territory. Reared on a slaveholding plantation, Harrison considered the institution benevolent when properly administered. Though he had been a member of an anti-slavery society while in Philadelphia, it had also been his philosophical differences with Dr. Benjamin Rush about slavery that had contributed to his decision to leave the University of Pennsylvania. A constant source of tension, his stand became more controversial after 1809 when the western half of Indiana Territory, whose residents generally favored slavery, was reorganized into Illinois Territory. Afterwards anti-slavery forces in Indiana became increasingly critical of Harrison.

The War of 1812 came at a good time for Harrison. With political opposition in Indiana growing, the war provided new opportunities for him. By virtue of his office as governor, he commanded the militia of Indiana. Powerful supporters, most notably Henry Clay, maneuvered an appointment as brigadier general in the U.S. Army for him. Like the Kentuckian, Harrison advocated an aggressive policy toward the British. For almost a decade he had been complaining about the British influence on Indians throughout the region. Like Clay he had concluded that a war would provide an opportunity to remove the British from Canada altogether. His appointment into the Army required that he resign as governor but brought him command of the 10,000-man northwestern force and a chance to oust the British. His immediate goal was to retake Detroit and then to invade Canada. Eager to attack, he underestimated the importance of naval support in Lake Erie; overestimated the capabilities of his untrained, poorly equipped volunteers; and disregarded obvious supply problems. Launching an ill-conceived fall campaign, his initial efforts failed dismally. The assault culminated in an embarrassing encounter at Fort Meigs in northwestern Ohio. However, despite the failure, his supporters in Washington had him promoted to major general, which significantly expanded his command.

After the fiasco at Fort Meigs, Harrison postponed plans for any future offensives. Finally in September 1813, with most of his supply problems resolved and shortly after Perry had secured Lake Erie, he was able to at last retake Detroit. Pursuing a sorely weakened British army into southern Canada, he soon overtook them. In the Battle of the Thames that followed, Harrison's army easily subdued the remaining enemy force. The victory ended concern about a future British offensive in the region and rehabilitated Harrison's reputation as a military leader. More importantly, during the encounter Tecumseh, the powerful Indian leader, was killed. The void undermined any immediate Indian plans to attack, thus further securing the Northwest for American occupation. After the battle, though still the target of sharp criticism, Harrison's supporters hailed him as one of the war's heroes.

His war experiences sapped Harrison's enthusiasm for military command. After the encounters with the British, he was no longer convinced that a conquest of Canada could be quickly achieved. The poor condition of his army and shoddy discipline of his men also frustrated him. Likewise, he was disillusioned by the political winds that swirled through Washington. Particularly upsetting was President Madison's appointment of John Armstrong as secretary of war. Armstrong had reprimanded Harrison's inactivity during the spring of 1813 and remained critical of his command decisions even after Detroit was retaken. Additionally, Harrison's greatest concern before the war, the threat of continuing Indian hostilities, ended with the death of Tecumseh. Anxious to return to his wife and eight children, he resigned his commission in May 1814 and began life as a gentleman farmer.

Returning to his North Bend farm just south of Cincinnati, Harrison, for the next two years, enjoyed a comfortable life, despite constant financial problems, as a gentleman farmer. Employing a small force of slaves, he was able to emulate the life that he had known as a child in Virginia. Additionally, he was periodically called upon by President Madison to negotiate postwar Indian agreements. Although displaying goodwill toward the region's tribes, he concluded that they were not capable of integrating themselves with American settlers. Consequently, he sought to splinter tribal lands. It was a maneuver that facilitated the forced removal of Native Americans from east of the Mississippi fifteen years later.

Politics remained a keen interest for Harrison. In 1816, encouraged by prominent local supporters, he won election to Congress. Although he was a minor participant in several debates, his primary interest as a congressman was strengthening and reforming the military. He also staunchly advocated internal improvements at government expense because it was a way to aid the military. On one other issue he took a notable stand. During the early debates about statehood for Missouri, he consistently opposed any efforts to limit the spread of slavery. On other domestic issues he played only a minor role, usually agreeing with Henry Clay. Foreign policy was another area of interest for Harrison. Generally he agreed with the increasingly nationalistic policies that characterized the period. Of special concern was the United States' relationship with the emerging independent states in Latin America. Harrison contended that the United States had a responsibility to nurture and lead the new nations politically and economically.

Disappointed that the Monroe administration had passed over him for appointments on a commission to Russia and as secretary of war, Harrison left Congress in favor of a seat in the Ohio State Senate. During his two-year term, economic problems dominated political matters. By 1819 the state, like much of the West, was struggling with ever-worsening fiscal conditions. Most in Ohio blamed the Bank of the United States (BUS). Harrison had supported the BUS when it was created in 1816, in part because a branch was to be located in Cincinnati. However, as economic hard times swept through the West, he deftly revised his stance. Reflecting the mood of his constituents, he worried that the BUS unfairly regulated credit and collected debts. Likewise, he complained that the bank infringed upon the rights of the state to tax. By 1819, he had become a vocal opponent of the institution, calling for its dissolution.

Always an ambitious politician, Harrison between 1820 and 1825 repeatedly tried to parlay his military record and political experience into high office. Riding a wave of anti-BUS sentiment, in 1820 he ran for governor but was defeated. The following year he unsuccessfully maneuvered within the state legislature for a spot in the United States Senate. In 1823 he was again defeated for the Senate as well as for Congress. Despite the string of election setbacks, he quietly campaigned for nomination as vice president in 1824. A primary source of his defeats was his stand on slavery. After the Missouri statehood debates in 1819 and 1820, Ohio residents in steadily growing numbers came to oppose the institution. Meanwhile Harrison staunchly resisted any limitations upon the expansion of slavery. Finally in 1825, with the help of Clay supporters in the state, he won a seat in the U.S. Senate.

In the Senate, Harrison generally supported the Adams administration. He was an energetic advocate of internal improvements, especially roads, at government expense. Though still wary of the BUS, his overt opposition melted away as the economy stabilized during the early 1820s. Military readiness, as always, remained one of his interests. Meanwhile he was also quietly maneuvering politically. For a time he set his sights upon the 1828 vice presidential nomination. Finally in 1827 Adams, who considered him an unabashed opportunist, appointed him minister to Colombia.

Harrison's brief tenure in Colombia proved difficult. He arrived in the midst of the country's struggle to adjust to recently won independence from Spain. Instructed to observe political conditions and press American commercial interests, he soon collided with the South American liberator Simon Bolívar. Harrison worried that Bolívar, with either French or British support, intended to declare himself monarch. Taking an inflexible stand, he criticized Bolívar for working against the rights and liberties of the South American people. Instead, Harrison argued that a democratic republic like that in the United States should be created. Likewise, he expected Bolívar to acknowledge the United States as the new nation's protector, thus preventing European powers from becoming entrenched in the continent. Underlying most of the American's efforts were the commercial interests of the United States. Fortunately, the increasingly charged relations between Harrison and his Colombian counterparts ended when he was replaced shortly after Andrew Jackson came to the presidency. Despite the recall, Harrison continued to press his hosts and on the eve of his departure was accused of conspiring to overthrow Bolívar.

Harrison's return to the United States began a period of personal disappointment. Plagued by debts, including unpaid taxes and $19,000 that he owed to the BUS, he spent much of the next five years working his Ohio farm. Hopes that he would be offered a lucrative political position went unfulfilled. Though his name was mentioned for several prominent posts, there was little interest in him as a candidate. Clay forces who controlled many offices within the state were content to have Harrison's influence contained. Debts further limited his ability to pursue political activities. Finally in 1834 he was appointed clerk of Common Pleas Court in Hamilton County, a post he considered well beneath his qualifications but the only office available to him. He accepted the position more because of the salary it offered than as a way to continue his political career.

Despite his problems and frustrations, Harrison maintained contacts with political leaders in several states. Though personally disheartening, his years out of politics ultimately worked to his benefit. He remained unscarred by the contentious partisan battles during Jackson's last term in office. Meanwhile, his status as the "hero of Tippecanoe" still commanded respect. As the election of 1836 approached, a few organizers in Ohio suggested him as one of numerous possible Jackson successors. Shifting regional alignments enhanced his appeal. Fed by a general disillusionment with Henry Clay, Ohio leaders initiated a Harrison movement. In early

1835 Pennsylvania Whigs joined the effort and nominated him as their presidential choice. Soon after, Maryland, New York, New Jersey, Delaware, and Kentucky, Clay's home state, joined the effort, adding significant momentum to the candidacy. Although there was still much competition, by 1836 Harrison began to emerge as one of the front-runners.

Surprised by the startling change in his political fortunes, Harrison prepared quickly. Riding the growing tide of popularity, he embraced a platform of familiar issues. As he had throughout his political career, he proposed that the national government should facilitate road building and internal improvements. Still an opponent of a national bank, he was able to dodge controversy by promising that he would approve such an institution if it were in the public's best interest. He also remained consistent with his lifelong stand on slavery, staunchly defending the institution and its expansion. Adhering to campaigning traditions, Harrison claimed to have little personal interest in winning election. Instead he relied upon ambitious supporters to promote his candidacy. Able to outmaneuver his Whig rivals, he nevertheless lost a close election to Jackson's vice president, Martin Van Buren. However, even though he had lost, he demonstrated great popular appeal.

Maneuvering for the 1840 election began within months of Van Buren's inauguration. Although numerous names were mentioned, the obvious front-runners were Harrison and Henry Clay. In April 1837, as the early effects of the Panic of 1837 struck the economy, Harrison's supporters began to organize. Projecting the prerequisite façade of disinterestedness, their candidate, nevertheless, quietly but eagerly assisted the efforts. Aiding his cause were two ambitious politicians, Thurlow Weed of New York and Pennsylvanian Thaddeus Stevens. Both saw in Harrison a popular figure who generally supported nationalistic policies but was free of the intense political opposition that Clay had generated over the years. Deftly guiding the candidacy through battles in their home states, the two orchestrated Harrison's selection as the Whig nominee. To appease Clay and the South, John Tyler from Virginia was added to the ticket.

The campaign that followed was unlike any the nation had experienced. Guided by Weed and Stevens, prominent Whigs, including Daniel Webster and Henry Clay, were enlisted to promote Harrison. Meanwhile, an army of stump speakers was recruited to drum up grassroots support throughout the country. Among them was a young lawyer from Illinois who had political aspirations of his own: Abraham Lincoln. Friendly newspapers were fed a steady stream of rhetoric portraying the candidate, despite his aristocratic background, as a simple folk hero. A log cabin and jug of hard cider became the campaign's symbols and, tapping into the nation's evolving commercial culture, a vast array of trinkets was used to advance the Whig cause. Banners, ribbons, medallions, soap, hats, ties, mugs, and bottles were among the paraphernalia distributed throughout the country.

Songs were composed, massive rallies organized, and barbecues held to further excite the constituency. Throughout it all, a crew of savvy aides helped Harrison maintain an appropriate image and avoid any misstatements.

When campaigning, Whigs usually chose innuendo over substance. With the nation still mired in the grip of its worst depression yet, Harrison made statements that implied both opposition and support for the creation of a new central bank. He took the same tact when discussing slavery and expansion. A longtime defender of slavery, he deftly avoided any firm stance on the institution's future, thus reassuring proponents without alienating anti-slavery voters. Texas was another potentially explosive issue that was carefully avoided. In one of his few definitive statements, he took a subtle swipe at both President Van Buren and former President Jackson, promising to curb the power of the executive and to serve only one term. Countering charges that at sixty-eight he was too old for the office, he energetically traveled throughout the country delivering twenty-three speeches in which he exhorted listeners to vote "Tippecanoe and Tyler Too."

Enlivened by the new campaign methods, almost twice as many voters cast ballots in 1840 as had in 1836. Harrison was the beneficiary of the expanded participation in most ways. Though the popular vote was surprisingly close, his electoral margin was significant. Only in the South and Southwest, where Jackson's influence remained a determining factor, did he experience any significant opposition. On the other hand, in the Midwest and East Harrison lost only two states.

Physically drained by the campaign, Harrison was nevertheless eager to assume his new office. He spent the months between the election and his inauguration visiting powerful supporters including Henry Clay, preparing a Cabinet, and listening to requests from ambitious office seekers. Inauguration day was cold and dank, and his address dragged on for almost two hours. By the end of the ceremonies, the new president had caught a cold. During the next three weeks the cold grew into pneumonia, and a week later Harrison became the first president to die in office.

The nation mourned Harrison's death as it had mourned only George Washington's before. Though his accomplishments fell far short of Washington's, Americans embraced him for other reasons. Most importantly, he seemed to embody many of the interests and attitudes of his fellow Americans. Though his military service was brief, he was considered a hero. He was a nationalist who had promoted expansion throughout his life. He had made his mark through persistence rather than fortune. Affable and not exceptionally sophisticated, he seemed to embody the common origins shared by most Americans. At the same time, he projected a patriarchal image that harkened back to Jackson and Washington.

BIBLIOGRAPHY

Freeman Cleaves, *Old Tippecanoe: William Henry Harrison and His Times* (New York: American Political Biography, 1990); Dorothy B. Goebel, *William Henry Harrison: A Political Biography* (Indianapolis: University of Indiana Press, 1926); Robert Gray Gunderson, *The Log-Cabin Campaign* (Lexington: University of Kentucky Press, 1957); Michael Holt, *The Rise and Fall of the American Whig Party* (New York: Oxford University Press, 1999); Daniel Howe, *The Political Culture of the Whigs* (Chicago: University of Chicago, 1979); and Norma Peterson, *The Presidencies of William Henry Harrison and John Tyler* (Lawrence: University of Kansas Press, 1989).

JOHN TYLER
(1790–1844)

There was no more committed defender of states' rights and southern tradition than John Tyler. He was a strict constructionist who challenged the constitutionality of a central bank and internal improvements funded by the federal government. He supported states' right to nullify federal legislation and, ultimately, to secede from the Union. An independent Democrat who criticized Jackson's nationalistic stand on the tariff and Van Buren's bank reforms, Tyler was elected vice president as a Whig in 1840. When William Henry Harrison died just four weeks into his presidency, Tyler became the first to ascend to the office. Unwilling to compromise his principles, he soon collided with Whig leaders. His one term in office was a politically turbulent time that in some ways set the stage for future sectional debates. His most notable accomplishment, the annexation of Texas, accelerated the nation's march into civil war.

John Tyler was part of the Virginia tidewater gentry. His family had emigrated from England during the British Civil War. Over the next five generations, the family established itself among the more prominent in Virginia. They acquired significant land holdings, including the land in Williamsburg upon which the provincial governor's mansion was built. The Tylers also held numerous colonial legislative and administrative posts. John's father, John Sr., a lawyer by trade, held various important offices during the late eighteenth century. At a time when the colony was polarized between British officials and American insurgents, the elder Tyler left no doubt that he was a patriot. A friend of Thomas Jefferson and Patrick Henry, among other Revolutionary leaders, Tyler helped to lead the state through the darkest days of the Revolution. During the two decades after the war he became a Virginia judge, was a member of the state's General Court, was a federal judge, and in the early nineteenth century served three terms as governor.

The sixth of eight children and the second of three sons, John Jr. was an amiable child. Born in 1790, he enjoyed a comfortable and generally uneventful childhood despite the death of his mother when he was just seven. As was expected of an upper-class tidewater male, he was formally educated at a prep school near his southern Virginia home and at fourteen enrolled in William and Mary College. As a student he was considered bright and a strong, though not flamboyant, orator. His greatest academic achievement was an invitation to deliver his class graduation address, which proved to be a great success. He graduated from William and Mary in 1808, the same year his father was elected governor. For the next three years he read law and apprenticed with Edmund Randolph, who was one of the most renowned lawyers at the time and was secretary of the state of Virginia, serving under Tyler's father. John Jr. was admitted to the bar in 1810.

Upon opening an office in Richmond, Tyler soon built a comfortable law practice. He also began a career in politics. In 1811 he was elected to the first of five one-year terms in the Virginia legislature. Even at this early stage, his political philosophy was fully formed and would remain consistent throughout the rest of his life. He was a traditional Jeffersonian Republican as his father had been. Most importantly, he took a strong states' rights position on most issues. He viewed the federal government as a confederation of states with no more power than the state. He opposed the growing nationalism that gripped many Americans during the decades following the War of 1812. Likewise, he opposed any federal interference in a state's right to administer slavery. True to his creed, he was also a strict constructionist who steadfastly denied the constitutionality of the national government funding internal improvements or creating a central bank. Although over the next fifty years he occasionally accepted compromise, he never wavered from the fundamental stands that he took as he entered the political arena.

Two years after entering politics, Tyler married Letitia Christian. The Christian family was also part of the tidewater gentry, and the marriage proved to be an exceptionally happy one. Letitia was well prepared for her role as the wife of a promising young Virginia aristocrat. She was attractive, intelligent, a gracious hostess, had a well-developed sense of style, and was a capable supervisor of the family's slave staff. The union also brought a bit of new wealth to Tyler. His new father-in-law, in addition to having many prominent cohorts who periodically needed legal services, held considerable property. Letitia inherited a portion of her father's property not long after her marriage. Through eight children and almost thirty years of marriage, the Tylers enjoyed a warm and satisfying relationship.

In 1816 Tyler was elected to complete the congressional term of John Clopton, who had died. Only twenty-six when he came to the House of Representatives, he immediately began defending his political principles. He promised to resist what he considered the growing nationalistic mood of his new colleagues. Instead he intended to maintain the traditional values of republicanism. In one of his first speeches, he opposed a proposal by Calhoun to provide government funding for internal improvements. After winning reelection in 1817, he labeled the recently established Second Bank of the United States (BUS) unconstitutional and argued that it had violated its charter. Tyler also clashed with Jackson in 1818. He convincingly argued that the general had exceeded his orders by invading Florida and executing two British trappers. It was a bold stand that Jackson did not forget.

By 1819 Tyler's constituency was so satisfied with his representation that he was able to run unopposed for reelection. Two important issues confronted Congress during his third term. One was a proposal to place a tariff on numerous commodities. Supporters argued that the legislation would provide protection for nascent American industry. A grand advocate of Jefferson's agrarian vision for the nation, Tyler made a well-reasoned argument that a high tariff would benefit the industrial sector of the economy at the expense of the nation's farmers. Although he reluctantly recognized the power of the national government to impose a tariff, he felt that the federal government should not be allowed to burden one region for the benefit of another. Effectively organizing Virginia's opposition to the tariff, he added to his growing political stature.

Another more immediately threatening issue further reflected Tyler's states' rights philosophy. In 1819 he became embroiled in the debate concerning Missouri statehood. A slave holder himself, he had always held that slavery was an issue for the state, not the federal government, to determine. He argued that if Congress imposed its will on Missouri, it would be treating Missouri differently than the states already in the Union because those states had decided about slavery themselves. Additionally, since the nation was composed of both slave and free states, to prohibit slavery in Missouri was to uphold the interests of one group of states while disregarding the interests of the other. The only just policy, therefore, was to allow Missouri to decide for itself about slavery. Tyler's arguments helped to defeat the initial statehood bill. However, when Henry Clay offered a compromise calling for a line separating potential slave and free states, Tyler, like some other states' rights advocates, cautiously agreed to it. Though concerned that the compromise would encourage sectionalism, Tyler nevertheless considered the bill to be a way to temper the current tensions between pro-slavery and anti-slavery forces.

After the Missouri statehood debate, Tyler chose to leave Congress. Considered part of a shrinking states' rights minority in Congress, he was frustrated that he did not have a greater impact on legislation. He was also having some financial difficulties. Service in Congress did not provide the income that a young planter/lawyer required to sustain his family's standard of living. To do that he needed to focus on his legal practice, his business dealings, and his plantation. Finally, he had a series of nagging health problems that seemed to intensify while he was in Washington. With all this in mind, he decided not to run for reelection in 1821 but instead to take a hiatus from elective office.

Two years later, Tyler resumed his political career. He was elected to return to the Virginia House of Delegates and in 1825 his fellow state legislators elected him governor, the office his father held fifteen years earlier. Though it carried political stature, the post of governor was not a particularly powerful one. Nevertheless, Tyler was able to promote some notable initiatives including improving the state's infrastructure. While in Congress, he had agreed that the infrastructure throughout the nation needed to be updated. However, he strongly disagreed that the federal government should have a role in that modernizing. Inspired by New York's Erie Canal project, he hoped to demonstrate further that states were capable of implementing major internal improvements on their own. Education was another of his priorities. Though his efforts ultimately failed to get approval, he promoted a discussion about state-funded public schools. Regardless of the issue, during his almost two years as governor he tried to avoid binding factional alliances, instead pursuing consensus whenever possible. As a result he earned support from all sides.

With his political status rising, Tyler was selected by the Virginia legislature to succeed one of the state's more powerful and controversial figures, Senator John Randolph. The cousin of Chief Justice John Marshall, Randolph had served in Congress since 1799. During that time he had earned a reputation for his idiosyncratic behavior and his biting defense of traditional republican values including states' rights. One of his infamous congressional escapades ended in a duel with Henry Clay. These legislative adventures had alienated a growing number of leaders in the state. When it became clear that he would be replaced, Tyler, who had always respected Randolph's stand on issues, reluctantly allowed his name to be offered as an alternative.

In the Senate, Tyler quickly established himself as an independent Democrat. Elected the same year that Jackson came to the presidency, the Virginian did not become part of the Jackson party. Neither was he part of the evolving opposition led by Clay and Webster. Instead he adhered to his own strict constructionist, states' rights philosophy. When that included supporting Jackson, as it did during the Maysville Road and the BUS re-charter debates, he did. When it meant opposing Jackson, as was the case during the nullification crisis, he did. His primary goal as a senator was to maintain what he considered traditional republican values.

Tyler's independence inevitably drew him into a clash with Jackson. Though he had supported the general during the 1828 election, he was always wary of the president's motives. It was the nullification crisis, how-ever, that ultimately separated the two. An opponent of a protective tariff, Tyler vehemently opposed the Tariff of 1828, or "Tariff of Abominations" as many in the South called it. He considered Jackson's passive acceptance of the legislation unacceptable. Instead he agreed with South Carolina's claim that the states had a right to nullify federal legislation. He also sup-ported South Carolina's contention that each state had the right to with-drawal from the union of states though he disagreed that secession was an action South Carolina should take in 1832. Jackson's Force Bill, which attempted to compel South Carolina's compliance, further troubled Tyler. He argued that the bill exceeded the limits of the president's executive power as described by the Constitution. Though he was not as concerned as some that the nullification debate might lead to civil war, Tyler was anxious to resolve the dispute even if it meant offending Jackson. When presented with Henry Clay's tariff compromise, he readily supported it. The bill proposed a tariff that Tyler considered too high but nevertheless offered a way past a potentially explosive episode.

On one other important issue, Tyler again aligned with the administra-tion's opposition. Although he agreed with Jackson that the BUS was un-constitutional, he joined Clay, Webster, and others in condemning the president's efforts to remove deposits from the bank. Tyler had chaired an investigation into corruption charges against the bank and found that in fact the BUS and its president, Nicholas Biddle, had done a commendable job. Additionally, in Tyler's opinion Jackson's instructions to withdraw deposits far exceeded his constitutional authority. After the president dis-regarded Congress and persisted with his withdrawals, Tyler joined the effort to censure Jackson.

Despite his growing criticism of the president, Tyler was able to maintain just enough backing in his state legislature to win reelection. That changed midway through Jackson's second term. Virginia Democrats were bitterly divided in their support of the administration. Though not yet identified as part of the evolving Whig Party, neither was Tyler considered a true Dem-ocrat. Consequently, in 1835 when Jackson Democrats gained control of the Virginia legislature Tyler was immediately requested to resign from the Senate. Though there were still four years left in his term, he remained true to his belief that governmental power flowed from the state. Reluctantly he complied and was replaced in the Senate. As a consolation, he was again elected to the Virginia legislature.

The number of southern Democrats, especially states' rights advocates such as Tyler, disenchanted by Jackson policies grew during Jackson's last two years in office. Martin Van Buren's election in 1836 heightened the southern discontent. Though Calhoun was their obvious leader, many disgruntled Democrats also looked to Tyler for direction. Likewise, Whigs eagerly courted Tyler as old political coalitions unraveled and new ones emerged. When Calhoun returned to the Democratic Party, he took with him many fellow southern Democrats. Tyler, however, was not one of them. Instead he joined the Whigs in challenging Van Buren. As much as anyone, Henry Clay was responsible for Tyler's switch. Although the two took very different stands on various issues, Tyler respected Clay and intended to help him get elected president in 1840. Likewise, Clay implied that Tyler would have a place of leadership in a Clay administration.

The Whig nomination of William Henry Harrison in 1840 dramatically changed the fates of both Tyler and Clay. Tyler was added to the ticket in an effort to placate Clay and his supporters. Whigs also expected the Virginian to attract southern Democrats by providing a balance to traditional Whig policies. As always, Tyler maintained his states' rights philosophy, continued to oppose internal improvement by the federal government, challenged the creation of a new central bank, and criticized a protective tariff, all key elements in the Harrison platform. Because the campaign was not issue oriented but rather a folksy celebration of slogans and mementos, the differences between the two candidates were easily circumvented. When issues were discussed, Tyler usually agreed that the Van Buren policies were wrong but rarely did he suggest alternatives. The strategy helped the Whig ticket win a surprisingly close election. However, it backfired badly during the following four years.

When Harrison died just four weeks into his presidency, Tyler became the first vice president to ascend to the office. His new and unclear constitutional status immediately became an issue. Many were concerned that the new president was simply a recalcitrant southern Democrat who would use his new authority to block key Whig programs. Some argued that Tyler should serve as an interim president until a new election could be held. Others expected him to defer to Harrison's Cabinet and Congress. Clay, who had unsuccessfully tried to impose his leadership upon Harrison, attempted to dictate policy to him. Few recognized Tyler as the leader of their party. In the months that followed, a nasty struggle for power and political control evolved among Whig leaders.

The first important battleground involved the new administration's fiscal policy. Like most Whigs, Tyler opposed the subtreasury plan that Van Buren had pursued. However, he also opposed the creation of a new central bank as called for by Clay, Webster, and others. Not long after coming to the presidency, he was presented with a bill that would have created a new bank. Whigs, who controlled Congress, had quickly passed the bill and expected its approval. Instead he vetoed the bill. He justified his action by claiming that the proposed bank was unconstitutional because it would have operated within the states but beyond any state controls. If that problem could be rectified, he implied that he would accept the creation of a new bank. Angry Whigs, led by Clay, soon had on the president's desk a revised bill that they believed met his requirements. However, again it was vetoed. This time Whigs launched a full-scale attack upon the president. Whig newspapers lambasted him. There were protests outside the White House. Numerous Whig congressmen indignantly argued that the Supreme Court had long ago declared a central bank constitutional. In an ultimate display of opposition, all but one Cabinet member resigned.

Debate about a new tariff widened the breach between the president and Whig leaders. Tyler warned that he would not approve tariff legislation if he felt it used the power of the national government to protect one segment of the economy at the expense of others. On the other hand, he promised to accept a tariff that equitably raised revenues that would be used to pay the ever-growing national debt. Congress responded by passing two tariff bills, but both were vetoed. Again Whig leaders, led by Clay, railed the president for what they considered his duplicity. He was condemned by Congress and some called for his impeachment. Derided as "his Accidency" by various newspapers, his waning public support eroded ever more rapidly. In less than a year after coming to the presidency, Tyler was abandoned by the Whig Party and had become the target of both media and public scorn.

On foreign policy issues, the Tyler administration was credited with several notable accomplishments. Secretary of State Daniel Webster, the only Harrison appointee not to resign after the president's second bank veto, was able to negotiate with the British a permanent border between Canada and Maine. The agreement ended growing border troubles and brought to the United States a large piece of the disputed land. Likewise, problems created by Canadian insurrectionists who used western New York as a place of refuge were successfully resolved. The Tyler administration also initiated formal relations with China. However, more important and more threatening than any of these achievements was the annexation of Texas.

Tyler was an advocate of annexation but, like most, recognized the complexities that surrounded the issue. For five years Texas had functioned as an independent republic. When Tyler came into office, he immediately experienced pressure from Sam Houston to acquire the Republic. In Congress powerful voices joined the call for immediate annexation. There were also some who opposed the acquisition until several issues, most importantly the slavery question, were resolved. Secretary of State Daniel Webster was among those who staunchly opposed annexation. However, with Houston adeptly countering American reluctance by encouraging British interests in Texas, Tyler felt pushed to action. He soon concluded that when all circumstances were considered, annexation was in the nation's best interest. His primary fear was that annexation would sacrifice the slowly improving relations with Mexico. On the other hand, annexation would benefit the American economy in numerous ways. Likewise, a vast majority of Texans were of American descent and a reunion seemed natural. Finally, and most controversially, Tyler proposed annexation as a way to protect slavery. He warned that the British ulterior motive was to abolish slavery in Texas. A free Texas would provide a grand refuge for American runaway slaves as well as a staging place for slave insurrections.

Tyler himself was a lifelong slaveholder. He defended the institution as a system of labor upon which the southern economy was dependent. He also believed slaves were inherently inferior to whites and that emancipation would create significant economic and social problems throughout the South. However, like Henry Clay among many other slaveholders, he had a basic philosophical problem justifying the institution. He criticized the abolitionist movement but at the same time served as the vice president of the Virginia colonization society. Although he applauded the manumission of slaves, he nevertheless advocated maintaining the institution into the foreseeable future. For him, slavery in Texas or in any other state was a question that should be answered by the state rather than the national government.

After completing border negotiations with Great Britain, Tyler's secretary of state, Daniel Webster, resigned. The move enabled the administration to ease the nation toward annexation. Quiet discussions with Sam Houston were initiated and the president promised that once a treaty was signed, the United States would protect the Republic against a Mexican attack. At the same time, a diplomat was sent to Mexico City to assure the Mexican government that the United States did not intend to seize other lands in the Southwest. The next obstacle was Congress and more specifically the Senate. Although the House approved an annexation proposal, the Senate initially rejected it. In responding, Tyler benefited from the 1844 election. James K. Polk, the Democratic candidate, had campaigned aggressively in favor of annexation while his opponent, Henry Clay, avoided the issue. After Polk's election, Congress appeared resigned to the inevitability of annexation. Meanwhile, earlier that year Tyler had appointed John C. Calhoun, an outspoken advocate of annexation, as his secretary of state. Although Calhoun's link between Texas and slavery alarmed a few, his stature and political leadership carried others. Tyler and Calhoun were able to maneuver a joint resolution through Congress that allowed the president to use his executive authority to annex the Republic. Finally, just hours before leaving office, he officially added Texas to the American domain. The acquisition, for better or worse, proved to be Tyler's ultimate legacy.

Amidst Tyler's political battles, his wife Letitia died. In 1839 she had suffered a paralyzing stroke. Once a gracious hostess, she was unable to fulfill those duties during the first year of her husband's presidency. Eighteen months after her death, Tyler married Julia Gardiner, the daughter of a New York senator. Thirty years younger than her husband, she brought new energy and life into the White House. Even before her marriage she was a Washington favorite, but as the nation's First Lady she was simply captivating. Intelligent, vivacious, attractive, and with a style of her own, she reveled in the swirl of the city's social life. Despite their age difference, the Tylers were well suited for each other and had a happy eighteen-year marriage. During that time, Julia added seven more children to the eight that Tyler already had with Letitia.

Passed over by his party for the 1844 presidential nomination, Tyler, disgruntled and angry, began preparing for retirement well before his term in office ended. Upon leaving the presidency, he moved to an estate near Williamsburg and lived comfortably as a gentleman planter. Returning to the Democratic Party, he maintained hopes for a return to high elective office, but the hostility that had been attached to his presidency did not truly abate until the last years of his life. In the 1850s, as the nation wrestled with ever-growing sectional issues, Tyler steadfastly supported the traditional southern positions. During the two years prior to the Civil War, he attempted to mediate the differences between North and South, but when faced with secession agreed with his state's decision to leave the Union. Elected to serve as a Virginia representative in the first Confederate government, he died in January 1862 before beginning his new legislative duties.

BIBLIOGRAPHY

Oliver Perry Chitwood, *John Tyler: Champion of the Old South* (New York: Appleton-Century, 1939); Robert J. Morgan, *A Whig Embattled: The Presidency under John Tyler* (Lincoln: University of Nebraska Press, 1954); Norma Lois Peterson, *The Presidencies of William Henry Harrison and John Tyler* (Lawrence: University of Kansas Press, 1989); and Robert Seager, *And Tyler too: A Biography of John and Julia Gardiner Tyler* (Norwalk, CT: Easton Press, 1963).

NICHOLAS BIDDLE
(1786–1844)

For almost twenty years during the Jacksonian era, Nicholas Biddle served as the nation's unofficial banker. A Philadelphia aristocrat and intellectual, he skillfully directed the economy past numerous potential pitfalls, thus helping to facilitate a period of unprecedented commercial growth. In so doing, however, he also became embroiled in a fundamental ideological debate with Andrew Jackson concerning the national government's role in managing the economy. In some ways a continuation of the debate between Jefferson and Hamilton a generation earlier, the dispute was one of several that characterized the era and significantly aggravated existing divisions within the nation. Often haughty and condescending when responding to his critics, Biddle was also a shrewd and brilliant fiscal manager who unhappily found himself at the center of a political firestorm.

Nicholas Biddle was the son of a prominent Philadelphia family. His forebears had been among the first settlers in Pennsylvania. During the century that followed, Biddle ancestors had regularly held positions of authority within the province. His father, Charles, served as vice president of the Supreme Executive Council of Pennsylvania, was elected to the Assembly, and was a prosperous maritime merchant in Philadelphia. Family friends included many of the city's revolutionary leaders, including Benjamin Franklin and Robert Morris. Young Nicholas, born in 1786, was reared to expect deference and to accept the responsibilities that came with social status.

From adolescence, Biddle's intellect set him apart. At ten he followed his brother William, who was five years older, to the University of Pennsylvania. Three years later, he enrolled at Princeton and at fifteen graduated at the top of his class, delivering the valedictorian address. Throughout his days at Princeton, Biddle was a model student. Diligent, thorough, and very committed to his studies, he did little socializing or entertaining. Instead his time was consumed pursuing his school's classical liberal arts coursework. Upon graduation he immediately continued his academic endeavors, studying law at the University of Pennsylvania. Again his prodigious intellect and a somewhat contrary spirit set him apart from older classmates. However, while studying law he joined a group of young, upper-class Philadelphians who, over the next few decades, would become some of the city's preeminent commercial and political leaders. He also contributed several pieces to *Port Folio*, a popular literary journal.

In 1804, as he prepared to begin his own law practice, Biddle was invited to assist a friend of his father's, George Armstrong, who had recently been appointed by Jefferson as the American ambassador to France. Though an unpaid position, it enabled the eighteen-year-old Biddle to travel and study in Europe. Over his parents' mild objections, he accepted the post and spent much of the next three years in Europe. In France he watched as Napoleon plotted out an empire, thereby complicating relations with the United States. Biddle also traveled extensively throughout Italy and Greece, soaking up ancient cultures wherever he went. The experience heightened his appreciation of the classics, particularly architecture, but also affirmed his budding sense of American nationalism. His journeys ended in London, where he briefly served as James Monroe's temporary assistant.

Back in Philadelphia, Biddle joined his brother's law practice. William had been elected to the Pennsylvania Assembly and welcomed his younger brother's assistance. Though not passionate about the law, Nicholas was a capable attorney and expanded the practice. When not involved with legal activities, he contributed to literary journals, eventually assisting with the editing and publishing of the *Port Folio*. In 1810, with his reputation as a writer growing, he was invited to edit the journals of the Lewis and Clark expedition. It was a task that had been languishing in the hands of Meriwether Lewis since the adventurer's return. Though the project was far more involved than Biddle had anticipated, he methodically pursued it. Aside from his law practice and literary endeavors, Biddle also resumed law school acquaintances and embarked on a full calendar of social activities.

Shortly after accepting the Lewis and Clark journal assignment, Biddle again followed the path of his oldest brother. He was elected to the state legislature. In the same election, his father won a seat in the state Senate as well. Since his days at Princeton, Biddle had embraced Hamiltonian ideals; as a legislator, he promoted policies that reflected his Federalist stance. Because a majority of his colleagues in the state Assembly were Jeffersonian Republicans, he expected to accomplish little. Nevertheless, he took an unusually active role in various legislative deliberations. He encouraged the state to assist with internal improvements. Creation of a canal system similar to the one being dug in New York was an especially important issue to him. He also sketched out an initial plan that twenty-five years later became a state system of public schools. A protective tariff was another issue he endorsed.

For Biddle the most important issue that confronted the legislature in 1811 was the recharter of the Bank of the United States (BUS). Most Republicans, consistent with a Jeffersonian philosophy, opposed the bank and wanted the state to reject the recharter. Biddle was a staunch bank defender. In a notable three-hour speech, he skillfully dissected criticism of the bank, analyzed BUS strengths, and advocated the recharter. He maintained that contrary to Republican claims, the middling sort needed the BUS far more than did the wealthy classes. The wealthy had investment options not available to the average American and would acquire wealth regardless of whether the BUS existed or not. On the other hand, the bank provided credit and fiscal security to the average American that would not be available otherwise. Only BUS bank notes provided the nation with a stable currency. Without the notes, state banks could issue credit and speculate with virtually no limits. This would eventually undermine the nation's economy and promote aristocracy. Biddle realized he had little hope of winning the debate, but even his opponents respected his efforts.

After just one term in the state legislature, Biddle was frustrated by what he considered the lack of vision of many of his fellow representatives. He also had another priority that became the focus of his activities. Shortly before his election, he had met seventeen-year-old Jane Craig. Immediately Biddle began spending his free time with Jane and her mother. Separated from her by his term in state government, which met in Lancaster, upon his return he formally courted Jane. In October 1811, they were married. The years that followed were generally happy ones for Biddle. Already free from any financial worries as a result of his father's commercial success, his union with Jane further enhanced his wealth. Her father, who died a year before she met her future husband, had owned the largest estate in Philadelphia, Andalusia. After their marriage, Biddle and his bride joined her mother there. He also took over management of the estate's farm operations as well as his mother-in-law's finances. Additionally, he accepted the editorship of *Port Folio*, which included a comfortable salary. The various incomes enabled the Biddles to entertain regularly, and they soon became an entrenched part of Philadelphia's high society.

Unlike five of his brothers, Biddle did not serve in the military during the War of 1812. Instead, despite some reservations about the war, he used his journal to rally support and to criticize partisan New England Federalists who openly opposed it. He also spoke out about the floundering state of the economy after the demise of the BUS in 1813. As he had predicted, with the bank gone, money was drawn out of the nation and into European banks. Meanwhile, some currency used in one region of the country was not accepted in other regions. By the end of the war, with the national treasury verging on bankruptcy, Biddle joined a growing call for the creation of a new central bank. Elected to the Pennsylvania Senate in 1814, he continued his efforts, applauding the establishment of the Second Bank of the United States (BUS) in 1816. He also renewed his call for a nationalistic program that included government-sponsored internal improvements and a protective tariff.

Calling upon his political connections, in 1819 Biddle maneuvered an appointment as one of twenty-five BUS directors. His reason for pursuing the post was a growing concern that the bank's initial president, William Jones, was mismanaging the BUS and therefore undermining the nation's economy. As did a growing number of others, Biddle worried that Jones had extended too many loans to unsound state banks, thus providing a variety of opportunities for devious speculators. Lacking competent BUS management, the nation's economy was tumbling into a deep economic panic. Adding momentum to the fall, the BUS left the federal government with insufficient specie to pay its debts. What was needed was a tighter fiscal policy imposed by the BUS. From his seat on the board, Biddle intended to push the bank in that direction. Shortly after he came onto the board a new bank president, Langdon Cheves, who replaced Jones in early 1821, endorsed his views.

Initially Biddle and Cheves agreed upon a similar course for the bank. The new president announced tighter credit policies that included suspending the issuance of new bank notes in the Southwest and West, where speculation and credit had soared. Also the BUS began foreclosing on existing loans to state banks. This, in turn, required state banks to call in their loans and forced overextended banks to go out of business. Unfortunately, many depositors and debtors throughout the country, and especially in the nation's interior, were also pushed into bankruptcy. Further, the policy eventually drew much needed specie away from the interior and into the Northeast. Despite roaring protests from banks and politicians in the West and South, the new BUS strategy began to fortify the national economy. Within six months Biddle, who served as Cheves's deputy, was satisfied that there had been enough recovery to allow some loosening of the imposed constraints. True to his basic Hamiltonian philosophy, he argued that the remaining debt if carefully regulated could be used to promote economic growth. Cheves disagreed. Instead, amidst a chorus of complaints that the BUS was saving itself at the expense of the American public, he maintained his austere fiscal program. Biddle, during the remaining two years of his term on the board, regularly but unsuccessfully challenged the bank president's course of action.

When Cheves announced his retirement in 1822, Biddle quietly began campaigning to become his successor. Again calling upon powerful backers, including his friend President James Monroe and Secretary of the Treasury William C. Crawford, he was able to override significant opposition in replacing Cheves. Once installed as the new bank president, Biddle successfully lobbied for new board appointees who shared his vision of the bank. In assuming his duties, Biddle was both the beneficiary and victim of his predecessor's legacy. Cheves had brought the bank to a very secure financial position but had also generated bitter opposition throughout the country. Biddle generally sympathized with the detractors and, as he had proposed while a board member, began to loosen the bank's restrictive fiscal policies. He also pursued a more cooperative relationship with state banks rather than the adversarial relationship that had existed under Cheves. To achieve that goal, he began issuing new bank notes and significantly expanding credit. This, he expected, would allow state banks some autonomy but, through close monitoring, the BUS could still restrain excessive and unwise local lending. Within six months, Biddle had won guarded approval from many of the bank's critics.

Biddle understood the important role that the bank could play in the nation's economic well-being. He also enjoyed the power that he had as the BUS president. Though responsible to his board, there were few limitations over his authority. With eighteen branches throughout the country, his bank was by far the largest financial institution in the nation. Though the BUS was essentially a private, for-profit enterprise whose stockholders expected regular dividends, Biddle was at the same time keenly aware of his bank's responsibility to the general public. In balancing these two priorities, he skillfully steered the BUS through several potential domestic and international economic dilemmas during mid-1820s.

As BUS president, Biddle attempted to keep his bank apart from the political arena. However, during the 1828 election the bank became the source of much debate. The Jackson campaign encouraged complaints that some, especially in the West, had been leveling against the BUS since its inception. Though Jackson himself said very little, his supporters accused the bank of actively opposing Jackson candidates in Kentucky, New Hampshire, and Louisiana. Biddle initially considered the charges to be simply campaign rhetoric, but after the election he investigated and found little valid substantiation. Though the specific circumstances were different, in each case he concluded that the problems were a combination of local political struggles and personality clashes. Reporting his findings to Jackson's secretary of the treasury, Samuel Ingham, he felt confident about the government's continued cooperation with the BUS. He was further assured by the number of bank supporters in powerful positions throughout the new administration. What he did not realize was the degree of Jackson's abiding opposition to all banks.

Though Jackson and Biddle clearly reflected opposite poles of American society, an air of mutual respect marked their initial formal meeting. Biddle was the polished, formally educated, calculating eastern aristocrat; Jackson the untrained, self-made, instinctive backwoods Indian fighter and populist. In November 1829, the two men met to discuss the bank. Biddle hoped to allay any remaining concerns Jackson might have about BUS support. Additionally, he offered Jackson assistance in paying off the national debt. Acknowledging Biddle's achievements, the president nevertheless described a deep hostility to banks in general. He also questioned the 1819 *McCulloch v. Maryland* decision, which affirmed the constitutionality of the BUS. Despite the reservations, Biddle left the meeting guardedly optimistic.

His optimism disappeared quickly. Two months after the meeting, Jackson implied in his annual address to Congress that he had no intention of rechartering the bank. Instead he had an alternative bank plan. This put Biddle in a difficult situation. On one hand he wanted to help the new administration succeed, but on the other hand he feared success included elimination of his bank. Hoping to end the controversy quickly and fortified by the knowledge that a majority in Congress supported the bank, Biddle prepared to apply for rechartering in 1831, five years early. However, in so doing he unexpectedly guaranteed that the BUS would remain a divisive political issue throughout the rest of the Jackson presidency and beyond.

Though anxious to resolve the rechartering problem, Biddle nevertheless agreed with advice from Henry Clay and others to delay his application until 1832, an election year. The delay would provide more time to solidify support. It was the first of several strategic blunders made by Biddle. Focusing on Pennsylvania and New York, he directed agents to lobby for the bank within the two states' legislatures. In Pennsylvania all went as planned and a resolution was passed endorsing the recharter. The campaign in New York did not go as well. Along the way, the BUS was again accused of aiding anti-Jackson factions. Several ill-advised loans to key figures in the debate further undermined Biddle's efforts. Eventually the legislature resolved to deny the rechartering. Meanwhile the administration mounted its own attack. Fearing the wrath of Jackson, congressional Democrats and Cabinet members who supported the bank were quietly encouraged to remain silent. Newspapers were also enlisted to expose alleged BUS abuses. Ultimately, Biddle's delay backfired and enabled opponents of the bank to organize more effectively.

Perhaps Biddle's biggest mistake was underestimating the depth of Jackson's opposition. Though he had little doubt that the president would veto the recharter, Biddle believed the president could be convinced to accept a congressional override. Most importantly, he was willing to implement reforms that the president required. Some important Jackson supporters, including Martin Van Buren, were reportedly ready to endorse the recharter if the reforms were made. Likewise, John Jacob Astor and numerous other prominent entrepreneurs were organized to defend the recharter. Meanwhile, congressional bank proponents seemed to be operating a successful political campaign. However, Jackson considered the efforts merely another example of bank interference in his administration. Biddle was accused of using bank money to buy influence in Congress and dupe the public. A hasty congressional investigation exonerated Biddle but did nothing to dissuade the president or his small corps of ardent BUS opponents that the bank's tactics were not devious. Jackson labeled the institution undemocratic, called it a tool of the rich and powerful, and officially denounced the Supreme Court decision that declared it constitutional. He also considered Biddle the instigator and personally responsible for challenging his authority. Despite his opposition, the House approved the recharter in mid-June. The Senate approved on July 3, but Jackson unequivocally denounced the bill and vetoed it immediately.

Biddle's hope for an override died slowly. Continuing charges against the bank and the election dominated the fall. After the election, buoyed by his impressive victory, Jackson stepped up his effort to eliminate the BUS even before its charter expired in 1836. In a campaign that became increasingly personal, new charges and investigations of Biddle and the BUS were launched. The president had opponents of the bank appointed as the government's representatives on the BUS board. Questions about the bank's solvency were used to justify withdrawing government deposits without congressional approval. Though the investigations ultimately validated Biddle's administrative tactics and demonstrated that the bank was fiscally sound, the administration's efforts continued. When his new secretary of the treasury, William Duane, refused to withdraw government deposits from the BUS, Jackson replaced him with Roger B. Taney. A staunch bank opponent, Taney agreed to withdraw deposits and place them in pro-Jackson state banks that were soon dubbed "pet banks." However, even this very controversial maneuver did not overwhelm the BUS.

Increasingly frustrated, angry, and belligerent, Biddle nevertheless skillfully navigated the bank past the Jackson obstructions. Denied government deposits, he initially tightened BUS loan policies. Within weeks, the American economy began a downward slide but the bank remained fiscally sound. Later, concerned about a possible financial panic, the bank president cautiously eased the loan policy balancing the fiscal needs of one region against those of others. Though demonized by Jackson and Democratic newspapers, Biddle kept both the BUS solvent and the national economy stable.

Adding to Biddle's frustration, the BUS became a central piece in the Whig party's maneuvering throughout Jackson's second term in office.

Whig leaders agreed that the slow demise of the BUS would soon under-mine the fragile economic stability that Biddle had engineered. They also agreed that a floundering economy would not bode well for Democrats. Vice President Martin Van Buren, Jackson's probable choice as a successor, appeared especially vulnerable. They disagreed, however, on what to do about the imminent problems. The three most influential anti-Jackson lead-ers, Clay, Webster and Calhoun, each had a solution of their own, and each solution included enhancing the sponsor's individual power. Clay ad-vocated extending the BUS charter by twenty years, in essence undoing Jackson's veto. Webster proposed a four- to six-year charter extension; and Calhoun called for maintaining the BUS for twelve years but with signifi-cant reforms including the use of gold to back currency. For Biddle, who needed immediate support and assistance, the political wrangling was ag-gravating.

The last hope to save the BUS was the 1834 congressional election. Ever more aggressive in his partisan duel with Jackson, Biddle became a polem-ical figure with virtually no chance of undermining the president's popu-larity. The election results were expected but discouraging nevertheless. Resigned to the bank's fate, Biddle began preparing for the end of the BUS and exploring his options. He instructed branch banks quietly to transfer their assets to the main bank in Philadelphia, after which the branches were put on the market. Meanwhile, with encouragement from friends and trusted associates, he pursued a bank charter from Pennsylvania. Resorting to the kind of unsavory tactics that he been accused of for almost a decade, he secured a very favorable arrangement with the state government and by the time the BUS charter finally expired on March 4, 1836, Biddle had the new United States Bank of Pennsylvania operating and ready to make ma-jor European investments.

When the Panic came, Biddle was prepared. Through judicious invest-ments in England and a tight credit policy, and by maintaining enough specie to satisfy demands, he enabled his bank to weather the crisis com-fortably. So successful were his efforts that his bank was able to help sta-bilize the national economy. The Panic had started when the cotton market collapsed. By gaining control of the cotton supply, Biddle restored a sat-isfactory market for farmers. His bank also helped to restore profitable trade with Great Britain and maneuvered currency rates in a manner that assisted the national government in paying its debts. Still harboring hopes that his new bank might eventually become a replacement for the BUS, the United States Bank temporarily served as the national government's unof-ficial bank. However, Van Buren had no intentions of recreating the BUS. Once the crisis subsided, the administration initiated plans to create a sub-treasury rather than a new BUS.

In March 1839, with another financial crisis looming, Biddle retired. In declining health and frustrated by what he considered the demagoguery of both the Democrats and the Whigs, he left the public arena. Though he continued to advise his bank, he turned over its operation to others. Within two years, the bank went out of business. He also could no longer tolerate the fundamental ideological differences and bitter political debates that had become a part of charting of the nation's economic future. It was a debate that he as much as anyone was responsible for creating but one that he could no longer endure. In February 1844, after a brief illness, he died. Reviled by many and respected by some, at the time of his death few denied his achievements as president of the BUS. In the time since his death, scholars have generally confirmed his reputation as a capable, hardworking fiscal administrator whose vision helped to steer the nation's economy through an important transitional period.

BIBLIOGRAPHY

Thomas Payne Govan, *Nicholas Biddle: Nationalist and Public Banker, 1786–1844* (Chicago: University of Chicago Press, 1959); John M. McFaul, *The Politics of Jacksonian Finance* (Ithaca, NY: Cornell University Press, 1972); George Taylor, *Jackson v. Biddle's Bank: The Struggle over the 2nd Bank of the United States* (New York: D.C. Heath, 1972); and Peter Temin, *The Jacksonian Economy* (New York: W. W. Norton, 1969).

WRITERS AND REFORMERS

WILLIAM LLOYD GARRISON
(1805–1879)

In an age of reform, William Lloyd Garrison was the era's preeminent social activist. In many ways, he was responsible for transforming an ineffective anti-slavery movement into an abolitionist crusade that dominated all other Jacksonian reform efforts. From a modest background with little formal education, Garrison apparently possessed few qualifications expected of an influential leader. However, gripped by a profound religious belief and unbending commitment to rid American society of sin, he became a compelling and zealous advocate for change. A printer by trade, he used his vocation to force the nation to confront the slavery issue and in so doing he emerged as one of Jacksonian America's most powerful reformers.

During his boyhood, Garrison developed the unbending religious beliefs and strong will that later characterized his crusading efforts. He was born on December 12, 1805. Seven years earlier his parents had migrated to Newburyport, Massachusetts, from Nova Scotia. His father worked as a seaman and eventually became a merchant ship pilot. By sailing under the American flag, he hoped to avoid growing hostilities between the British and the French. Ironically, in 1807 Jefferson's Embargo, which halted most American shipping activities, made it nearly impossible for the transplanted Canadian to ply his trade. Not long after, the elder Garrison, distraught and in debt, abandoned his family. William's mother, aided by the local Baptist Society, was able to sustain the family until a devastating fire swept through Newburyport and burned down the Garrison home. Afterward five-year-old William was left with a family from the church while his mother, older brother, and two younger sisters moved to Lynn, thirty miles away, where Mrs. Garrison found work.

During the next five years, young William spent far more time away from his mother and siblings than with them. For the first three years, he rarely saw his mother. Eventually he joined the family in Lynn and they then moved to Baltimore, where he and his brother were apprenticed in a shoe factory. However, within a year William was back in Newburyport. Despite the long absences, Mrs. Garrison had a strong influence on her son. Throughout her life, she was a devoutly religious woman. Consumed by the evangelical passion of the Second Great Awakening, she instilled in William strong religious beliefs. When they were together, she usually took him to three church meetings each week. When they were apart, she expected him to continue his religious instruction. She also arranged for her son to acquire vocational training rather than a formal education. She insisted that as a craftsman he would have a secure future. Eager to please and quick to learn, young William almost always abided his mother's wishes.

Just eleven years old when he returned to Newburyport, Garrison was soon apprenticed to a local printer. Work as an apprentice printer, or "printer's devil," was filthy, odious, and physically grueling, but the youngster proved capable. Within a few years he had matured into a skillful printer and valuable worker. Though he received little formal education, his apprenticeship provided him with access to a range of books and enabled him to discover a passion for literature. He also tried his hand at writing. He anonymously penned several humorous commentaries that the paper's readers enjoyed. Encouraged by the success, he sent copies to his mother. She was not impressed and warned that he would not be able to support himself as a writer. Heeding her admonition, he temporarily curtailed his writing.

In 1823 Garrison's mother died in Baltimore. Only two months earlier, the boy's master had permitted him to visit her for the first time since William had returned to Newburyport. It was a sad visit. For months his mother had been in poor health, and both she and her son knew that she was dying. Additionally Garrison's one surviving sister had recently died and his brother, who had been in and out of trouble for several years, finally disappeared, probably going off to sea. Reticent about the passing, Garrison published a brief notice of his mother's death.

Shortly after his apprenticeship ended in December 1825, Garrison was given the opportunity to begin a print shop of his own. A local printer, looking for a buyer, offered to sell his business to Garrison. With help from his former master, the young man acquired the shop and began operation of his own press. While printing various materials, his primary production was a newspaper that he named the *Free Press*. Well organized and attractively designed, the paper in most ways was typical of early nineteenth-century newssheets. Political news and commentary comprised a major component of the paper. Promising to maintain a high moral standard and integrity, Garrison took a stand critical of Jeffersonian policies. In addition to commentary, much of which Garrison wrote, the *Free Press* included excerpts of important speeches, advertisements, community announcements, tide charts, and other assorted lists, remedies, and information. What set the paper apart from others was its literary content. Readers were offered a wide range of poetry that the publisher had collected. Among the paper's notable achievements was the publication of poetry by a young local shoemaker, John Greenleaf Whittier. So impressed was Garrison by the work of the as yet unpublished Whittier that he tried to convince the young man's parents to free their son of other obligations so that he could develop his writing. The response was much like Garrison's mother's response to his initial commentary. Nevertheless, Garrison could later claim to have been the first to recognize the genius of John Greenleaf Whittier.

Gliding into political activism, Garrison through the *Free Press* became increasingly bold. At times abrasively attacking Democrats, he soon became a victim of changing political allegiances. After less than a year in operation, the paper was silenced by a coterie of opponents organized by Caleb Cushing, son of a local shipping merchant. Cushing planned to unseat the incumbent Federalist congressman. Encountering barbs from the *Free Press*, he enlisted the support of Garrison's former master and forced the young printer to sell his print shop. Disgruntled, angry, and in need of work, Garrison moved to Boston. There he worked temporarily as a journeyman for several of the city's publishers. A pious man excited by the intellectual swirl of Boston, he was immediately drawn to reform movements that had begun to sprout throughout the city. The temperance movement was especially appealing to him for two important reasons. On a personal level, Garrison attributed many of his family's problems to alcoholism. Both his brother and father's lives had been scarred by heavy drinking. Intellectually, he was inspired by the Reverend Lyman Beecher's emotional call for temperance. A year after committing himself to Beecher's cause, Garrison was invited to publish the movement's paper, the *National Philanthropist*.

It was during his brief time running the *Philanthropist* that Garrison first met Benjamin Lundy. In March 1828, Lundy came to Boston to promote the anti-slavery cause and his paper, the *Genius of Universal Emancipation*. Garrison was familiar with the publication and impressed by its zealous tenor. Lundy also impressed him. In some ways, he saw the Quaker reformer as a kindred soul. Both men had lost their parents early in life. Both had taken up trades; Lundy had been a harness maker rather than pursue a formal education. And both were driven by deep spiritual convictions. The manner through which Lundy pursued his cause also impressed Garrison. Unlike some of his contemporaries, Lundy advocated reform for purely humanitarian reasons. Garrison, not long before meeting Lundy, had lamented that some reform leaders were becoming partisan and promoting themselves as much as their cause. Instead, he proposed that reformers should strive to set a moral tone that transcended partisan limitations and self-aggrandizement. To Garrison, Benjamin Lundy was the model of a committed, conscientious reformer.

Somewhat disenchanted with the temperance movement and the *Philanthropist*, Garrison left Boston in mid-1828 to run a paper in Bennington, Vermont. Funded by National Republicans, the paper, the *Journal of the Times*, was created to aid John Quincy Adams in his quest for reelection. Garrison also used the paper to advocate reform, particularly a call for anti-slavery. Printing commentary, which was often abrasive, interspersed with poetry, Garrison employed the confrontational style that had characterized his previous publishing endeavors. His work quickly stirred local passions but failed to generate significant support. After the election, when the paper's funding ended, Garrison returned to Boston, where he intended to establish an anti-slavery paper of his own. More confident and committed than ever, he expected to find sponsors for his venture but discovered that the city was still not ready to embrace his cause. Frustrated, he stridently chastised the city's reformers, claiming that they displayed a moral cowardice for not embracing the anti-slavery campaign. Addressing audiences whenever given the opportunity, he established himself as an effective speaker. Though his speeches lacked the power of Daniel Webster's, they were tightly reasoned, illustrative, and evenly delivered. His most notable effort was a Fourth of July speech in 1829 in which he masterfully reinterpreted the Declaration of Independence to include slaves. Soon after, Benjamin Lundy invited Garrison to join him in Baltimore and run his paper. Garrison immediately accepted the offer.

Garrison's transformation from social activist to moral crusader was completed during his time in Baltimore. Lundy allowed him to run the *Genius for Universal Emancipation* with few limitations. Meanwhile, Lundy spent much of his time traveling to promote the anti-slavery cause. Garrison redesigned the paper, bringing to it a more attractive appearance and a bold new masthead. He also sharpened the content while incorporating some of the literary devices, including poetry, which had characterized his earlier publishing efforts. Immediately becoming the paper's chief writer, he again employed a confrontational, aggressive style. Demanding that the only solution to the slavery question was the immediate abolishment of the institution, he denounced gradual emancipation, a concept that Lundy accepted, as impractical. In a regular column entitled "Black List," he sought to shock readers into a moral outrage by describing explicit atrocities committed against slaves throughout the country. He denounced local slaveholders in specific terms and relished publicly dissecting any defense they offered. Political leaders from the founding fathers to Henry Clay and Andrew Jackson were also targets for his barbs. Unconcerned about the enemies he might make, Garrison was intent upon establishing the paper as a vehicle capable of single-handedly ending slavery throughout the nation. Although offering suggestions about content, Lundy generally allowed his new associate to steer the paper's course as he saw fit.

Denouncing slavery was controversial but when Garrison expanded his crusade to include civil rights for blacks, Baltimore officials joined slave traders in opposing him. Adding to their concern was an independently published pamphlet, written by free black David Walker and known as *Walker's Appeal*, which advocated black liberation through insurrection. Alarmed locals feared that armed with the pamphlet, Garrison might push the city's sizable free black population to rebellion. Though the *Genius* did not republish any part of the pamphlet, the paper did acknowledge the potential of slave rebellion. Searching for a way to silence Garrison, his opponents arranged for him to be indicted. He was charged with criminal libel for accusing Baltimore's most notorious slave trader of brokering a shipment of slaves to New Orleans. Legally the charge was easily refuted but, prodded by an unsympathetic judge, the jury found Garrison guilty and sentenced him to pay a substantial fine or spend six months in jail. Choosing the latter, the publisher stridently entered the Baltimore jail in April 1830. He considered incarceration merely a further demonstration of the extent to which he would go for his cause. Spending his time in jail writing letters and editorials, he encouraged other abolitionists to follow his lead. After serving two months, he was released when a wealthy New York City reformer, Arthur Tappan, paid his fine. Though the *Genius* temporarily ceased operations, Garrison emerged from jail as the nation's preeminent abolitionist and an acknowledged crusader.

Ready to start his own paper, Garrison traveled along the East Coast giving speeches and looking for a home. He initially considered taking over a press in Washington but could find no sponsors. His plans received equally chilly receptions in Philadelphia, New York, Hartford, New Haven, and Newburyport, his hometown. Even social activists were skeptical about Garrison's reform and hesitant to endorse his inflexible style. Though not warmly greeted in Boston, he was able to convince a childhood friend and fellow printer, Issac Knapp, to help him. The two borrowed a press and acquired enough supplies to begin printing. Armed with a few small advances and loans, they began publishing the *Liberator* on January 1, 1831. With circulation of the paper slowly growing, Garrison and Knapp, a month after their first issue, bought a small print shop and inexpensive press of their own.

From its first edition and throughout its thirty-five years of publication, the *Liberator* served as the clarion call of the abolitionist movement. In look and style, the paper was similar to the other papers Garrison had printed. Along with a great deal of commentary, it included anecdotal accounts of slave abuse, religious excerpts, and, of course, some poetry. Garrison intended for his new paper to pick up where his efforts at the *Genius* had ended. Strenuously advocating the immediate emancipation of slaves throughout the United States, he vowed to tolerate no compromise. He also attacked the racial prejudice that permeated American society and the political hypocrisy that denied free blacks constitutional rights as citizens. Targeting black readers, he promised that his paper would provide a forum for black activists and a means to build a biracial political coalition. Within several months, he gained important financial support from a few prominent black merchants and had begun to win over some reluctant Boston reformers.

A little more than six months after Garrison's paper began operating, the nation was shocked by a bloody slave insurrection, the Nat Turner rebellion, outside Richmond, Virginia. Horrified, some southern officials blamed the *Liberator* and its publisher for instigating the uprising. Garrison was upset by the episode but not surprised. Although he never advocated violence, he had predicted that as long as slavery existed such an attack would eventually occur. Likewise, he warned that the potential for new and equally destructive assaults was likely. In response, several major newspapers condemned him. A number of southern communities banned the *Liberator*, and a few tried him in absentia, finding him guilty of various crimes. In Georgia a reward of $5,000 was offered for his arrest. President Jackson was so angered that he forbid the Post Office from delivering antislavery material. However, rather than deterring Garrison, the various actions energized him and propelled his paper to new prominence.

For the next two years, Garrison worked tirelessly at creating his own abolitionist organization. Tapping both newspaper colleagues as well as fellow activists, he diplomatically appealed for support. In January 1832, he assembled eleven cofounders and established the New England Anti-Slavery Society. With others to help drive his crusade, Garrison focused on the *Liberator* and convinced readers that immediate emancipation was the only solution to the slave problem. Expanding the size of the paper, he provided additional accounts of abuse as well as coverage of other anti-slavery societies. He also initiated a series of speaking tours designed to recruit members and discredit the gradualists, especially those who proposed creating colonies of freed slaves in Africa. On both counts he succeeded. A firebrand as a speaker, many found him unexpectedly mild-mannered and congenial away from the platform. His well-reasoned conclusions about slavery and the contradictions implicit in the colonization alternative also appealed to many listeners. Though still considered a mere rabble-rouser by some, Garrison proved very effective in attracting followers.

With his paper and Society securely established, Garrison traveled to England in early 1833. Parliament was on the verge of abolishing slavery and Garrison hoped that the tides of the British movement would carry Americans along as well. Through a series of speeches, he impressed British audiences with his ability and sincerity. Meeting with prominent British anti-slavery advocates, including William Wilberforce who was the movement's acknowledged leader, Garrison enlisted significant assistance from British writers and reformers. He also further undermined the American Colonization Society, whose adherents had been portraying their organization as America's dominant anti-slavery effort. Armed with new abolitionist pamphlets, speeches, and tracts that could be printed in the *Liberator*, he returned to the United States as the acknowledged American anti-slavery leader. The trip also reinforced to Garrison how difficult it would be to completely end slavery in the United States. The sheer numbers of slaves held in the United States compared to those held in the British Empire was daunting. Likewise, British owners were separated from their West Indies slaves by thousands of miles. Of course, American slaveholders lived alongside their slaves. Politically, unlike British officials, both major American parties avoided the issue. And finally, passions about slavery and race ran far stronger in the United States than in Great Britain.

Upon his return to the United States, Garrison was encouraged by the growing momentum of the abolitionist movement. Shortly after his arrival, the American Anti-Slavery Society (AAS), the first national anti-slavery organization, was founded in New York City. With Garrison's assistance, Arthur and Lewis Tappan and Theodore Weld establish the society. Spawned by the organization, local chapters began forming almost immediately. Within eighteen months, the New England Anti-Slavery Society also agreed to become a regional auxiliary for the AAS. From the beginning the *Liberator* served as the primary media outlet for the new society, providing Garrison with a broader audience than ever before. Weld was another source of encouragement. A young, dynamic abolitionist, he proved to be a brilliant organizer and was able to recruit thousands. Other committed reformers, including Englishman George Thompson who had accompanied Garrison back to the United States, added their abilities to the movement. Thompson had been one of the leading abolitionists in England, and his experience helped to guide the American movement during the next few years.

Amid the rush of promoting his paper, his abolitionist society, and his crusade, Garrison married Helen Benson. They had first met briefly during a visit Garrison made to her father, who was a successful merchant and anti-slavery proponent, and her brother George. Several months later, in January 1834, after much trepidation he began writing to her. Throughout the spring the two wrote each other regularly, though initially neither was completely certain of the other's intent. In April Garrison again visited the Benson home but this time spent three days courting Helen. Soon after, they began planning a September wedding. Demure and reticent, she provided a well-suited domestic counter balance for Garrison. Their union, which lasted forty-two years, was the beginning of an exceptionally warm, supportive family that included seven children.

The emergence of women's abolitionist societies further encouraged Garrison. Unwelcome in most traditional reform organizations, women nevertheless formed their own anti-slavery societies. As the abolitionist movement grew, the women's societies became an increasingly effective element. Garrison, unlike many of his colleagues, encouraged women's participation. He periodically addressed women's groups and attended their meetings. On several occasions, he actively assisted schoolmistress Prudence Crandell in creating and maintaining a school for black girls. When Crandell's school was burned, he helped her reopen it. When she was arrested for violating a Connecticut ordinance that declared her school illegal, he helped her avoid jail. Several years later, he used the *Liberator* to promote the Grimke sisters as both abolitionists and advocates of women's rights. He also pushed to revise the American Anti-Slavery Society charter to include women on the executive committee. By the late 1830s, Garrison had concluded that women in some ways were also compelled to endure injustices similar to slavery. Therefore he expanded his efforts to include women's rights.

Of course, the growth of the abolitionist movement did not come without fierce opposition. Southern hostility was expected, but there were also violent assaults in the North. Leaders of the American Colonization Society, struggling to compete for popular support, actively opposed Garrison who denounced colonization as merely a stratagem that reinforced white prejudices. Defenders of colonization used newspaper attacks, political blockades, and physical intimidation to deter the burgeoning growth of Garrison's movement. More menacing were the informal anti-abolitionist groups that formed in communities throughout the North. Often these groups initiated violent confrontations. In New York, anti-abolitionist gangs razed three black churches. Philadelphia, in reaction to an abolition appeal, experienced several days of rioting directed at free blacks in the city. Abolitionist speakers regularly were threatened and pelted with stones. At a meeting of the Boston Female Anti-Slavery Society in October 1835, Garrison himself barely escaped serious harm. Fleeing rowdies through a back window, he was dragged through the streets just ahead of an angry mob. Fortunately, Boston's mayor accompanied by two constables interceded and protected him from the frenzied throng. Two years later Elijah Lovejoy, an Illinois abolitionist, was not as lucky. Attacked and beaten to death, he became the movement's first martyr. Meanwhile Garrison, Thompson, and other leaders received thousands of death threats. The warnings, however, did not deter the movement.

Internal tensions also plagued Garrison's movement. At the core of these tensions was his uncompromising idealism. Embracing the era's concept of perfectionism, he demanded that slavery was sinful and exclusively a moral issue. He rejected the assumption that government should play the primary role in abolishing the institution. Instead he portrayed government as a vehicle of coercion and violence. The Constitution itself provided an explicit compact for preserving slavery and was simply a contemporary example of ruling through force. Coercion and violence were indispensable instruments of such a government and had scarred the entire body of American society. These tools could play no part in abolishing slavery; therefore, government would be unable to successfully eliminate the institution. In his challenge to the values, institutions, and power structure of American society, he also condemned the traditional clergy for perpetuating sin and violence by complying with an immoral government.

Garrison claimed his appeal for universal emancipation, which necessarily included the radical reformation of American society, was part of an encompassing effort to establish a more humane world civilization. He demanded that true moral cleansing transcended government. Abolishing slavery was, therefore, an essential step toward societal purification. Only through the twin ideals of selflessness and pacifism could such reform be achieved. Likewise, he defended moral independence and proposed that lasting reform could not be imposed upon the individual. Instead it had to be part of a spiritual maturation. Asserting strong, unyielding religious convictions, he declared that God could never sanction slavery, for slavery required violence. He further alienated established religious leaders throughout the country by advising abolitionists to withdraw from churches that did not fully embrace his crusade.

A growing challenge to the traditional role of women in society became another point of contention between Garrison and his critics. Embracing the incipient women's rights movement, he proposed that like slaves, women were restricted by violence and coercion. Remaining true to his abolitionist principles, he endorsed a defense of equal rights regardless of race or gender. He maintained that morality is not the domain of men alone. Rather, women are responsible moral beings and must be encouraged to play a leading role in reforming society. Individual convictions emanating from personal liberty and impartial judgment ought to prevail over social conventions. Further, Garrison demanded that women should be permitted to participate actively within male reform organizations, something that many male reformers opposed. Demonstrating his unflinching resolve, he attended but refused to participate in an 1840 international abolitionist convention in London because women had been refused admittance. Although his radical views factionalized the abolitionist movement, they strengthened his leadership role and reputation among supporters.

Rejecting partisan politics, Garrison shunned the formation of the Liberty Party in 1840 as a way to promote abolitionism. Instead, through the

Liberator and his many speaking engagements, he continued to pursue his own perfectionist methods. He maintained his campaign against fugitive slave laws that required the return of runaway slaves, who he referred to as "self-emancipated." The elimination of slavery in the District of Columbia was another regular target of his barbs. He also took on segregation in transportation and other public facilities. A fortunate encounter in 1841 gave his efforts additional impact. While attending an abolitionist convention on Nantucket, he met a young runaway, Frederick Douglass, who soon became a powerful abolitionist himself. Impressed by a speech that Douglass made, Garrison immediately began promoting him. Eloquent, intelligent, and charismatic, Douglass was the ideal contradiction of the racist attitudes that permeated most of American society. With Garrison's encouragement, Douglass polished his skills and soon became a popular abolitionist speaker. Garrison also used his press to publish Douglass's autobiography, which helped to transform him into an international abolitionist celebrity. In the coming years, Douglass's influence significantly aided Garrison's crusade.

The growing controversy about Texas provided another target for Garrison. Annexation, he warned, would entail an immoral war with Mexico to preserve slavery into the foreseeable future. From his point of view as both a pacifist and an abolitionist, a war to expand slavery was utterly abhorrent. In confronting the issue, he organized protest meetings, launched an encompassing petition campaign, and lobbied Congress. Immediately after war was declared, he also instigated an antiwar movement that garnered significant support throughout New England. The war and subsequent addition of Texas as a slave state further confirmed to him that the nation had separated into two incompatible sections: one that opposed slavery and one that supported it. Consequently, he proposed that the time had come for the nation to divide itself formally into two nations. It was a radical call that was echoed by some southern leaders, including John C. Calhoun. Though unable to curtail the nation's expansionist zeal, Garrison's demand that slavery be repealed in Texas brought new legitimacy to his abolitionist crusade. At the same time, his call for the peaceful separation of slave and free sections of the nation troubled many.

The conclusion of the Mexican War and Compromise of 1850 infused new intensity into the anti-slavery movement. Assessing the postwar debates, particularly the Wilmot Proviso controversy, Garrison concluded that the American public was swinging away from slavery. A new middle ground had opened up. Growing numbers of Americans were speaking out against slavery though they were not yet ready to embrace his radical abolitionist appeal. Hoping to build upon the momentum, Garrison launched an ambitious campaign in Ohio and the West. His offensive called for both the immediate elimination of slavery as well as the complete integration of free blacks into American society. He also staunchly maintained his call for

women's rights. Controversial as always, he was able to win new supporters despite stiff opposition wherever he went. The Compromise of 1850
further energized him. Condemning the Compromise as completely unjust,
he lambasted its primary supporters. His favorite targets were Henry Clay,
who he had never trusted, and Daniel Webster, who Garrison complained
had sold out to slavery in a desperate effort to win a presidential nomination. Ironically, Garrison seemed to share more opinions with John C.
Calhoun, who had begun proposing secession, than he did with Webster.
Despite his efforts, Garrison was not surprised by the passage of the Compromise but instead used the legislation as new ammunition for his crusade.

The most unacceptable element of the Compromise was the new Fugitive
Slave Act. During the months after its passage, Garrison filled the *Liberator*
with horror stories about the ordeal involved in returning runaways. He
also helped to organize unofficial patrols in Boston that monitored slave
catchers' activities and warned runaways when a catcher approached. Beyond encouraging civil disobedience, the Act fed Garrison's disdain for the
American legal system. At the core of his protest was a conviction that
the Constitution validated the nation's immorality. As he did throughout
the rest of the decade, he claimed that both the American political and legal
systems were unjust. Disregarding the electoral system, he steadfastly refused to endorse political candidates. Instead he chose to win his own spiritual constituents. Only by remaining outside of the political arena did he
feel that he could pursue his cause without compromise. For him, the 1857
Dred Scott decision served as an ultimate confirmation that the national
government as it then existed would never end slavery. Asserting that there
was a higher law than the Constitution, he concluded that disunion and a
new morally sound frame of government were required to before slavery
could be ended.

By the 1850s the anti-slavery movement had grown beyond the domain
of Garrison. He had become simply one voice, though still a powerful
voice, in an ever-expanding anti-slavery chorus. Spurred on by events and
circumstances, the opposition to slavery evolved in a variety of forms. Even
Frederick Douglass, who had been a loyal Garrison disciple for a decade,
broke from his abolitionist mentor and organized a campaign of his own.
The diversity, however, only intensified the movement. And with diverse
methods came polarization and a new potential for violence. While Garrison continued to advocate exclusively pacifist methods, he subtly fanned
the flames of the radical abolitionist fires. As much as any, his vitriolic
appeals encouraged violent anti-slavery activists including John Brown.
Condemning their methods, Garrison nevertheless applauded their convictions. After Brown's raid at Harper's Ferry in 1859, Garrison as much as
anyone was responsible for transforming him into an abolitionist martyr.

The secession of southern states after the 1860 election did not surprise
Garrison. On the other hand, although he expected a conflict, the carnage

and suffering entailed by the Civil War horrified him. It was, however, a conclusion that he felt was almost inevitable. Throughout the war, he continued to denounce slavery and promote the eventual integration of free blacks into American society. In December 1865, with the fighting over and slaves freed, Garrison ended publication of the *Liberator*. Though he recognized much still had to be done before black equality was achieved, he believed that the sin of slavery had been resolved. To challenge the ongoing constitutional adjustments and reforms would be counterproductive. His reforming efforts, however, did not end. Throughout the last fifteen years of his life, he actively supported women's rights as well as several other social reforms. He died in 1879 surrounded by his children.

BIBLIOGRAPHY

George Frederickson, *William Lloyd Garrison* (Englewood Cliffs, NJ: Prentice-Hall, 1968); Archibald Grimke, *William Lloyd Garrison the Abolitionist* (New York: A.M.S. Press, 1970); Henry Mayer, *All on Fire: William Lloyd Garrison and the Abolition of American Slavery* (New York: St. Martin's Press, 1998); Walter Merrill, *Against Wind and Tide: A Biography of William Lloyd Garrison* (Cambridge, MA: Harvard University Press, 1963); Russell Nye, *William Lloyd Garrison and the Humanitarian Reformers* (Boston: Little, Brown and Co., 1969); Vito Perrone, *William Lloyd Garrison* (Cambridge, MA: Harvard University Press, 1995); James B. Stewart et al., *William Lloyd Garrison and the Challenge of Emancipation* (New York: Harlan Davidson, 1992); and John Thomas, *The Liberator, William Lloyd Garrison* (Boston: Little, Brown and Co., 1963).

LUCRETIA MOTT
(1793–1880)

In an age marked by social change, no reformer was more active than Lucretia Mott. Hers was a life dedicated to humanitarian causes. From adolescence she questioned those aspects of American life that she considered unjust. Beginning with a challenge of the traditional Quaker Church, she embraced the anti-slavery movement and later helped to initiate the women's movement within the United States. Blessed with a bright, probing intellect, she became a compelling advocate for her causes. Though she was an unassuming, devoutly religious woman who in most ways conformed to the roles expected of her—wife, mother, and housekeeper—she also was among the first women to publicly campaign for political change. Her efforts had profound ramifications during and long after the Jacksonian era.

Lucretia Mott was born in 1793. Until she was eleven years old, she lived on Nantucket Island. Her father was a sea captain who spent much of his time away from home. Consequently, her mother, like most Nantucket women whose husbands made a living from the sea, played a particularly important role in rearing her children. Both parents were Quakers who steadfastly adhered to the requisites of their church, which included attending regular meetings and providing their daughters with a thorough education. When she was four, Lucretia was enrolled in a Quaker school on the island. A happy, gregarious child, she enjoyed her early years on Nantucket and throughout her life she referred to the island as her home.

After a near disastrous three-year voyage during which Spanish officials confiscated his ship, Lucretia's father decided to leave the sea and become a merchant. In 1804 he moved his family to Boston and began a prosperous business. Soon after the move Lucretia and her younger sister were enrolled in a Quaker coeducational boarding school, the Nine Partners School, in Duchess County, New York. Though initially unhappy at being away from her family, Lucretia soon adjusted. Her adroit mind, quick wit, and sharp intellect established her as one of the school's more capable students. An unusually self-assured child, she periodically challenged various school policies including the difference between the pay that her female and male instructors received. Influenced by one of the school's founders, Elias Hicks, she also developed what became a lifelong opposition to slavery.

It was while at Nine Partners that she first met James Mott. Five years older than she, he was the grandson of the school superintendent and brother of one of Lucretia's classmates. Upon completing his studies, James stayed on as an instructor and Lucretia became one of his students. When she was fifteen, Lucretia finished her own studies and was invited to remain at the school for almost two years as an apprentice teacher. However, in 1809 her parents, who had relocated to Philadelphia where they began a new business, called for her to return home. She agreed upon the promise that her father would provide James with a position in his business.

Soon after joining her parents in Philadelphia, eighteen-year-old Lucretia wed James. The marriage, which lasted fifty-six years until James's death in 1868, produced six children. In temperament and demeanor, Lucretia and James complemented each other. Both devout Quakers, they were well read and discerning. She was quietly aggressive and passionate about what she considered obvious inequalities. He was more constrained and less demonstrative but shared his wife's concerns. His willing support helped her to become a prominent social activist.

For Lucretia and James, the birth of two children and a series of financial difficulties marked their early years of marriage. Their first child was born in 1812. Soon after Lucretia's father's once-successful business failed, forcing James to find work elsewhere. Joining an uncle who operated a cotton mill, he moved his family back to New York, where a second child was born. Unfortunately the cotton trade was curtailed by the War of 1812 and James was again out of work. Meanwhile, after struggling to establish another business Lucretia's father died of typhus in 1815. Saddled with significant debts, her mother in true Nantucket fashion opened her own shop and quickly built it into a thriving enterprise. James and Lucretia, encouraged by the success, moved back to Philadelphia and James opened a shop of his own. To supplement the family income, Lucretia took a job as an assistant schoolteacher. Unfortunately, James was not as capable an entrepreneur as his mother-in-law and after a year had to close his business. Again seeking work, he was offered a position with a bank in New York City. However, Lucretia was unhappy about moving away from her mother and took it upon herself to find James employment in Philadelphia. She soon secured a position for him with a local merchant.

With her family's unsettled financial condition easing, Mott experienced the great tragedy of her life. Her two-year-old son, Thomas, died from a mysterious fever. Trying to understand the loss, she began studying various religious books and tracts. She found the printed sermons of William Ellery Channing especially revealing. The relationship between humanitarian concern, religion, and individual duty that he described profoundly moved her. About a year after her son's death, still unable to completely accept the loss, she experienced a personal epiphany while attending the Twelfth Street Quaker Meeting. Suddenly moved to share her revelation, she addressed the meetinghouse for the first time. The spontaneous message purged her spirit. During the months that followed, she became a regular contributor at monthly meetings. Her quietly delivered, succinct, and well-reasoned monologues made her a popular speaker among congregants. Her messages often proposed that if listeners obey their inner spirit, they would eventually find perfection. Convinced that she had a true gift, the meeting formally recognized her as a minister in 1821, a rare designation for a woman.

At the time that Mott began her ministry, a schism had begun to develop within the Philadelphia Meeting. At the center of the tensions was Elias Hicks, the seventy-year-old minister who had been so important to the Motts while they were at Nine Partners School. Hicks called for a return to a more traditional and evangelical method of worship. Opposing him were younger leaders who sought to tighten the rules and discipline within the Philadelphia Meeting. The Motts were caught between the two factions. The Twelfth Street Meeting, which was controlled by the new leaders or Orthodox Quakers, had provided them with a spiritual home during difficult times. It was there that Lucretia had begun her ministry and James served as the meeting's clerk. At the same time, the Motts disagreed with the Orthodox leaders on important points. Several times Lucretia had been gently warned about her preaching. Increasingly troubled by slavery in the United States, she had encouraged listeners to boycott products acquired through slave labor including cotton, molasses, and sugar. The Quaker elders, who included prosperous merchants, complained that such messages were more political than spiritual. Despite the warnings Lucretia, true to her character, discreetly defied the elders and continued to speak out against slavery.

As tensions between Hicksite and Orthodox Quakers grew, the Motts were forced to choose between the two factions. James quickly sided with Hicks but would not commit to him without Lucretia. She was more reluctant to leave the Twelfth Street Meeting. Although admiring Hicks, she was troubled by those who surrounded him. She particularly deplored their petty bickering and increasingly fiery rhetoric. She was also concerned that if she and James joined the Hicksites, relations with his mother, who staunchly supported the Orthodox faction, would suffer. Ultimately the deciding factor for Lucretia was her loyalty to James. Despite her trepidation, she agreed to follow Hicks. Once her decision was made, she immediately organized Hicksite Quakers in the Philadelphia area and extended her ministry as far north as New England.

Another reason the Motts left the Twelfth Street Meeting was because of their growing intolerance for slavery. Both had opposed the institution since adolescence and James was a member of the venerable Pennsylvania Abolitionist Society. Further moved by a visit from William Lloyd Garrison in 1830, they fully embraced the abolitionist appeal. The stand troubled some Quaker elders. Although they opposed slavery themselves, they considered Garrison's demand too confrontational. Recently released from a Baltimore jail where he had spent seven weeks for promoting his abolitionist crusade, Garrison had never been more passionate about his cause than he was when he visited the Motts. Though they had not previously met him, they knew his reputation and invited him to stay with them on his journey back to Boston. During his stay Garrison convinced his hosts that colonization and gradual emancipation in general, which they supported, was not an answer to slavery. Instead, the only solution was an immediate end of the institution throughout the nation. Impressed by the young reformer, Lucretia and James were converted and agreed to help his cause. Equally struck by Lucretia, Garrison immediately recognized her intelligence and commitment to humanitarian issues.

After Garrison's visit, Lucretia advocated abolitionism whenever speaking about slavery. However, organizing and promoting Hicksite Quakers continued to be her focus. To expand her ministry she made occasional trips throughout eastern Pennsylvania, New York, and New England. Whenever possible James accompanied her, but his business limited his travels. Aside from her journeys, Lucretia spent her time attending to her church and family. Always in demand as a minister, she also served as clerk of the local monthly meeting. Addtionally, her family, which now included four daughters and a son, required much attention. Despite her various church and community activities, she performed all the essential household activities. A frugal and demanding housekeeper, she refused to hire domestic help even though she and James could afford it.

In December 1833, Garrison again visited the Motts. This time he came to Philadelphia to attend a convention that he had called to form a national abolitionist organization. During the convention James, who was a delegate, and Lucretia transformed their home into an unofficial gathering place for attendees. Among the early guests, Garrison invited Lucretia, her mother, and her daughter to attend the convention even though officially women were prohibited. At the session Lucretia intended to sit silently and listen to the proceedings. However, as the delegates began to discuss the wording of the organization's Declaration of Sentiments, she quietly suggested several grammatical improvements. Though some were initially put off by her participation, others including Garrison encouraged her. By the end of the meetings, her contributions as well as her firm but gentle assurances won the respect of most delegates.

Mott's life, which was already quite active, acquired a new momentum following the convention. Inspired by the formation of the American Anti-Slavery Society she immediately called a meeting of her own to form a local women's anti-slavery organization. Employing skills honed while administering Quaker activities, she gathered together thirty local women, including several prominent black women, and established the Philadelphia Female Anti-Slavery Society. Unlike earlier women's societies that had been created for charitable and religious purposes, the Philadelphia society was the first truly political women's organization. As its corresponding clerk Mott was instrumental in drafting the society's constitution and determining its goals, which included challenging segregation throughout the city. For that purpose, she became increasingly involved in the local black community, often contesting the city's policies there. On one occasion she spearheaded a drive that kept a black school open. Later she led an effort to furnish poor blacks in the city with various essentials. Her organization also provided a refuge for runaway slaves. Although some applauded the efforts, others in the city were threatened by them. Less than eight months after the formation of the society, the opposition in Philadelphia instigated a destructive riot directed at the city's black population. Although the tumult frightened some of her supporters, Mott became even more committed to her cause.

The growing demands upon Mott's time took a toll on her health but did not slow her. In 1837, she was one of several women who organized the First Annual Anti-Slavery Convention of American Women. Held in New York City, the convention brought together for the first time women abolitionists from Philadelphia, New York City, and Boston as well as other communities in eight states. In all, seventy-one women attended. At the convention the delegates initiated a petition calling for an end to slavery in the nation's capitol. The goal was to collect 1 million signatures from throughout the nation and pressure Congress to pass appropriate legislation. The convention also agreed to publish two anti-slavery pamphlets written by Angelina and Sarah Grimke. The Grimke sisters, who were considered the first legitimate female abolitionist agents, were requested to travel to Boston and speak to women there. The convention also spawned the creation of new women's anti-slavery groups throughout the nation.

When Mott and the Grimke sisters met for the first time, it was in some ways the beginning of a women's movement in the United States. Their encounter also accelerated a growing division within the abolitionist movement. Though the Grimkes had briefly lived in Philadelphia and all three women were members of The Philadelphia Female Anti-Slavery Society, they had had no notable contact with each other prior to the New York convention. Mott completely agreed with the Grimkes' call for an end to racial prejudice and segregation throughout the United States. However, just as satisfying was their subtle argument that women should be considered equal to men. Since her childhood in Nantucket, Mott had questioned why society generally considered women less capable than men. One of the qualities that appealed to her about Quaker theology was the general belief in gender equality. Although she agreed that men and women had different natural roles, she did not agree that one gender should be considered superior to the other. Yet women in America were assigned a place subordinate to men. Mott applauded the way that the Grimkes enmeshed in their challenge to slavery an equally forceful challenge to the status of women.

Within a year, the controversy about allowing women to lead anti-slavery meetings threatened to divide permanently abolitionists into two opposing factions. During the Second Annual Anti-Slavery Convention of American Women, which met in Philadelphia in May 1838, one of the primary debates involved whether women abolitionists should be allowed to address men's meetings. Garrison, though he did not attend the convention, staunchly supported Mott and the Grimkes. At the same time there were women, including some influential leaders, who just as vehemently opposed mixed meetings. Midway through the weeklong convention, the debate came to dominate official discussions. However, before a policy could be determined delegates were confronted by a more immediate threat. Unruly Philadelphians, angry that black women were permitted to attend the convention, began to parade outside the meeting hall. Reviving destructive passions from several years earlier, a mob of more than 17,000 descended upon the delegates and set fire to the convention building. Not satisfied with merely breaking up the meeting, rioters next paraded off to attack two prominent black facilities within the city. Prematurely ending the convention, the ugly assault also delayed further formal deliberations about mixed abolitionist meetings.

During the next two years, the controversy intensified. For Mott and several others, the debate became intolerable in 1840 during the World Anti-Slavery Convention in London. Acknowledged as America's preeminent female abolitionist, Mott, along with her husband, was part of a Pennsylvania delegation that attended the convention. However, influenced by the split within the United States, British abolitionist leaders decided that women should not be permitted to participate. Despite a notable speech by Wendell Phillips supporting them, Mott and the other women were given seats in the back of the hall and were only allowed to observe the proceedings. When Garrison arrived midway through the convention, he demonstrated his unbending support for the women. Ignoring his assigned place at the front of the hall, he instead sat beside Mott throughout the rest of the convention. Whenever called upon to participate, he did so from the back of the hall with Mott and the other women by his side.

Outside the convention, Mott made several addresses challenging limits placed on women. It was the first time she had spoken specifically about women's rights and she made a lasting impression upon at least some of her listeners. Elizabeth Cady Stanton, who had accompanied Mott to London, was especially moved. Though the two women did not completely agree about how to end slavery, Stanton thoroughly admired Mott's defense of women's rights. Upon returning to the United States, Stanton increasingly focused her reforming efforts on women's rights. At the same time, there were others who attempted to obstruct Mott's efforts. Throughout her travels, British Quakers who refused to acknowledge Hicksites denounced her. Likewise, though she was applauded wherever she went, she was frustrated by the general disinterest of most British women. True to her character, though, their apparent apathy further impassioned her.

The years following the London convention were active and often trying ones for Mott. Upon returning to Philadelphia, she was more influential than ever before. Thoroughly committed to the abolitionist crusade, she resolutely carried her message as well as a growing concern about women's rights to new audiences including Congress and President Tyler. Adding to her reputation as the nation's foremost woman reformer, she embraced social causes ranging from opposing corporal punishment of children to anti-sabbatarianism. She lamented the plight of famine that struck Ireland and lambasted the meager living conditions that Irish immigrants were expected to endure within Philadelphia. The nation's growing tensions with Mexico and Great Britain also became targets of her dismay. As the United States marched to war with Mexico, she helped to organize an antiwar movement. Of course, as her reputation grew so too did her opposition. Rowdy individuals and groups physically threatened her numerous times. Even within the abolitionist movement, she felt the sting of reprisal. The controversy that swirled around Garrison stained her efforts as well.

In addition to her public battles, Mott encountered several trying personal matters. Particularly upsetting was an ongoing debate with Quaker leaders. They complained that her increasingly strident approach strayed from acceptable church behavior. Some warned that she had become too militant and should no longer be allowed to preach. Though still a popular Quaker minister, she was turned away and was denounced by some meetings. On one occasion while attending a yearly meeting in Ohio, local brethren denied her lodging and medical care. Despite the travails and a threat of banishment that Philadelphia Quakers regularly waved in front of her, she conscientiously continued to pursue reform. A couple of family matters also clouded her life. During the early 1840s James's business declined seriously, requiring her to again employ frugal household measures. More troubling was the death of her mother, Anna, in late March 1844.

Along with James, Anna had provided the emotional foundation and support that fortified Lucretia. Her mother's death was devastating and plunged her into six months of depression and very poor health.

In 1848 Mott, accompanied by her husband, made a momentous journey to upstate New York. After touring a Seneca Indian reservation and several runaway slave villages, the Motts visited Elizabeth Cady Stanton, who had recently moved to nearby Seneca Falls. On the first day of their visit, Stanton invited three local woman activists to join her and Mott for an afternoon tea. While discussing the status of women in the United States, Stanton proposed calling a convention to formally compile a list of women's grievances. The four women agreed and hastily scheduled a meeting for the following week. Expecting only a few other women to attend, the five organizers were amazed by the turnout. Nearly seventy women and thirty men trudged into Seneca Falls to join the deliberations. During the two-day convention, participants wrote a Declaration of Sentiments that paralleled the Declaration of Independence but included women. They also devised resolutions challenging the inequalities and indignities that women suffered from government and the law. Among the primary reforms called for was women's suffrage. Mott, who was the most notable attendee, was the first to sign the Declaration.

The Seneca Falls Convention became a landmark event for women in the United States and established Mott as one of the movement's founders. However, the initial reaction to the convention added to her controversial reputation. Some critics labeled the meeting as frivolous whereas others warned that it threatened to undermine American society. As always, Mott defended her position. Though she was disillusioned by the political system and therefore had some trepidation about suffrage, she nevertheless argued that if women were to have equal status with men, they must be able to participate politically. Education was also necessary for women to achieve equality. Since adolescence, she had questioned restrictions that prevented women from receiving professional training. She maintained that such obstacles were unjust and should be removed. Finally she advocated economic equality for women including fair wages and the legal rights necessary to operate businesses.

During the 1850s, Mott split her time fighting against slavery and for women's rights. After the Fugitive Slave Act in 1850, many in the North who had not previously taken a stand joined the anti-slavery movement. Though she was still considered a radical abolitionist, the change facilitated Mott's crusading efforts. It also allowed her to assist runaways more overtly and to confront slavery proponents more directly. The course of the women's movement, on the other hand, experienced many setbacks during the decade. The criticism that followed the Seneca Falls convention grew stronger and nastier. Though frustrated by the lack of support, Mott steadfastly continued to promote the cause in general and suffrage in particular.

She helped to organize conventions; she spoke regularly and attempted to recruit new, young leadership.

True to her Quaker beliefs, Mott opposed the Civil War, and although suspicious of Lincoln she did not question his motives as did Garrison. Throughout the war and afterwards, she helped emancipated slaves adjust to freedom by collecting donations, clothing, and other essentials and sending them to former slaves. She also spoke out about the travails faced by the newly enfranchised population whenever given the opportunity. Like some other women's rights activists, she recognized an opportunity to include women's suffrage as a part of the civil rights amendments that were designed to bring full citizenship to freedmen. Unfortunately, not all in the women's movement agreed and, as had happened within the Quaker church and the anti-slavery movement, a schism split the women's movement. Mott, as usual, was identified with the more confrontational faction.

Despite her age, health problems, and the loss of many beloved family members, including her husband in 1868, she actively continued to promote her causes through the 1870s. Until well into her eighties, she regularly attended women's rights conventions, spoke in support of suffrage and other reforms, and preached in Quaker meetings. Until the time of her death in 1880, she remained an icon of social reform within the United States.

BIBLIOGRAPHY

Margaret Hope Bacon, *Valiant Friend: The Life of Lucretia Mott* (New York: Walker and Company, 1980); Jennifer Fisher Bryant, *Lucretia Mott: A Guiding Light* (Grand Rapids, MI: W. B. Eerdmans Publishing Co., 1996); Otelia Cromwell, *Lucretia Mott* (Cambridge, MA: Harvard University Press, 1958); and Eleanor Flexner, *Century of Struggle: The Woman's Rights Movement in the United States* (Cambridge, MA: Harvard University Press, 1959).

SARAH AND ANGELINA GRIMKE (SARAH, 1792–1873; ANGELINA, 1804–1879)

Sarah and Angelina Grimke were South Carolina sisters who during the Jacksonian era established themselves as the first two active women abolitionists. In their fight to end slavery, they also began a campaign for their own rights as women. Compassionate and persuasive writers as well as engaging speakers, they traveled widely for several years lecturing about their controversial twin crusades. Having witnessed slavery firsthand while growing up, they vividly described the horrors associated with institution. However, to effectively promote the anti-slavery cause, they also sought justice for women. Despite abuse and ridicule from predominantly male audiences, they steadfastly pursued their reforms. Eventually they helped to provide a foundation for the redefinition of women's roles in American society.

The Grimke sisters spent the first twenty years of their lives in South Carolina. Born in 1792, Sarah was the sixth of thirteen children. Twelve years younger than her sister, Angelina was the youngest of the Grimke children. The girls had relatively happy childhoods. They were reared in a fashion typical of wealthy southern gentry. The family spent half the year in Charleston and half the year on their cotton plantation near Beaufort. The household was characteristic of an antebellum southern planter's home. Their father, a judge and planter, directed the important family activities and had a squadron of slaves to attend to most essential needs. By adolescence, the Grimke boys had been channeled into professions through which they could eventually become part of their community's leadership. Meanwhile Sarah and Angelina were taught the domestic duties of a planter's wife. Beyond basic reading and writing, their education focused upon genteel activities including needlework, drawing, music appreciation, manners, and deportment. These skills would help them attract an acceptable husband.

Both girls were bright, outgoing, reflective children. Although neither was rebellious, they were not satisfied with their predetermined future as planters' wives. Sarah, who was the more introspective of the two, longed to follow the path taken by her father and brother, Thomas. Of French Huguenot ancestry, her father was a successful planter, merchant, and politician. Sarah revered him and felt that he respected her intellectual potential despite her gender. Thomas was one of her three older brothers and took a special interest in her education. He often shared books and lessons with her that otherwise would have been unavailable. After he left home to study at Yale, she became increasingly discontent because of the limits on her opportunities. Angelina's role models included the men in her family but also Sarah, who had assumed much of the responsibility for rearing her. A strong-willed child, Angelina was more outspoken and judgmental than her sister was. Even as an adolescent, she was not afraid to challenge circumstances that she found unjust.

Religion played an important role in both girls' lives. Reared as Anglicans, both girls spent a part of their early years doing church-related activities. As they grew older, the church became one of the few socially acceptable alternatives to a husband and children. Sarah, when she was twenty-four, experienced a religious conversion that had profound ramifications for both girls. In need of specialized medical care, her father asked her to go with him to Philadelphia. It was a great responsibility rarely offered to a woman, and she interpreted it as a confirmation of the respect her father had for her. During her three-month stay in Philadelphia, she began to explore the tenets of Quakerism. Her spiritual probe was heightened by the death of her father, which she in part blamed on herself. On her journey back to Charleston, she began reading the writings of John Woolman. Once back home, she began corresponding with Quakers in Philadelphia. Fortified by her inheritance and spiritually moved, she soon decided to return to Philadelphia and become a Quaker.

Like her sister, Angelina as a young adult began a spiritual search of her own. Breaking from the Anglican Church, she joined a Presbyterian congregation in Charleston when she was twenty-two. For several years afterwards, she operated the congregation's Sunday school and contributed in numerous ways to church life. Among the activities she initiated were daily prayer sessions for her family's slaves. When she tried to expand the slave services the church reverend, while quietly acknowledging the immorality of slavery, discouraged her efforts. About the same time, Sarah came home to Charleston for a visit. Listening to Sarah's descriptions of her experiences among Philadelphia Quakers, Angelina became intrigued by the simple life, the egalitarian theology, and the Quaker opposition to slavery. She soon began attending Charleston's Quaker meeting. Unfortunately, the congregation consisted of only two members who were feuding. Undaunted, she set out to establish a new meeting and began in her own household. Despite alienating her mother, siblings, and some in her former Presbyterian congregation, she persevered for more than a year. However, in late 1828 she decided to join her sister in Philadelphia.

Another quality that the two sisters shared was their opposition to slavery. As children, both girls had obviously observed slavery but had been sheltered from the worst of its horrors. Sarah's concern began during her childhood. Reared in part by a slave maid, Sarah as a child questioned why slaves were denied education and formal religious training. In a moment of youthful rebellion, she secretly began teaching a slave girl who attended her how to read. Her father's stern rebuke only heightened Sarah's curiosity. As she matured, she became increasingly upset about slave conditions. Her brother Thomas, who helped organize the American Colonization Society in South Carolina, inadvertently fed her emerging convictions. While admitting that it was unjust he, like many of his contemporaries, also defended its necessity in the South. Sarah was perplexed by the apparent contradiction. Instead she agreed with the Quakers' uncompromising portrayal of the institution as morally evil. Though she left Charleston for religious reasons, a growing opposition to slavery was an important part of her new spiritual convictions.

Angelina's opposition to slavery came a bit later in life but more forcefully than did her sister's. As the youngest child, she was insulated from the abuses of slavery because her doting siblings often attended to tasks that house servants would have performed otherwise. Not until she was a young adult did she understand the inhumanity of slavery. It was after joining the Presbyterian Church that she began to seriously question the institution. Of particular concern was the lack of religious instruction slaves received. Additionally, she was often confronted by the institution's harsh realities while visiting the homes of her Sunday school students. The father of one student operated a workhouse in which slaves were tortuously punished. Outspoken in her condemnation, she left the church primarily because it continued to defend the institution. Unfortunately the local Quaker meeting that she joined also tolerated slavery. By the time she left Charleston, she was obsessed by slavery. She considered her departure an act of protest and her relocation to Philadelphia as an exile.

Upon their arrival in Philadelphia, both women concentrated on becoming faithful Quakers. They were enchanted by the city and comfortable with their new church, even though the Orthodox Quakers they joined expected conformity from members. Sarah spent her initial years in the home of a Quaker friend, Catherine Morris. Eight years later, Angelina joined her in Morris's house. Living cloistered lives, the two sisters were unconcerned about contemporary political issues aside from slavery. Nor did they become involved in the tensions between their Orthodox Quaker meeting and evangelical Hicksite Quakers. Instead they strove to serve their meeting however they could. For Angelina, service included becoming a Quaker teacher. She hoped to study at Catherine Beecher's Female Academy in Hartford, Connecticut. However, after she had gained admittance, the meeting's leaders discouraged her from leaving Philadelphia.

After eight years in Philadelphia, a series of events transformed the Grimkes from obedient Orthodox Quakers into radical abolitionists. The death of their brother Thomas in late 1834 began a new period of intense personal reflection for Sarah. Ultimately she concluded that the source of her discontent was the rigid conformity required by her meeting. Particularly troubling was the church's reluctance to confront slavery. Although inwardly tormented, Sarah nevertheless continued to comply with Quaker elders. Angelina, however, reached a similar conclusion but as always was far more demonstrative about her convictions. Since the establishment of the American Anti-Slavery Society in 1833, the sisters had tried to push their meeting to oppose slavery actively. In March 1835 Angelina attended a lecture by George Thompson, a British abolitionist and a spokesman for William Lloyd Garrison. Swept up by the address, Angelina was no longer willing to restrain her opposition to slavery. In a letter of support to Garrison, she committed herself to the radical abolitionist crusade. Garrison recognized the effect that the letter might have on his readers and published it in *The Liberator*.

Publication of Angelina's letter infuriated Quaker elders. They condemned her and ordered her to demand that Garrison, who they considered a fanatic, withdraw the letter. Even Sarah suggested that she write a retraction. Despite the pressure, Angelina stridently refused to renounce her words. Instead she became more aggressive in supporting Garrison. Rather than a retraction, she allowed her letter to be reprinted in numerous abolitionist publications. Additionally, she wrote an appeal to southern women describing ways that they could actively oppose slavery. Further defying church elders, she joined the Philadelphia Female Anti-Slavery Society whose leaders included Lucretia Mott. Orthodox Quakers, troubled by the schism within their church, had already labeled Mott as an instigator and denounced those associated with her. They threatened to do the same to Angelina. Nevertheless, Angelina joined Mott in promoting a boycott of all products made by slave labor. She also entertained other woman abolitionists who had been drawn to her by her letter to Garrison. Reflecting her new energy and commitment, Angelina's reputation as a radical opponent of slavery grew rapidly.

The force of Angelina's convictions soon filled Sarah as well. Although initially hesitant about the extent of her sister's anti-slavery activism, she readily joined in boycotting goods produced by slave labor. After much contemplation and coaxing from Angelina, she began questioning a number of apparent contradictions within her church. She was disturbed by the segregation that characterized Quaker meetings. The limits that Orthodox Quakers imposed upon all members but especially women also troubled her. When the meeting forbade her sister from speaking to women abolitionist organizations in New York, Sarah again objected. A final rebuff came during a regular worship session. While sharing prayers with the congregation, she was silenced by the meeting's leader. An obvious personal insult, Sarah afterward severed her relationship with the meeting and prepared to leave Philadelphia.

Departing Philadelphia, the sisters began a new life as the first women abolitionist agents appointed by the American Anti-Slavery Society. Traveling to New York City, they trained along with forty male agents. It was there that they first met Garrison and the Tappan brothers, who generally presided over New York abolitionists. However, it was their trainer and mentor, Theodore Weld, who made the greatest impact on the two women. Weld had established himself as an abolitionist by organizing students at Lane Seminary in Ohio. The sisters were also familiar with his fearless work leading abolitionists in the West and his reputation as a compelling speaker. After three weeks of his encouragement and intense instruction, the sisters launched their own campaign. Scheduled to speak to women in small, informal groups, the Grimkes' initial audiences far surpassed all expectations. So well attended were they that assembly rooms had to be found. However, larger facilities entailed new problems. Some churches and civic organizations refused to allow radical abolitionists to use their buildings. Likewise, many local officials were concerned about large gatherings of women without male supervision. Despite the obstacles, the sisters continued to draw large crowds.

As speakers, the Grimkes became an exceptionally effective team whose abilities and interests complemented each other. Combative as ever, Angelina was a fiery orator. Capable of moving listeners with her passionate appeals, she focused on current political conditions. Sarah was more analytical, more theoretical, and a thorough researcher. Soft-spoken and unassuming, she usually linked contemporary issues with the perfectionist reform philosophy of the era. For instance, it was Sarah who first paralleled the rights of women with slave conditions. She also provided an intellectual foundation from which the two sisters challenged segregation. Although they both blossomed into compelling advocates, Sarah's growth was profound. Once filled with self-doubt, she bristled with new confidence when describing the reforms that she concluded were necessary to save American society.

From New York, the sisters moved on to the Boston area. The center of reform activities, the city generally received them warmly. However, with Angelina promoting the abolitionist agenda and Sarah increasingly advocating women's rights, some anti-slavery leaders, including Weld, worried that they were becoming too radical. Already critical of Garrison's extremism, Weld feared that the sisters would further divide the movement. Church officials had their own concerns. They complained that the Grimkes challenged the patriarchal order of society and church authority. Several ministers launched campaigns against them. Commentary was published in local papers, congregations were instructed to disregard the sisters, and churches closed their doors to them. Nevertheless, the sister's audiences, which included both men and women, grew steadily. When denied church facilities, they found alternative buildings, including barns, for their meetings. When verbally attacked, they often responded directly, unwilling to be intimidated. So great was their appeal that during a grueling eight-week period in the fall of 1837, they spoke to hundreds of listeners almost every day. Audiences were drawn to them for a variety of reasons. A few were simply curious about their growing notoriety. Many women, in addition to sharing a concern about slavery, came to endorse the Grimkes' appeal for women's rights. Others, both men and women, wanted to hear them speak about ending slavery. Regardless of the motive, listeners were presented with well-reasoned, clearly argued addresses that combined both emotion and logic.

The rigor of their campaign finally took its toll in late October. Physically drained, Angelina contracted a fever and became gravely ill. To recuperate, both sisters spent the winter in Boston being cared for by friends. They briefly resumed their crusade in early 1838. Accepting an invitation to speak to the Massachusetts State Assembly, they became the first women in the nation to formally address a state legislature. The speeches were so well received that supporters claimed they did more to promote the abolitionist cause than any previous event had. The sisters also delivered four speeches on behalf of the Boston Female Anti-Slavery Society. With audiences of up to 2,800, the series concluded a stunningly successful nine-month journey. In spite of scurrilous personal attacks and controversy, since coming to Boston they had spoken to tens of thousands and enlisted hundreds into anti-slavery societies. They had also begun an important debate about women's rights.

Shortly after the sisters' last speech in Boston, Angelina married Theodore Weld. Since their first meeting two years earlier, they had silently nurtured a passion for each other. Even when Weld criticized her for including women's rights in anti-slavery speeches, Angelina maintained her ardor for him. Each admired the other's ability to inspire and lead. They were also attracted to the other's selfless pursuit of social reform. They had, however, rarely discussed personal matters. That changed during Angelina's illness. Writing each other regularly, they cautiously, almost accidentally, began describing their growing emotional attachment. After exchanging a series of increasingly personal letters, they agreed to wed. Angelina's only reservation was that she and her sister would have to part. Weld, who deeply respected Sarah, allayed the concern by insisting that Sarah should live with them. In May, the two reformers were wed. True to their reforming spirits, the civil ceremony was attended by a racially integrated gathering of guests.

Two days after the wedding, the Welds and Sarah briefly resumed their crusading efforts. Traveling to Philadelphia, the sisters addressed the Anti-Slavery Convention of American Women in Philadelphia. From the beginning, the convention was the target of rough opposition. By the third day, when Sarah and Angelina spoke, the attacks had become dangerous. Nevertheless, the sisters carried on. The following day, the hall was ransacked and set afire. Afterwards mobs descended upon other black facilities throughout the city and threatened several abolitionist leaders, including Lucretia Mott. Shaken by the destruction, the sisters returned to their new home just up the Hudson River from New York City. For the next few months, their lives focused upon setting up house and learning to perform essential domestic tasks, something they had never had to do, and recuperating from various health problems. They also contributed to an exposé about slavery that Weld was writing. When published in 1839 the book, *American Slavery as It Is*, significantly added to growing anti-slavery passions.

During the Grimkes' hiatus, a schism among abolitionists broke the movement into two factions. The split troubled the sisters and Weld. Although they endorsed the radical approach of Garrison, they disagreed with his rejection of the political system. On the other hand, orthodox abolitionists, led by the Tappan brothers, refused to support the sister's stand on women's rights. Complicating the situation, Theodore had long been a Tappan supporter but he too was troubled by the Tappan faction's reluctance to promote women's causes. Rather than attach themselves to one side or the other, the three reformers delayed resuming their crusading. Instead they continued to work quietly from their home writing anti-slavery tracts. Theodore and Angelina also had two children in the space of thirteen months.

In June 1840, the sisters were invited to attend the World Anti-Slavery Convention in London. Concerned about lingering health problems and growing debts, they chose not to make the trip. However, Elizabeth Cady Stanton kept them well informed about the proceedings. Stanton had met the sisters for the first time six months earlier. She too was the daughter of a judge and like the Grimkes was troubled by the limited legal rights of women. Her experience in London began a personal transformation that eight years later culminated in the formal launching of the American women's rights movement. During the years that she contemplated organizing a women's rights campaign, she often sought the advice and help of the Grimkes. Because the sisters were confined by various circumstances, they did not actively assist Stanton. They did, however, encourage Stanton's efforts. Angelina, who had a third child in 1843, suffered from an almost constant series of health problems. Sarah, as always, remained her sister's keeper through the health problems and in child rearing. Meanwhile, Theodore struggled with severe throat problems caused by years of bellowing out long, impassioned abolitionist speeches. Financial problems also plagued the trio and forced Theodore to serve as an abolitionist lobbyist in Washington for several years.

Plagued by continuing health concerns and financial problems, and frustrated by the pace of the anti-slavery movement, Weld and the sisters began to withdraw from reform activities. It was also during this time that Sarah briefly left the household. Absent for several months, she was invited to rejoin her sister's family and continue her role assisting Angelina with child-rearing duties. In 1840 the family bought a small farm and opened a school in Belleville, New Jersey. Consumed by the abolitionist crusade, Weld neglected the school during its initial years, but by the mid-1840s had begun to focus on it. After struggling for almost a decade to maintain the school, he was invited to become the education director of the Raritan Bay Union, a utopian cooperative. The offer provided the Welds and Sarah with a degree of financial security and appealed to their idealism. Though the experiment failed, the school endured. The trio remained at Raritan until shortly before the Civil War, when they moved to Perth Amboy and then to the Boston area.

After moving to Raritan, the two sisters no longer participated as actively in reform as they once had. They did, however, continue to advocate women's issues. Both served in women's organizations and as chairpersons for national committees. Sarah resumed her writing, focusing on issues ranging from practical child rearing to women's legal and economic rights. Her primary concern was the condition and status of working women. Though she never again completed a full manuscript, her letters and tracts were published widely. Along with Lucretia Mott and Elizabeth Cady Stanton, the two sisters helped to inspire the next generation of women's leaders.

The two sisters also continued to support the abolitionist campaign, though they became somewhat disillusioned with the increasingly violent character of the movement. Steadfastly holding to a peaceful solution to slavery, they were resigned to the realization after the Dred Scott decision that violence was probably inevitable. They greeted the beginning of civil war with despair, though assisted with various peaceful community efforts to aid the northern army. After the war, they worked in various ways to help freed slaves adjust to their new status. Anticipating the three civil rights amendments to the Constitution, their activities included promoting legislation that would guarantee the freed population constitutional rights. Their efforts to promote racial equality became personal shortly after the war when they discovered they had two mulatto nephews who had been fathered by Henry Grimke, their brother. Warmly accepting the two nephews, the sisters during the rest of their lives assisted the two young men in many ways and proudly included them in the Grimke-Weld family. Sarah died in 1873 and Angelina six years later, in 1879.

BIBLIOGRAPHY

Stephen Howard Browne, *Angelina Grimke: Rhetoric, Identity, and the Radical Imagination* (East Lansing: Michigan State University Press, 1999); Dwight Lowell Dumond, *Antislavery: The Crusade for Freedom in America* (Ann Arbor: University of Michigan Press, 1961); Robert Durkin, *Before Equal Suffrage: Women in Partisan Politics from Colonial Times to 1920* (Westport, CT: Greenwood Press, 1995); and Gerda Lerner, *The Grimke Sisters from South Carolina: Pioneers for Woman's Rights and Abolition* (New York: Oxford University Press, 1998).

RALPH WALDO EMERSON
(1803–1882)

Ralph Waldo Emerson provided a vital intellectual foundation for the Jacksonian era. The vigor of his writings and force of his ideas profoundly influenced the way that Americans viewed their world and themselves. He, more than anyone else, was responsible for projecting an idealized vision of the national character and society that Jacksonians sought to achieve. Through his observations and writings, he was able to integrate the rugged individualism that characterized Americans with the quest for perfection that permeated their society. A man of words rather than actions, his ideas and brilliant prose helped explain and justify the deeds of various reformers including William Lloyd Garrison, Margaret Fuller, and the Grimke sisters, among others. In his pursuit to establish a uniquely American culture, he became part of a group of writers, scholars, and philosophers who are recognized as the first generation of American literature.

Poverty, religion, and education characterized Emerson's early life. His forebears had been in Massachusetts since 1635, and for most of those years the family patriarchs had served as ministers. Continuing the tradition, his father was a Unitarian clergyman and part-time schoolteacher in Boston. Born in 1803, Ralph was the fourth of eight children and the third of six sons. The death of his father when Emerson was eight added to the family's financial woes. However, his mother was an intelligent and particularly forceful woman who provided for her children by taking in boarders. Aside from constant money problems, the family was in most ways typical of other New England families during the early nineteenth century.

One quality that did separate the Emerson boys from many of their peers was the family's emphasis upon education. Despite constant financial difficulties, Ralph and his brothers were educated at one of the finest schools in New England, the Boston Public Latin School. From there they went on to Harvard, Ralph pursuing religious studies. At Harvard he was a mediocre student, eventually graduating in the middle of his class. Avoiding mathematics and science classes, Ralph instead focused upon classical languages, history, and rhetoric though there was little hint of the literary stature that he would eventually achieve. Upon graduation in 1821, he joined his older brother William who had opened a school for young women which he operated out of the family home. After a year, William left to pursue theological studies in Europe while Emerson maintained the school for the next three years. A voracious reader throughout his lifetime, he filled his spare time writing essays and poetry.

Increasingly restless and anxious to establish himself, Emerson entered Harvard Divinity School in early 1825. Almost immediately, he was struck by a variety of maladies ranging from an eye disease to hip problems and chest pains. Laboring through the problems for eighteen months, he was sanctioned to preach. However, still in poor health he decided to spend the winter of 1826–27 in the South. Traveling first to Charleston and then to Florida, his journey included a great deal of soul searching and study. Much of his time was spent reading classical philosophy, preparing sermons, and writing poetry. In Florida he stayed with Achille Murat, a young French intellectual and nephew of Napoleon. A European exile, the Frenchman combined a brilliant mind with eclectic interests, which Emerson found intriguing. Encouraged by Murat, he returned to Boston with rejuvenated spirits and his health restored.

In addition to Murat, several people had a strong influence on Emerson's intellectual development. His mother, a devoutly religious woman in the Puritan tradition, constantly encouraged his academic endeavors. His aunt, Mary Moody Emerson, more than anyone else helped to shape her nephew's intellect. For thirty years, the two maintained a regular correspondence. He considered her one of best writers and brightest minds in his world. A frequent visitor in the Emerson house, her presence included various peccadilloes. She was, for instance, obsessed with death and slept in a coffin-shaped bed. Despite obvious talents and skills, she chose to live an austere life of penury and painful limitations. Self-educated and a demanding critic, she constantly challenged her nephew intellectually. Emerson's brother William in some ways served as a surrogate father and role model. Two years older than Ralph, William first traveled the academic path that his brother would follow. Soon after Ralph had graduated from Harvard, William, feeling that his family responsibilities had been fulfilled, pursued a theology degree in Germany. Upon his return, he turned to the law and began a successful practice in New York City. Among Emerson's mentors were Edward Everett and William Ellery Channing, both of whom had a profound effect upon him.

In December 1827, Emerson was invited to deliver a Christmas sermon in Concord, New Hampshire. There he met Ellen Tucker. Though only sixteen, she captivated the twenty-four-year-old preacher and they began a nine-month courtship. They were married in September 1828. By that time, Emerson had become the junior pastor to Boston's Second Church. The congregation, which had once been served by Cotton and Increase Mather, provided a comfortable salary for the newlyweds. Unfortunately throughout most of their brief marriage Ellen suffered from tuberculosis. Initially her bouts with the disease were mild, but they soon worsened. By the end of their first year of marriage, Ellen's decline was irreversible. She succumbed in February 1830. Here death shattered Emerson's otherwise comfortable life.

The two years following Ellen's death were a dark and uncertain period in Emerson's life. During that time, his activities included a daily visit to the mausoleum where his deceased wife was interred. So remorseful was he that on one visit eighteen months after her death, he opened her casket to confirm that she was gone. His faith also wavered during this time. While continuing to carry out church duties, he began to question conventional Christian theology. It was an intellectual probing that had begun before his marriage but was significantly accelerated after his wife's death. Voraciously reading philosophy and science, he contemplated ever more seriously the relationship between God, humanity, and nature. Intrigued by Eastern philosophy and religion, he concluded in mid-1832 that he could no longer conform to all formal Christian rites and rituals and that unless his church allowed him to perform services as he saw fit, he must resign. Though accommodating, the Second Church was not able to satisfy all Emerson's wishes and in September 1832 he resigned as junior pastor. The decision freed him from any restraints upon his conscience, but relatives and friends questioned his rationale for leaving a secure and prestigious position to pursue his own personal philosophical dilemmas.

Two months after resigning, Emerson embarked on a ten-month journey to Europe. Half his time was spent wandering through the cities of Italy, inundating himself in the country's classical art and philosophy. Inspired, he traveled north through Switzerland and into France. In Paris he focused upon the city's centers of natural science, visiting numerous botanical gardens. Then he went on to England, where he visited the writers Samuel Taylor Coleridge, Thomas Carlyle, and William Wadsworth. The trip further confirmed the theological doubts that he had been contemplating for several years. By the time he returned to the United States in the fall of 1833, he had broken completely from conventional Christianity and had begun to formulate his own understanding of the relationship between humankind and nature.

Upon his return to the United States, Emerson set out to support himself as a lecturer. He was financially aided by a modest inheritance from his wife's estate. The money also allowed him to continue his religious and scientific studies. Moved by the tenets of Quakerism as well as his evolving understanding of nature, he met a German-trained Unitarian minister and philosopher, Frederic Hedge, whose work he came to admire. Hedge's assessment of various contemporary thinkers, particularly Immanuel Kant, impressed Emerson and further stimulated his own understanding. Intellectually integrating these three elements—Quaker theology, natural science, and Hedge—Emerson began to define the concept of transcendentalism for which he was to become associated.

Lydia Jackson provided another necessary element to Emerson's evolving views about the world. In early 1834 while addressing a congregation in Plymouth, he first met Lydia. A year older than he, she had heard him speak several years earlier and had been enthralled. After hearing him again in Plymouth, she concluded that his ideas were hers as well. Likewise, she shared his love of literature and the spoken word. Soon after his lecture, they began a relationship that would blossom during the next eighteen months and bring a real joy to his life for the first time since Ellen's death. In September 1835, they were married. Though the relationship with Lydia, or Lidian as he called her, was never as passionate or demonstrative as was his first marriage, she nurtured him intellectually and encouraged his academic endeavors. She became both a partner as well as a quiet but necessary collaborator. During their forty-six years of marriage, they had three children, two of whom survived both parents. Fortified by his new happiness, Emerson began to formally forge the precepts of transcendentalism.

A year after his marriage Emerson published his first book, *Nature*. The work is an outgrowth of the author's observations and understanding about the relationship between nature and humankind. He proposes that all experience is essentially a product of nature and that experience elevates the spirit. Emerson contends that on the most basic level, nature obviously provides the raw materials necessary for life, but it also educates, informs, and endows through aesthetics and beauty. Extending his thought, the author idealistically proposes that there is a natural order that transcends science, civilization, and humanity. Rather than a tangible product such as a law or behavior, for Emerson it is the idea or plan that is most important. He insists that thought, action, ethics, religion, and art ought to be grounded in individual experience and that the source of experience is found in nature. In prose his contemporaries described as dazzling, he engages the reader with self-validating explanations about nature and humanity. His effort marks a formal rethinking of classic philosophers, particularly the Stoics, and established him as the principal spokesman for the evolving New England transcendentalist movement.

About the same time that *Nature* was published, Emerson joined several other New England thinkers in a casual symposium designed to challenge what they considered the prosaic intellectual climate in the United States. The ten attendees included Frederic Hedge, educator Bronson Alcott, George Ripley who later founded the Brook Farm commune, as well as several Harvard divinity students. By providing a stimulating forum for new ideas, the meeting soon led to somewhat regularly scheduled get-togethers in which various specific topics were discussed. A few participants comprised the society's core, but others joined or left the group from one meeting to the next. Referring to themselves as the Transcendental Club, Emerson and his fellow thinkers ultimately held thirty similar meetings over the next four years. As with the first symposium, these encounters became sounding boards where current issues were discussed within a philosophical context. To further promote their evolving views, the club began a quarterly magazine, the *Dial*, which Emerson helped to edit. Though he never considered the Transcendental Club more than an informal gathering, it did invigorate and energize him.

The twelve years following *Nature* were Emerson's most productive. His reputation as the preeminent transcendentalist grew steadily. In demand as a lecturer, he was able to support his family comfortably on his speaking fees. By the 1840s, he was delivering as many as eighty lectures a year. Likewise, his circle of friends broadened to include other notable intellectuals. Among them was a young Harvard student, Henry David Thoreau, whose observations and thoughts Emerson found compelling. Activist Margaret Fuller was another whose ideas nurtured his intellect. As a lecturer, he was in ever-greater demand. Presenting numerous lecture series, he also gave several important and very well-received discourses. Among them were two major addresses at Harvard that further solidified his reputation as one of the era's great thinkers. Because all his lectures were carefully written out before they were delivered, his speaking fed his writing. As always, writing remained at the center of his endeavors. In addition to many articles for the *Dial* as well as other publications, he produced much poetry and essays, including two volumes of collected essays published between 1841 and 1844.

Throughout his endeavors, Emerson continued to refine transcendentalism. At its core was a defiant rebellion against convention and orthodoxy. Challenging eighteenth-century rationalists and rejecting traditional Christian attitudes, Emerson optimistically stressed individualism. He proposed that basic concepts, including God and freedom, are inborn in all persons and that regardless of education, social status, or wealth, each person is equally capable of pursuing truth and knowledge. Relying heavily upon spontaneous insight, he contended that beyond science, there is a state of understanding that combines knowledge and intuition. He urged people to be self-reliant and to look within themselves for truth. Likewise, each person should act upon their own convictions regardless of societal dictates or public opinion. He maintained that inner truth inspires a reverence for self and others, which, in turn, promotes efforts to perfect civilization. The time had arrived, according to Emerson, for the young, democratic United States to establish its own culture and lead the world to a higher level of civilization. For him, transcendentalism was a movement that, by encouraging individualism and self-awareness, could provide an intellectual foundation for improving human culture.

Though his purpose was not to promote the economic expansion that had come to characterize the American experience, his work mirrored the ebullient, democratic nation in which he lived. Seeking to encourage a spiritual realization within each individual, he provided unintended momentum to the various forces of change swirling through Jacksonian society. The individualism that was at the core of his philosophy complemented the ever-growing ambition and self-image of his fellow Americans. In praising intuitive understanding, he was commending a quality ideally suited for a nation that had begun to embrace personal achievement rather than inherited status. The wisdom attained by balancing civilization and nature as described by Emerson was consistent with the kind of basic understanding Jacksonians aspired to achieve. Although it was not his primary intention, Emerson through his philosophical enterprises tapped into the mood of the country and in so doing fed the evolution of a national character. In response, his growing American audience eagerly anticipated further observations and revelations, thus heightening his popularity.

In addition to his carefully crafted prose, the quality that separated Emerson from his literary peers was his ability to relate his philosophical conclusions to contemporary events and circumstances. Although not a part of mainstream American society, he was acutely sensitive to daily ebb and flow of life around him. Politically he was most comfortable with the simple agrarian traditions espoused by Jefferson and later by Jackson Democrats. For him, the government that governed least was the best government. However, consistent with his New England background, he, like many Whigs, did not trust the masses. He was suspicious of any government directed by what he considered the middling sort. Likewise, he was wary of leaders who established themselves by mobilizing popular sentiment. Instead he praised self-directed leaders who acted upon their own convictions. Beset by these contradictory attitudes, practical politics was, therefore, problematic for him. Instead, he functioned politically as a critic and commentator.

Although his ideas encouraged many of the era's social reformers, Emerson rarely participated in reform efforts. Uncomfortable as an organizer or in an activist role, he instead remained apart from his countrymen by immersing himself in cerebral pursuits. His world revolved around his home and family in Concord and visits from fellow thinkers. George Ripley, Margaret Fuller, Bronson Alcott, and young Henry David Thoreau were among those who regularly visited him. Thoreau in particular was the beneficiary of Emerson's philanthropy. It was on land near Walden Pond provided by Emerson that Thoreau built a cabin and spent a solitary year pondering and writing some of his most important works. Other less frequent visitors, including William Henry Channing, Theodore Parker, and Sarah and Angelina Grimke, were drawn to him by his ever-growing reputation as the guiding light of transcendentalism. With Lidian's help, Emerson encouraged visits by opening his home to those who he considered colleagues and friends. Visits could last from a day to several weeks, thus creating an environment that nurtured his intellectual activity. When not exploring ideas with colleagues, he spent much of his time writing essays, reading on a wide variety of subjects, preparing lectures, and editing various future publications. Only when he was away lecturing did he leave his relatively insulated existence in Concord.

When he did become involved in reform efforts, it was often the result of his wife Lidian's steady prodding. On women's rights in particular, she was well ahead of her husband. Emerson was generally ambivalent about the status of women. He contended that with a few exceptions such as Margaret Fuller and the Grimke sisters, most women did not want a place in society equal to men. Lidian, on the other hand, was a self-assured woman capable of intellectually challenging her husband in various ways. Assisted by Fuller, she was able subtly to convert her husband into an advocate of women's rights. Although Emerson always questioned the morality of slavery and encouraged Americans to eventually do away with it, Lidian again was ahead of him in calling for the institution's immediate elimination. She became an active opponent of slavery after a visit from the Grimke sisters in 1837. For him, it would be another seven years before he fully committed himself to ending slavery. Like many, he feared that William Lloyd Garrison, who he admired personally, was too radical and demanding. However, influenced by his wife, his readings, his abolitionist friends, and a Frederick Douglass speech, Emerson in 1844 openly joined the call to end slavery immediately. Afterwards emancipation became a regular theme in his writings. By the 1850s, the Emersons were energetically supporting various anti-slavery efforts, including the Underground Railroad and radical abolitionist John Brown.

Among the causes that Emerson was active in throughout his life were various peace movements. They included opposing Indian policies initiated by the Jackson and Van Buren administrations. Emerson publicly assailed the forced removal of Cherokee that became known as the "Trail of Tears." In an open letter to Van Buren, he angrily denounced the episode. Later he shifted his focus to Texas and annexation. Before most, he recognized the potential ramifications of acquiring Texas. In 1844 he organized a series of meetings designed to convince Massachusetts's voters to demonstrate their opposition to annexation. He also opposed the war with Mexico and feared the consequences of seizing California and the New Mexico Territory. After the war, he prophetically warned that the victory over Mexico would split the United States into two incompatible sections. The Compromise of 1850 further convinced him about the crisis looming in the nation's future.

The growing sectional tensions that characterized the nation during the 1850s obviously influenced Emerson. Upon returning from a lecture tour to London in mid-1848, he allowed himself to be drawn into the fiery national debate about slavery. Frustrated and increasingly intolerant of slaveholders, he began to denounce publicly defenders of the South's "peculiar institution." In great demand as a lecturer, his addresses often focused on emancipation and abolitionism. Though still engaged in philosophical endeavors, by the mid-1850s much of his time was spent denouncing the immorality of slavery and assisting various abolitionist causes. The extension of slavery into western territories acquired from Mexico was especially appalling to him. By the end of the decade, Emerson had completely rejected the South and supported the Union with a patriotic fervor throughout the war.

Revered throughout the western world as America's preeminent intellectual, Emerson spent much of his last twenty years enjoying the acclaim of his earlier successes. Immediately after the Civil War, he grew disillusioned by the changes that followed the war and the rapidly evolving industrial order. Retreating to literary endeavors, he remained a popular lecturer but was less willing to accept as rigorous a speaking schedule as he had during his prime. He did, however, make several ambitious tours, including one to California and another to Europe. Likewise, while he continued to publish, his production fell off noticeably. His home remained a gathering place for scholars and philosophers, but the length and regularity of visits declined significantly. Instead Emerson spent more time with Lidian and their children and grandchildren. In April 1882, surrounded by family, Emerson died.

BIBLIOGRAPHY

Harold Bloom, *Ralph Waldo Emerson* (New York: Chelsea House Publishers, 1985); Peter S. Field, *Ralph Waldo Emerson: The Making of a Democratic Intellectual* (Lanham, MD: Rowman and Littlefield, 2002); Lisa Lipkin, *Ralph Waldo Emerson* (New York: Book Sales, Inc., 2000); Joel Myerson, *Ralph Waldo Emerson: A Descriptive Biography* (Pittsburgh: University of Pittsburgh Press, 1982); Joel Porte, *Representative Man: Ralph Waldo Emerson in His Time* (New York:

Columbia University Press, 1979); Robert D. Richardson, *Ralph Waldo Emerson: The Mind on Fire* (Berkeley: University of California Press, 1995); and Lloyd Earl Rohler, *Ralph Waldo Emerson: Preacher and Lecturer* (Westport, CT: Greenwood Press, 1995).

CHARLES GRANDISON FINNEY
(1792–1875)

Charles Grandison Finney became the preeminent clergyman of Jacksonian America. Despite minimal formal theological training, he dominated the Second Great Awakening revival movement that swept through the Northeast during the 1820s and 1830s. Relying on an appeal to the conscience and an uncomplicated, plain-spoken doctrine, he attracted many middle- and working-class followers who traditional religious leaders were unable to reach. His message stressed that each individual is capable of salvation but is also responsible for sin. Likewise, even those who have been saved are required to reaffirm their salvation regularly. Further challenging the conventional church, he encouraged men and women to worship together. Finney's powerful message reflected and reinforced the evolving values of individualism, expanded democracy, and moral responsibility associated with the Jacksonian era.

Little is known about Finney's childhood. He was born in 1792, the seventh of nine children. His parents operated a small farm near Litchfield, Connecticut, but, lured by cheap land, they moved the family to Oneida County, New York, when Charles was two years old. Though the region soon earned the reputation as "the burned-over district" because of the religious fervor that gripped it, the Finney family was untouched by the evangelical passions. Instead, their energies were spent carving an existence out of the backwoods settlement.

Until he was fourteen, Finney's formal education consisted of learning basic skills at home and receiving irregular lessons from itinerants who periodically traveled through the region. In 1806, it appears that his parents enrolled him in the Hamilton Oneida Academy in nearby Clinton, New York. The school offered a respectable classical curriculum and included several notable faculty members. Though there are no extant records, there is some evidence that while at the academy, Finney did well. Blessed with a capable intellect, he seems to have had no problems meeting the school's academic standards. Outside the classroom he participated in several sports and discovered a lifelong love for music. Religion, however, remained beyond his realm of endeavors. Despite various church influences, he claimed to have remained ignorant about religion during his student days. His time at the academy ended after two years when his parents moved to Henderson, New York, a remote village on Lake Ontario.

Despite limited formal education, Finney's academic abilities and general knowledge impressed his new neighbors enough that they hired him to teach school in the village. During the next four years, he established himself as a capable and popular teacher. As well as an alternative to the family farm, the position provided him with an opportunity to further develop his own interests. In 1812, spurred by a growing thirst for additional academic training, he moved to an uncle's home in Warren, Connecticut, and renewed his formal studies. However, after a year spent preparing for the Yale entrance examinations, his mentor in Warren suggested that he forgo Yale. Instead Finney became convinced that he could learn in two years of directed self-study what would take four years at Yale to learn. It was a decision that the young man happily embraced at the time but would later regret. Rather than attending Yale, he accepted a position teaching in the New Jersey public schools. There he remained for four years until his mother's health required him to return to Henderson.

His home had changed little during his six-year absence. Aside from the family farm, there were few opportunities for an ambitious young man. At twenty-six, Finney was anxious to find a vocation that, unlike teaching school, provided a comfortable income as well as long-term security. Encouraged by friends and a growing local demand for lawyers, he chose to pursue the law. It was a career for which he seemed well suited. A captivating speaker who possessed a sharp, inquisitive mind, he could both charm and dominate a jury.

Finney began his studies apprenticing at a law office in a nearby town of Adams. During the next three years, he read law and served as a clerk assisting with various cases. The absence of trained attorneys coupled with a constant demand for legal services provided him with regular opportunities to practice even though he was not formally licensed. When not pursuing his studies and clerking duties, he enjoyed an active social life that included directing the Presbyterian Church choir. Admittedly skeptical about organized religion, he soon developed a close friendship with the church's young pastor, George Gale. Though unimpressed by Gale's oratorical skills, Finney was drawn to him intellectually. As part of his legal studies, Finney had become increasingly curious about numerous references to the Bible made by the legal scholars he read. To better understand the source of those references as well as Calvinism in general, he turned to Gale. Finney's lifelong Bible study subtly evolved from those conversations.

In October 1821, Finney experienced an epiphany. Through his broadening understanding of church doctrine, he had grown exceedingly perplexed about his own spiritual well-being. One morning, in an attempt to resolve his struggle, he walked into the woods just north of Adams, found a remote spot, and prayed for several hours. Purged of self-doubts, Finney spent the afternoon in his law office singing hymns and reflecting upon his experience earlier in the day. That evening, he claimed that Christ appeared to him and that the Holy Ghost baptized him. Filled with a new inner joy, he immediately decided that his life calling was to share his revelations with others. The next morning, he formally ended his law studies and began life as an evangelist.

The first step in Finney's new life was to identify his personal spiritual beliefs. In so doing, he acknowledged some basic differences with Gale and traditional Congregational theology. From his own studies and particularly his recent conversion experience, he was convinced that Calvinism, upon which church doctrine was established, was flawed. He found elements of Calvinism both polemical and contradictory. Most importantly, he disagreed with the basic premise that humankind possesses an essentially sinful nature and is inclined to evil. Instead he held that life is a series of personal choices that include sinful behavior. However, he contended that even when sinful behavior is chosen, each person has the opportunity to repent. Therefore, salvation is not exclusively a matter of predestination. Rather, every person has the power to earn salvation through good works and faith.

Despite these basic disagreements, Finney intended to remain within the church and immediately began formal studies with Gale. Appreciating his friend's new passion, Gale was concerned about his theology. Nevertheless, he encouraged Finney and, when necessary, defended him from local skeptics who questioned the recent convert's sincerity. After instructing Finney for several months, Gale became ill and was unable to attend his Adams congregation. Into the local spiritual void came a Universalist minister who attempted to win over some of Gale's followers. Finney was asked by his mentor to respond publicly to the newcomer's doctrines. Eagerly accepting the invitation, Finney delivered two compelling addresses, after which the challenger left town. As a reward the Presbytery, with Gale's endorsement, allowed Finney to conclude his studies after only six months and licensed him to preach. Though still weak on fundamental theology, he was assigned to fill in for the ailing Gale.

Within a few weeks, the Adams congregation recognized that Finney differed in significant ways from Gale. He was a more spontaneous and extemporaneous speaker. Likewise, his lack of rudimentary theological understandings troubled some, including Gale. Responding to the growing discontent, the Presbytery reassigned Finney to missionary service in a sparsely populated region east of Lake Ontario. Though a difficult task, he pursued it aggressively. Convinced that he was part of a holy mission against Satan, he sought to save souls however possible. To do this, he developed a style that included both the emotional outbursts associated with evangelists and the quiet reasoned manner of more traditional ministers. The efforts, despite some initial reservations, won him general acceptance. Soon his reputation alone began to attract new followers.

Amid his early success, Finney married Lydia Root Andrews in October 1824. Their families had known each other long before Finney came to Adams but Charles, who was twelve years older than Lydia, had little contact with her. Shortly after he moved to Adams, Lydia began visiting her sister, who also lived in the village. The handsome law clerk and choir director captivated her. Months of casual encounters preceded a more committed relationship and eventually a formal engagement. A pious young woman, Lydia became a significant influence in her future husband's conversion experience. Their marriage lasted for twenty-three years until her death in 1847 and produced six children. Throughout Finney's rise to prominence, Lydia provided constant support and encouragement to him.

Immediately after his marriage, Finney left his bride with her parents and returned to his missionary work. Though he had planned to be away for only a few weeks, he was in such great demand that he spent the entire winter attending to settlements near the St. Lawrence River. When in the early spring he was finally able to reunite with Lydia, he brought her back north and resumed his work. Traveling from village to village, his following as well as his reputation grew steadily. Soon he was requested to lead a series of revival meetings in more established communities around Rome and Utica in the central part of the state. The success of those efforts during the summer and fall of 1825 earned him an invitation from a few clergymen in Rome. By 1825 Rome was a rapidly growing commercial center along the recently completed Erie Canal. The town was characterized by a burgeoning economic base and a diverse population. For Finney, who had been preaching for less than two years, the invitation offered a great opportunity to further expand his evangelical ministry and, during the first four weeks of 1826, he industriously stoked local revival fires. His efforts proved a resounding success. Local clergymen attributed hundreds of new members to his activities. All elements of the community, from commercial and political leaders to unskilled laborers, were among those moved by the evangelist.

From Rome, Finney moved on to Utica. Another booming canal town, Utica had a larger population than Rome. Most of the town's clergy received Finney warmly with hopes that he would outdo his recent successes. They provided him with more help and assistance than anywhere he had been. As a result, the Utica revival was better organized, more encompassing, and longer lasting than any of Finney's previous ventures. Beginning in early February, the campaign continued for over three months. It included a coordinated schedule of regular prayer meetings throughout both the town and neighboring villages. At the center of all the activity was Finney. Preaching, praying, organizing, and advising, he built a revival unlike any the region had ever experienced. The results were spectacular. Church membership swelled as hundreds committed themselves to their faith. After the Utica revival, Finney was considered one of the nation's preeminent evangelists.

By the time he left Utica, Finney had developed the essential elements of both the style and the message that became his professional trademarks. At the core of his message was the belief that sinners are responsible for their own salvation. Unlike the traditional clergy, he contended that conversion is immediate rather than an evolving condition. It is emotional and demonstrable, often through physical manifestations such as the spontaneous fainting spells that occasionally occurred during Baptist and Methodist services. To Finney there was no middle ground between the saved and the unsaved. Reinforcing this belief, he concluded each revival session by calling upon converted listeners to join him in front of the audience and accept their new commitment to the church. Drawing upon his understanding of scripture and past theologians such as Jonathan Edwards, he contended that once saved, true believers demonstrate salvation through assiduous morality and benevolence. However, rather than the controlled, restrained behavior typical of traditional churches, Finney encouraged passionate displays of faith. Likewise, worship is a unifying and fulfilling experience rather than one that segregates populations. The message was a relatively simple proposal that salvation is not predestined and does not require deep study or scholarly analysis.

When organizing revivals, Finney adapted the camp meeting techniques typical of western revivals to an urban setting. At the same time, he employed his training as a lawyer when addressing congregations. A keen judge of his audiences, he learned to evaluate instantly what they wanted and how much they would accept. Depending upon his listeners, he adjusted the degree of showmanship he used much as a lawyer would when addressing a jury. He also used language that he felt would be comfortable to his audience rather than the platitudes often employed by his peers. As circumstances required, he could broaden his intellectual content or tone it down. In either case, his easy yet confident demeanor usually assured listeners. He could also be imposing physically. Tall, athletic, and handsome, he became particularly animated when he felt conditions required it. His most notable physical assets were his steely blue eyes. Many claimed that his eyes had an almost hypnotic effect. They commanded attention and would not release a listener until the speaker's message had been delivered. The end result was that Finney, whether through gentle persuasion or abrupt confrontation, could usually maneuver his audience into embracing his discourse regardless of the circumstances.

Finney's appeal was well suited to the evolving ideals and attitudes of Jacksonian America. His emphasis on self-determination reinforced a growing belief that success was proportionate to an individual's abilities, enterprise, and worth. He also addressed the conflict between traditional communal values and the new self-serving standards required by the developing market economy. Sensitive to the stresses upon the emerging entrepreneurial class, he advocated an alternative method for maintaining order. At the heart of that order was a cooperative relationship between the community and the church. Finney proposed that the church should provide a way for traditional community leaders to share responsibilities and authority with the emerging entrepreneurial class. The role of the church was to determine moral standards while community commercial and political leaders implemented those standards. This in turn would encourage conformity and maintain harmony throughout the community as a whole.

Women were especially drawn to Finney's message. With early industrial pursuits taking men away from the household, the role of the woman changed in many ways. Increasingly women were expected to manage domestic responsibilities, especially child rearing, with limited guidance or assistance from the family patriarch. At the same time, with manufactured goods available, the status of women as a skilled family craftsperson eroded. Consequently women were generally excluded from much of the expanding market activity. Even those women who did work outside the home had at best minimal opportunity to participate commercially. Improved transportation and increased mobility further challenged the traditional role of women. Decline of extended families meant less support from mothers and sisters and greater isolation within the household. These profound changes had a disconcerting effect upon many women.

Finney proposed a role for women to play in the evolving American society. He contended that because they were less likely to be contaminated by the evils associated with urban and industrial growth, women should serve as the moral protectors of their family and community. Likewise, new opportunities to influence their communities, especially as educators, should be opened to women. To fulfill their new responsibilities, he felt that women must be considered capable of salvation, which in turn required religious instruction equivalent in most ways to males. Therefore, he encouraged mixed congregations that included both men and women. As an alternative to the traditional family support system among women, he encouraged the formation of sisterhoods, especially among entrepreneurial-class women. Acting cooperatively, sisterhoods could help focus communities on the moral issues within their community.

Although Finney converted thousands in just a few months, many traditionally trained church leaders vehemently disagreed with him. Their chief concerns were that he misled the faithful, threatened church organization, and challenged theological wisdom in general. At the same time, the opposition reflected a growing competition for followers with the evangelist. Finney's method was another source of anxiety. Detractors complained that his language was coarse and often inappropriate. His unbridled zeal, frantic manner, and overly emotional appeals constituted unacceptable behavior. Likewise, his superficial interpretations denigrated the scholarship and education of the clergy. Denounced for instigating a growing split within the church, he was accused of invading congregations for the purpose of building his own church organization. Rather than tolerating church differences, he was criticized for attempting to crush those who resisted his movement. Although some charges ebbed with time, Finney, throughout his career as an evangelist, regularly had to defend his methods and message.

Of course there were church leaders who enthusiastically supported Finney. His former mentor George Gale had initially been wary of his apprentice's efforts but was soon assisting him. Gale was one of a coterie of ministers who regularly helped Finney fan revival fires. Another important convert was young Theodore Weld. A man of passion, energy, and innate intelligence, Weld initially disapproved of Finney's endeavors. However, after attending several revival sessions, he was won over, eventually providing invaluable service by recruiting and training college men. Lyman Beecher, though never an active Finney supporter, also came to tolerate the evangelist's work. Beecher was one of the preeminent church leaders in the nation at the time that the revival movement began. Early on, he was among the more outspoken critics of Finney. However, eventually he came to acknowledge the evangelist's passion and commitment though never completely embracing his message. Beecher's reluctant approval nevertheless brought new status to Finney and added strength to his movement.

With his popularity soaring, Finney carried his message beyond central New York for the first time. In December 1827, responding to several requests, he began a yearlong revival in and around Philadelphia. The city was a Presbyterian bastion, but some local church leaders felt their congregations needed the sort of a spiritual reawakening that New York was experiencing. For that purpose they called upon Finney. Accepted cordially even by those who disagreed with him, the evangelist eagerly pursued the challenge. However, in the end he was not satisfied by the outcome of his efforts. Although congregations grew in size with converts numbering in the thousands, the campaign lacked the passion and enthusiasm of his earlier revivals. In assessing the results, he concluded that he was becoming a bit jaded and vowed to recapture the verve and fervor that previously had characterized his revival meetings.

His opportunity came soon after leaving Philadelphia. His surging popularity irresistibly pulled him to New York City. A group of wealthy city merchants, led by brothers Arthur and Louis Tappan, were anxious to create an alternative to the New England church hierarchy that directed many New York City congregations. They concluded that Finney could provide a bold, dynamic new spiritual direction and invited him to the city even though most local church leaders did not share their enthusiasm. Finney accepted the offer but worried that without assistance from the city's churches, he would have no pulpit from which to launch a campaign. His merchant hosts quickly solved the dilemma by purchasing a church building of their own, the Union Presbyterian Church, and installing Finney as its temporary pastor. News that the evangelist would be attending his own congregation immediately attracted large audiences that, in turn, initiated a spiritual revival within the city.

Finney's tenure in New York initiated a period of significant religious activity and social reform in the city. At the heart of the effort was a free church movement. Eager to reach the city's ever-growing poor and laboring populations, his sponsors intended to attack growing urban problems with Christian principles. To help accomplish their goal, they organized a new free church that eliminated long-standing traditions that separated congregations along social, economic, and racial lines lines. Services steeped in intellectual content were discouraged in favor of emotional pleas. Finney's simple messages and passionate appeals made him ideally suited to lead the church. Since beginning his evangelical career, he had promoted open worship services and had challenged church authority. His fire and brimstone message had an obvious emotional effect upon listeners. Likewise, his addresses had always been sprinkled with a call for social reform. Temperance, basic women's rights, and opposition to slavery were regularly integrated into his appeals. Demonstrating a command over his congregants regardless of their class, Finney once again successfully converted hundreds.

For more than a year, Finney attended the spiritual needs of his ever-growing congregation. However, despite his success, increasingly he felt confined by the organization building around him. During the summer of 1830, despite some reservations, he accepted an invitation to come to Rochester. For several years, the city had experienced unprecedented growth as a result of the access that the Erie Canal provided to New York City. However, the new business also brought a new and diverse population, including avaricious entrepreneurs and unruly laborers. Concerned about the deteriorating moral climate within the city, Josiah Bissell, one of Rochester's leading merchants, sought out Finney's services. Bissell hoped that the evangelist could bring to his town the same sort of spiritual and social reforms that he had brought to New York City.

Finney's six-month revival transformed Rochester. As always he set an ambitious schedule for himself with sessions every day, some that began at dawn and concluded after dark. To assist him he enlisted a squadron of effective assistants, including Theodore Weld. However, Finney always remained the main attraction. His eager audiences came from well beyond the city's borders to hear him speak and experience his spiritual guidance. Whether leading prayer sessions or delivering sermons, he was polished, powerful, and compelling, reaching his full potential as an evangelist. The results were beyond his hosts' expectations. Thousands were converted and congregations of all denomination swelled. Likewise, a new atmosphere of harmony among churches replaced the divisions that had characterized church relations prior to the visit. The city's efforts at social reform also benefited. Most notably, the local temperance movement gained new momentum. For Finney, the success in Rochester brought an avalanche of new requests for revivals from other communities and established him undeniably as the nation's preeminent evangelist.

From Rochester, Finney decided to invade one of his harshest critic's territory. For several years, Lyman Beecher had voiced grave reservations about Finney's methods and theology. Responding to an invitation from a Boston congregation, the evangelist embarked upon his first New England revival. Although eventually he completely won over Beecher, his audiences were far less enthusiastic than he had hoped. His basic contention that every person is endowed with a free will and has the power of moral choice, which had previously been so attractive to listeners, troubled many in Boston. Local church leaders closely scrutinized his work and regularly challenged his theology. Nevertheless, despite mixed results, Finney considered the revival a success simply because he had earned Beecher's approval.

Fearing that Finney might accept an offer to establish a seminary in Ohio, Louis Tappan implored the evangelist to return to New York City. Growing reform efforts needed the kind of encouragement that only he could provide. As an enticement, Tappan promised a new building that would hold 2,500. Finney agreed and in September 1832, prepared for installation at the Chatham Street Chapel, a former theater that Tappan, as promised, had converted for him. Unfortunately, he was struck with the cholera that gripped the city. Though he survived, he was so weakened that he was unable to resume preaching until the following spring and even then only on a limited schedule. Almost as disconcerting was the growing opposition to the Tappan brothers and their reform efforts, particularly their stand against slavery. Finney, who shared most of the Tappan's anti-slavery views, and his church became easy targets for discontented mobs.

With his health slowly improving, Finney decided to make a pilgrimage to Europe and the Holy Lands. It was a miserable trip. Lonely and unaccustomed to the rigors of ocean travel, he quickly tired of Europe and the Mediterranean. The six-month sojourn proved to be among the unhappiest periods in his life. When he did return, he found that circumstances on Chatham Street had changed. The chapel was located several blocks from the notorious neighborhood later known as the "Five Points." The area was characterized by a broad collection of unsavory characters and readily available vices. Periodically, ethnic and racial tensions fed by wandering gangs of rowdies spilled onto the streets. Living conditions were harsh, thievery was a constant, prostitutes were easily procured, and drinking houses were abundant. In short, it was a tough place to live and was growing tougher. The Tappans had hoped that Finney could help to reverse the neighborhood's fortunes. It was a challenge that Finney had welcomed. However, in July 1834, just before his return from Europe, his new church was damaged in a riot that at the time was the most destructive in the city's history. Racial attacks, spurred by the church's integrated congregation and call to end slavery, spread throughout the lower Manhattan. Although relatively minor damage was done to the chapel, numerous residents, especially blacks, were beaten, some were killed, and dozens of buildings were destroyed.

Finney resumed his duties at the Chatham Street Chapel in November but by the spring of 1835 he was contemplating leaving. Discouraged that his mission to the city remained largely unfulfilled and frustrated by the potential violence that surrounded his church, he questioned his effectiveness. His health also remained a concern, which was heightened by the deteriorating living conditions in lower Manhattan. Additionally, he concluded that the abolitionist crusade was beginning to sap the vitality of his evangelical revival movement. The Tappan's promise to construct yet another new church building for him did ease his doubts a bit but not completely. More appealing was an invitation from another evangelist, John Jay Shipherd, to get his help in establishing a seminary in northern Ohio.

True to their word, the Tappans built a colossal new church, the Broadway Tabernacle, and in early 1836 installed Finney as its first pastor. However, the evangelist by that time was deeply involved with the creation of Oberlin College in Ohio. Grateful to the Tappans, he agreed to serve half of each year at their new church while spending the rest of the year teaching theology at Oberlin. Nevertheless, his life and activities increasingly focused upon the school. Combining intellectual and spiritual growth with a program of manual labor, the curriculum pleased Finney. Several outstanding students, including Theodore Weld, who had left the Lane Seminary in Cincinnati after a prolonged dispute with that school's administration, also surrounded him. Oberlin's bold stand to admit women and black students further pleased Finney. Additionally, his health began to improve once he was away from New York City.

At Oberlin, Finney concentrated upon teaching and further developing his own theological interpretation. Labeled "Oberlin Perfectionism" and "Oberlin Theology," it challenged traditional Presbyterian doctrine. At the core of the evolving creed was the proposition that to maintain a holy life, an individual must steadfastly obey God's moral laws. Salvation comes from a virtuous life of disinterested benevolence. Accomplishing this requires a person to accept self-denial and to avoid behaving out of self-interest. However, once achieved, salvation is not necessarily a permanent condition. It is, therefore, an ongoing lifetime struggle to achieve and retain. As expected, Finney's controversial theology generated significant criticism from church leaders. It also subtly questioned the increasingly confrontational methods of what he considered to be self-indulgent abolitionist leaders and their movement. Rather than disinterested benevolence, Finney felt that abolitionists such as William Lloyd Garrison had begun to develop factions designed as much to promote themselves as their causes. On the other hand, the evangelist continued to embrace social reform and the anti-slavery movement as demonstrations of righteous moral commitment.

As Finney's allegiance to Oberlin grew, his relationship with the Tappans faded. He lamented that the brothers' abolitionist tactics were becoming too radical and too political. He especially questioned the potential for violent confrontations that abolitionists seemed to be encouraging. Likewise, he was concerned that the abolitionist crusade was about to smother all others reform efforts. To him, the quest for spiritual purity ought to have been the primary goal of all reform including efforts to end slavery. Additionally, though his health had finally returned, he felt drained by his arduous travel schedule between Oberlin and New York City. Finally, in April 1837 he reluctantly resigned his position as minister at Broadway Tabernacle, thus severing forever his active relationship with the church.

During the next few years, Finney focused completely upon sustaining Oberlin and its message of perfectionism. The difficult economic times brought on by the Panic of 1837 had a potentially devastating effect upon the school. Many once generous contributors, including the Tappan brothers, were no longer able to provide adequate financial support. Consequently, there were times when faculty went without salary and school activities had to be reduced or suspended. Equally threatening in many ways were challenges to Oberlin's perfectionism. Evangelist John Humphrey Noyes, who had been inspired by Finney several years earlier, devised his own perfectionist message. Advocating shared sexual relations among his followers, Noyes became a target for moral outrage wherever he went. Though Oberlin certainly did not promote Noyes's ideas, some people nevertheless questioned the school's mission. Presbyterian and Congregationalist church organizations also derided Finney, his theology, and his school, labeling his perfectionist teachings simplistic and misleading. Local proponents of slavery served as yet another source of disapproval. They considered the school to be a breeding place for abolitionists. The more aggressive of these pro-slavery critics resorted to menacing threats of violence against both faculty and students. At the same time, radical abolitionists criticized Oberlin for not doing enough to end slavery. Finney and his school were caught in the middle. Although Oberlin continued to embrace the anti-slavery movement, it did not share the abolitionist fervor of Theodore Weld and the other Lane Seminary students who had followed him to Oberlin. Through it all, Finney worked tirelessly to sustain the institution.

One of the reasons that Oberlin was able to survive its early travails was the reputation of Finney. Using his influence he eventually found new benefactors, most notably abolitionist Gerrit Smith, to replace the Tappan brothers and others. More importantly, he attracted an ever-growing number of students to the school. From an initial enrollment of 200, the school's population doubled within five years and grew to more than 1,000 in 1852. Many of those students came to study with Finney. Just as his reputation as an itinerant evangelist had attracted followers during the 1830s, so too did his reputation as a teacher of future ministers attract apprentices after he came to Oberlin. At the same time, his appeal from the pulpit remained compelling. Though he mellowed a bit after leaving New York City, he never lost his power or near mystical allure over congregations. Twice on Sundays and again once during the week, he preached to school and community alike, always attracting large audiences.

During Oberlin's early years, one of Finney's closest friends, Asa Mahan, served as the school president. The two men had met in 1830 during the Rochester revival. Later as a trustee at Lane Seminary, Mahan had supported Theodore Weld and several other disgruntled students in their protest against Lyman Beecher. Mahan had been instrumental in bringing them to Oberlin. With Finney's backing, Mahan soon after became the new school's first president. However, in the years that followed his caustic and egotistical demeanor alienated both trustees and faculty. Finally in 1850, amidst growing tensions, he agreed to resign. Finney was the obvious choice as Mahan's replacement. His international reputation easily established him as the best-known person associated with the school. However, he was not comfortable with succeeding his longtime friend. He was also concerned that the requirements of the position would limit his teaching and revival activities. Faced with these concerns, the school's trustees were so eager to have him as president that they allowed Finney to devise an administrative method that allowed him significant time away from the school and included few actual responsibilities. In return, he somewhat reluctantly accepted the position in August, 1851. It was a post that he held until 1865.

In addition to his duties at Oberlin, Finney remained an active evangelist. During the school's early years, his itinerant activities focused upon the Northeast. Periodically he returned to New York City and occasionally preached at the Broadway Tabernacle Church. In 1842 he became involved in revivals in Boston, Providence, and Rochester. Late the following year and through early 1844, he was back preaching in Boston. The death of his wife in 1847 and remarriage a year later curtailed his travels briefly but in the autumn of 1849 he launched a major campaign to England. A challenging but very successful journey, it kept him away from Oberlin for almost two years. In 1852 he went to Hartford, and three years later returned once again to Rochester. Amidst an economic Panic and with the Civil War looming, he began a very successful journey to Boston in 1858, which he again followed with a long trip to England and Scotland, his last significant revival campaign. These ongoing efforts, though they kept him away from Oberlin for considerable periods, further heightened both his reputation as an evangelist and his school's prestige.

The Civil War years were for Finney, as they were for most Americans, especially trying times. The war forced him to suspend his evangelical travels and limit the college's activities. Health problems also began to plague him. Since his bout with cholera in 1832, he had been bothered periodically by fevers and ailments. During the early 1860s, these episodes became more frequent and intense. The death of his second wife, Elizabeth, who had been an exceptional helpmate, in 1863 added to his travails. That pain was eased a year later when he married for a third time. Though he continued to teach, he resigned as the Oberlin president in 1865. He spent much of the last years of his life writing theological tracts, compiling his voluminous papers, and preparing his memoirs. He died on August 16, 1875, shortly after attending the Oberlin August commencement.

BIBLIOGRAPHY

Marion Bell, *Crusade in the City: Revivalism in Nineteenth Century Philadelphia* (Lewisburg, PA: Bucknell University Press, 1977); Clifford C. Griffin, *Their Brothers' Keepers: Moral Stewardship in the United States, 1800–1865* (New Brunswick, NJ: Rutgers University Press, 1960); Keith J. Hardman, *Charles Grandison Finney, 1792–1875: Revivalist and Reformer* (Syracuse, NY: Syracuse University Press, 1987); Paul Johnson, *A Shopkeeper's Millennium: Society and Revival in Rochester, New York, 1815–1837* (New York: Hill and Wang, 1978); and Carroll Smith-Rosenberg, *Religion and the Rise of the American City: The New York City Mission Movement, 1812–1870* (Ithaca, NY: Cornell University Press, 1971).

JAMES FENIMORE COOPER
(1789–1851)

During the Jacksonian era, James Fenimore Cooper established himself as the first great American novelist. Though before publishing his first novel he avoided writing even short letters, he became a prolific author, publishing more than two dozen works. An enigma personally, he was nevertheless able to capture the American character as no one before him had. He began writing to satisfy his own longing for personal adventure. In the process, he created a romantic American archetype. His most important works, the five-volume Leatherstocking Tales, provided a mythical figure that loosely resembled Andrew Jackson and inspired readers. Cooper's success also encouraged a generation of great American writers, including Hawthorne, Melville, and Poe, that followed.

Born in 1789, James Fenimore Cooper was the twelfth of thirteen children. His father, William, was a prominent New York politician and successful businessman. The source of the family wealth was land. Aided by his wife's inheritance, William, shortly after the Revolutionary War, purchased a large tract of land adjacent to Lake Otsego in central New York. During the next decade, he sold lots and established the village of Cooperstown. The year after the birth of James, the family moved from the comforts of Burlington, New Jersey, to the backwoods settlement. There William built a formidable estate that immediately became the community focal point. Soon William's authority within the region became almost unlimited. His council was regularly sought by the state's political leaders and, despite having no formal legal training, he was appointed as judge. Twice during the 1790s, he was elected as a Federalist to Congress. A scrupulously honest entrepreneur who was blessed with an exceptionally sharp mind and a commanding physical presence, Cooper was well suited for life in the emerging community. It was in this setting that James spent his childhood.

The forest and Lake Otsego served as young James's first classroom. A free-spirited child, he and several brothers spent much of their early years roaming through the backwoods surrounding Cooperstown. His initial formal education came at a local academy. With the basics mastered, he was sent to Albany to study with a noted mentor in 1801. There he met and became friends with several boys who later served as leaders within the state. After two years in Albany he was admitted, at age thirteen, to Yale. An avid reader with a quick, inventive mind, he was also an acknowledged prankster. During his junior year, his quest for amusement became more than Yale officials would tolerate. After using gunpowder to blow open a classmate's door and sneaking a mule into a classroom, Cooper was expelled. He returned home where he briefly studied with a local clergyman. However, the elder Cooper was distressed by his son's apparent lack of ambition and in 1806 sent him off as a common sailor to prepare for a career in the navy. For the next fourteen months, the young man traveled throughout the Atlantic as a crew member aboard a merchant ship. When he returned to America he was, with his father's assistance, commissioned as a midshipman in the United States Navy.

Cooper was first assigned for a year to Fort Ontario at Oswego in upstate New York. The following year he was reassigned to a navy ship, the *Wasp*, anchored in New York harbor. While Cooper was stationed in New York, his father was killed by an angry political opponent. Just nineteen, James inherited $50,000, a grand sum that promised financial security thus making a career in the navy unnecessary. Nevertheless, he remained in the service for another eighteen months during which tensions with the British built almost to the point of war. Though he resigned his commission in early 1811, he fantasized and periodically wrote about a life at sea throughout the rest of his life.

Cooper left the navy to marry Susan De Lancey. At one time, the De Lancey family had been among the most prominent in New York but Susan's grandfather, James De Lancey, led the state's Loyalist opposition during the Revolutionary War. As a result, the family's name was badly tarnished and a sizeable portion of their property was confiscated. In the decades that followed, Susan's father was able to rehabilitate the family reputation and a significant portion of its wealth. Thus when Susan and James were married, on New Year's Day, 1811, it became a union of two prominent families. The De Lancey wealth also provided a further degree of economic stability for James.

For Cooper, the years following his marriage were spent searching for an acceptable lifestyle. His most satisfying work involved serving as a colonel in the New York militia and as aide-de-camp to Governor DeWitt Clinton during the War of 1812. Meanwhile, he bought land near Cooperstown and built a house, Fenimore, in an effort to establish himself as a gentleman farmer. Later he also built a home on De Lancey land outside New York City. By 1819 his growing family, which included four daughters (a fifth died in infancy) and a son, split time between their De Lancey home and Cooperstown. Unfortunately, throughout his endeavors the family fortunes slowly shrank. Several events during the late 1810s added to Cooper's financial concerns. The economic hard times that struck the nation after the War of 1812 significantly reduced the size of the Cooper accounts. Likewise, the death of four older brothers transferred to James responsibility for what remained of his father's estate and, therefore indirectly, the welfare of his deceased brothers' families. To recoup his and his family's losses, he invested in several unsuccessful speculative ventures, including the purchase of a whaling ship.

Under ever-growing financial pressure, Cooper was pushed into an unconventional speculative gamble. After criticizing a recently published English novel, he was challenged by his wife to write one himself. Though he did not consider himself a writer, he took up the challenge. Several months later he read his finished work to her, claiming it was by an anonymous author. With the help of an old schoolmate, John Jay, Jr., the manuscript, entitled *Precaution*, was published in 1820. Though disregarded in the United States, the work received enough attention in England to encourage Cooper to write a second novel. Finishing the manuscript in just a few weeks, he published *The Spy* in December 1821, and it was an immediate success. Set in Westchester County, New York, during the American Revolution, the book loosely portrays the divided loyalties and inner conflicts that his in-laws as well as other local families were subjected to during the war. With translation into more than half a dozen languages, the book instantly established Cooper as a successful author and a notable literary personality.

Though his second novel was well received, the revenues did not stem the tide of Cooper's growing debts. Publication of his anxiously anticipated third work, *The Pioneers*, the first of what became his Leatherstocking Tales series, barely slowed his financial problems. The pressures only added intensity to his writing. A pair of sea novels, *The Pilot* and *Lionel Lincoln*, followed in 1824 and 1825.

The next year, Cooper published the second and the most popular of his Leatherstocking tales, *The Last of the Mohicans*. Set in the New York forests that he knew so well, the story established some of the themes that characterized the series. The hero, Natty Bumpo (also known as Hawkeye), combines a well-developed understanding of nature with the order and control spawned by an evolving American civilization. He is a modern man with rough edges who is able to function successfully in both the natural world and human society. He takes from nature only what he needs to survive and avoids excesses. Bumpo is innately just and virtuous while maintaining the individualism necessary to exist in a wilderness. He is humble and confident about his decisions and abilities, and he generally views humanity from a democratic perspective. Heartened by the intrinsic qualities of his fellow man, he also recognizes inherent shortcomings. Addressing his own flaws resolutely, he strives for a personal perfection that he realizes he will never achieve.

Readers were able to draw parallels between Cooper's fictional heroes and contemporary figures. Among the more obvious was Daniel Boone, whose saga became popular legend in the 1820s and 1830s. Andrew Jackson was another who seemed to possess many of the traits that characterize Natty Bumpo. Jackson had been reared in the wilderness. He claimed to put ideals before interests. He was also an Indian fighter who professed to be a protector of civilized Indians. At the time the early Leatherstocking Tales were written, Jackson had become the symbol of democracy and an egalitarian society. Of course, Cooper insisted that his heroes were completely fictional. Nevertheless, readers were able to make many favorable comparisons to Jackson as well as several others. Additionally, though his father had been an ardent Federalist, Cooper himself embraced the Democratic ideals associated with Jackson. The author was particularly upset by the "Corrupt Bargain" that Clay and Adams had allegedly concocted to defeat the general in 1824.

Aside from his idealized hero, Cooper's depiction of Native Americans helped to create one of the popular myths about nineteenth-century America. Reflecting the attitudes of many Americans, he portrayed Indians as either "noble savages" or as ruthless, untamed forest warriors. In either case, when coming in contact with white society they are doomed. His "good" Indians, which are glorified representations of several eastern Woodlands tribes, are either conquered by their hostile counterparts or drained by white society of the nobility that they acquired by living in harmony with nature. Ultimately they are sad victims of expanding European civilization. Hostile Indians, portrayed as Iroquois though in fact possessing few specific Iroquois characteristics, are in part simply less civilized and in part an undesirable product of contact with avaricious white commercial interests. Only rarely do these "bad" Indians reveal admirable qualities. What Cooper acknowledges is that although Native American civilization possessed worthy characteristics in its pure form, it could not endure contact with European civilization. Ultimately, Native Americans were doomed by the ever-expanding white society and its transforming technology. It was an attitude that in many ways reflected the nation's Indian policy during the Jacksonian era.

Another recurring theme at the heart of Cooper's works is his nostalgic

vision of nature and the inevitable changes that his civilization was imposing upon it. Cooper's happiest days were spent during his childhood roaming the woods around Cooperstown. In his works he implies that if
perfection is possible, it is by living a solitary life in harmony with nature
but at the same time cognizant of human society. The heroes in his early
novels experience the transforming effect that an expanding nineteen-
century, technological society has on nature. In the final volumes of the
Leatherstocking Tales, written in the early 1840s, the quest for a pure life
leads West. At that time, the West was idealized as a region where nature
remained unaltered and a place where a man (Cooper does not portray
women in a particularly favorable light) could live virtuously. However,
society's migration ultimately required that nature be subdued and transformed as had occurred in the East. Therefore, the opportunity for virtue
is limited. Cooper rather pessimistically laments that as the nation moves
west, it destroys those qualities that give the untouched West its true significance. It is an inevitable process that ultimately does little to elevate
American society. Here again the author taps into both the vigorous expansionistic nature of Jacksonian Americans as well as the concern among
some about the effect that rapid expansion was having on American civilization.

After publishing *The Last of the Mohicans* in 1826, Cooper and his
family began a seven-year adventure through Europe. In part, they made
the trip to prevent unauthorized European publication of his novels. He
also hoped to parlay his success into an expanded readership. Of course
he continued writing throughout his travels, completing five more books.
The works, two of which were encouraged by the Marquis de Lafayette,
were intended to correct misunderstandings about Americans. However,
the novels instead demeaned various national populations, particularly the
British. Also the American press complained that he had become too involved in European matters. In response, the author forthrightly attacked
American journalists thus initiating a struggle with the media that plagued
him for the rest of his life. By the time he returned to the United States in
1833, his appeal with his American audience had eroded significantly.

During the years following his return, Cooper wrote political satire and
nonfiction. He was especially disillusioned by the apparent demise of Jacksonian Democracy that seemed to be accompanied by the rise of the Whig
Party. He bemoaned that the nation had veered away from the Jeffersonian
ideals upon which he believed it had been established. Instead, new Jacksonian leaders had produced a general leveling within American society that
erased valid distinctions based on intellect and ability. Swelling numbers of
immigrants encouraged demagoguery as well as the formation of political
machines, which were interested exclusively in attaining power. Likewise,
the quest for profit and wealth had supplanted the concept of civic responsibility. American civilization was, in Cooper's opinion, feeding upon itself

and needed to recapture the ideals of its past. The hope for the nation lay in the unspoiled West.

In 1840, after writing a history of the American navy, Cooper returned to his Leatherstocking Tales. Adding an expansionistic dimension to his previous themes, he completed the five-volume series with publication of *The Pathfinder* (1840) and *The Deerslayer* (1841). Written fourteen years after *The Last of the Mohicans*, at a time when Americans were fiercely debating the annexation of Texas and future settlement in the Southwest, Cooper's works subtly suggest values that ought to guide the nation's westward growth. Further developing the romantic image of the frontier that he had begun in his earlier works, his efforts, along with paintings by George Caleb Bingham and John Gast among others, encouraged the nation's enthusiastic embrace of manifest destiny. Cooper's central character, Natty Bumpo, is portrayed as an almost mythical figure free of the corrupting influences of civilization. At the same time Bumpo is a typical man, of average intellect, unimposing physically, and unsure about personal relationships. It is the wilderness that enables him to discover his best qualities. Cooper's new novels again became the favorites of American readers, though he remained a target for both personal and professional criticism.

Even before publication of *The Pathfinder*, Cooper had retreated to the refuge of his upstate home. It was there that he spent most of his time during the last decade of his life. Maintaining a prodigious production pace, he published more than a book a year, several of which again explored maritime themes and others that lamented the decay of American republican ideals. In 1850, while writing a history of New York City his health began to fail. Incapacitated by chronic liver problems, he deteriorated quickly. Within eighteen months, Cooper was dead. At the time of his death, although he was not particularly popular personally, his works were revered by American and European readers alike. Having written more than twenty books, he had firmly established himself as the first great American novelist. Likewise, his characters reflected the ideals of Jacksonian Americans that shaped the quintessential American character of the era.

BIBLIOGRAPHY

Robert Clark, ed., *James Fenimore Cooper: New Critical Essays* (New York: Barnes and Noble, 1985); Robert Emmet Long, *James Fenimore Cooper* (New York: Continuum, 1990); Donald A. Ringe, *James Fenimore Cooper* (Boston: Twayne Publishers, 1988); Warren S. Walker, *James Fenimore Cooper: An Introduction and Interpretation* (New York: Barnes and Noble, 1962); and James D. Wallace, *James Fenimore and His Audience* (New York: Columbia University Press, 1986).

APPENDIX: BRIEF BIOGRAPHIES

Astor, John Jacob. John Jacob Astor was born in Waldorf, Germany, in 1763. He immigrated to the United States in 1784, arriving in Baltimore penniless. Moving to New York City, within two years he opened a fur shop and became involved in the China export trade. His fortunes improved upon his marriage to the daughter of a prominent New York merchant. Soon after the Lewis and Clark expedition to the Pacific, Astor hired two fur trappers to establish a trading post, Fort Astor, on his behalf. From that base, Astor created a fur-trading monopoly that by 1810 made him one of the wealthiest men in America. Investing his profits in New York City land, his fortune became one of the greatest in American history. Astor became the nation's first true rags-to-riches story. He died in 1848. *Bibliography*: Axel, Madsen. *John Jacob Astor: America's First Millionaire*. New York: John Wiley and Sons, 2001. Chittenden, Hiram Martin. *The American Fur Trade of the Far West*. Lincoln: University of Nebraska Press, 1986.

Austin, Stephen Fuller. Stephen F. Austin became known as "The Father of Texas," after establishing the first Anglo-American colony in the Mexican province of Texas. Born in 1793 in southwestern Virginia, he moved with his family moved to Missouri when he was five years old. In Missouri he was a merchant, ran the family mining business, and was the director of a failed bank. He also served as a militia officer, as a member of the

Missouri territorial legislature, and as a circuit judge in Arkansas. In 1820 he assisted his father Moses in a speculative effort to establish an American settlement in Texas. Moses died a year later, and Stephen assumed responsibility for the venture. As the colony's administrative authority, he became the official liaison between the settlers and the Mexican government. Growing troubles between the ever-expanding American population and the Mexican government put Austin in an increasingly difficult position. Jailed by the Mexican government for two years from 1833 to 1835, he nevertheless hoped to resolve the problems through diplomacy. Reluctantly, he supported the Texas independence movement and afterward, though losing the presidency to Sam Houston, Austin became the new republic's first secretary of state. He held the position for several months until his death in late 1836. *Bibliography*: Barker, Eugene Campbell. *The Life of Stephen F. Austin, Founder of Texas, 1793–1836: A Chapter in the Westward Movement of the Anglo-American People*. Temecula, CA: Classic Textbooks, 1925. Cantrell, Greg. *Stephen F. Austin: Empresario of Texas*. New Haven, CT: Yale University Press, 2001. Hendrickson, Kenneth. *Chief Executives of Texas from Stephen F. Austin to John Connelly, Jr*. College Station: Texas A & M Press, 1995.

Beecher, Lyman. Trained at Yale under Timothy Dwight, Beecher (1775–1863) became one of the preeminent theologian during the Jacksonian era. He began his ministry in 1799 but attracted national attention after initiating an anti-dueling campaign in reaction to the Hamilton-Burr duel. Moving to Litchfield, Connecticut, in 1810, he embraced the New Haven Theology, which sought to bring new optimism and hope to Calvinistic doctrines. Initially Beecher fought hard to maintain the traditional church but eventually came to respect evangelical leaders such as Charles Grandison Finney. By 1830 Beecher himself was considered to be a "New School" advocate. In 1832 with the financial support of the Tappan brothers, Beecher opened Lane Seminary in Cincinnati. The school promoted "New School" theology and included a corps of committed students, including Timothy Weld. Beecher was also involved in several social reform movements including the temperance crusade and the anti-slavery movement. His children, Harriet Beecher Stowe and Henry Ward Beecher, were well-known activists in their own right. *Bibliography*: Cross, Barbara M., ed. *The Autobiography of Lyman Beecher*, 2 vols. Boston: Little, Brown and Co., 1961; Rourke, Constance. *Trumpets of Jubilee: Henry Ward Beecher, Harriet Beecher Stowe, Lyman Beecher, Horace Greeley, P. T. Barnum*. New York: Harcourt, Brace and Co., 1927.

Birney, James. Born in Kentucky in 1792, he moved to Alabama as a child and was elected to the state legislature. An outspoken opponent of slavery, Birney served as an executive of the American Anti-Slavery Society. Unlike

William Lloyd Garrison, Birney sought to use political action and pressure to end slavery. An influential anti-slavery alternative, he ran for the presidency on the Liberty Party ticket in 1840 and 1844. Throughout the rest of his life, he continued to denounce slavery while resisting a call for extremism. He died in 1857. *Bibliography*: Birney, William. *James G. Birney and His Times*. New York: New Library Press, 1969. Fladeland, Betty L. *James Gillespie Birney*. Baton Rouge: Louisiana State University Press, 1984.

Blair, Francis. Born in Virginia in 1791, Francis Blair moved to Kentucky as a child. His father served as attorney general of the state and Blair and was admitted to the bar in 1817, though he never practiced law. Instead he became involved in politics. During the tensions surrounding the Panic of 1819, Blair became a leader of the so-called Relief Party, contributing opinions to local newspapers. Initially a supporter of fellow Kentuckian Henry Clay, Blair became disenchanted with Clay and instead switched his allegiance to Andrew Jackson. During the election of 1828, his editorial abilities on behalf of Jackson gained him a national reputation. When Jackson sought a loyal editor for an administration journal, Blair was called to Washington, where he established the *Washington Globe* in 1830. He remained editor throughout the presidencies of Jackson and Martin Van Buren. However, with the election of James K. Polk, Blair was forced to sell his interest in the paper in 1845. Later, Blair was instrumental in organizing the Republican Party and promoting the 1860 candidacy of Abraham Lincoln. He died in 1876. *Bibliography*: Smith, Elbert. *Francis Preston Blair*. New York: Free Press, 1980. Smith, William E. *The Francis Preston Blair Family in Politics*. New York: Macmillan Co., 1933.

Brownson, Orestes. Born in Vermont, Brownson (1803–1876) moved to upstate New York as a boy. There he received a modest formal education before going to work in a printer's office. An avid reader, he began teaching when he was twenty, and three years later became a Universalist preacher. His religious studies led him to philosophy and eventually to the transcendentalist movement. The author of numerous philosophical papers and articles, he emerged as an important transcendentalist voice. Along with Emerson and Margaret Fuller, among others, he became an active participant in the Brook Farm commune. Eventually he became disenchanted with transcendentalism and converted to Catholicism, for which he received much criticism. Throughout his philosophical journey, Brownson also supported numerous social reforms, including women's rights and the anti-slavery movement. *Bibliography*: Gilhooley, Leonard. *Contradictions and Dilemma: Orestes Brownson and the American Idea*. New York: Fordham University Press, 1972. Maynard, Theodore. *Orestes Brownson, Yankee, Radical, Catholic*. Ann Arbor, MI: Books on Demand, 1943.

Crittenden, John Jordan. A native-born Kentuckian, Crittenden (1787–1863) graduated from William and Mary College and served briefly as attorney general in Illinois Territory. Returning to Kentucky, he was elected to the state legislature in 1812 and within three years became speaker of the state House. In 1817 he was selected to fill a vacancy in the U.S. Senate, a post he held for two years. Through his political activities, Crittenden became a friend and supporter of Henry Clay and in 1824 actively campaigned for his fellow Kentuckian. Upon Adams's election, he was appointed U.S. district attorney for Kentucky, but was replaced when Jackson came into office. After several years in private practice, Crittenden was elected to the Senate in 1835. There he opposed Jackson's banking policies and Van Buren's subtreasury scheme. In 1840 Crittenden vigorously campaigned for William Henry Harrison and was rewarded with appointment as Harrison's attorney general. He resigned his post when Tyler came into office and instead returned to the Senate in 1843 to fill Henry Clay's seat. An opponent of admitting Texas to the Union, he was also skeptical about the stated reasons for war with Mexico. In 1848, his long friendship with Henry Clay ended when he backed Zachary Taylor for the Whig presidential nomination. During the 1850s, he served as the governor of Kentucky, attorney general for Millard Fillmore, and again as a senator. Best known for the proposed Crittenden Compromise, he feared the evolving sectional tensions during the decade, and on the eve of the Civil War he tried to resolve the differences through his proposal. The plan called for compensation to owners of runaway slaves, a constitutional amendment prohibiting the federal government from interfering with slavery in southern states, repeal of northern personal liberty laws, and a constitutional amendment restoring the Missouri Compromise line, south of which would be protected. With the outbreak of the Civil War, he vigorously advocated that Kentucky remain part of the Union. *Bibliography*: Coleman, Ann Mary Butler. *Life of John J. Crittenden*. Philadelphia: Lippincott, 1871. Kirwan, Albert. *John J. Crittenden: The Struggle for the Union*. Westport, CT: Greenwood Publishing, 1974.

Crockett, David. Born in the Tennessee backwoods in 1786, Davy became a frontier legend. During the Creek Indian War in 1813–1814, he commanded a Tennessee battalion. Seven years later, portrayed as a brave Indian fighter and a backwoods hero, he was elected to the Tennessee legislature, where he served until 1824. He was elected to Congress in 1826, reelected in 1828, and after losing in 1830 was again elected in 1832. Though he generally remained independent in his actions, Whigs at one point considered him for high national office because of his opposition to Jackson and his obvious earthy appeal, an appeal that he nurtured by periodically wearing buckskins and backwoods garb. Disillusioned by politics, Crockett joined the Texas independence movement in 1835. He died at the Battle of the Alamo in 1836. *Bibliography*: Lofaro, Michael. *Davy Crockett: The Man, the Legend, the Legacy, 1786–1986*. Knoxville: University of Tennessee Press, 1985. Rourke, Constance. *Davy Crockett*. Lincoln: University of Nebraska Press, 1998.

Dallas, George Mifflin. Dallas (1792–1864) was the son of secretary of the treasury Alexander J. Dallas. In 1813 his father arranged for him to serve as a private secretary to Albert Gallatin on a diplomatic mission to Russia to negotiate an end to the War of 1812. After working for his father in the Treasury Department and with the legal staff of the Second Bank of the United States (BUS), he entered Pennsylvania politics. Four years after being elected to the Senate, in 1831 he was appointed minister to Russia. After Polk's nomination for president, the Democratic Party sought to balance its ticket and offered the vice presidential nomination to Dallas. Like Polk, he was an ardent supporter of American expansion and annexation of Texas. After his term as vice president, he served as minister to Great Britain. *Bibliography*: Belohavek, John M. *George Mifflin Dallas: Jacksonian Patrician*. State College: Pennsylvania State University Press, 1877; Dallas, George Mifflin. *Brief Memoir of George Mifflin Dallas*. Philadelphia: Lippincott, 1893.

Evans, George Henry. Born in upstate New York, Evans (1805–1856) became an early labor activist. While serving as an apprentice printer, Evans embraced the thoughts of Thomas Paine and began to apply them to labor conditions. Soon he and Thomas Skidmore founded the Workingman's Party as a way to promote the interests of the growing laboring population. His *Workingman's Advocate* became an influential labor newspaper and helped to unite workers. The Panic of 1837 had a very negative effect upon Evans's appeals, and for several years in the early 1840s Evans's efforts were somewhat dormant. However, in 1844 he revived the effort with some success. A decade later, he used his status as a labor organizer and leader to promote the new Republican Party on behalf of his working supporters. *Bibliography*: Pilz, Jeffrey J. *The Life, Work and Times of George Henry Evans, Newspaperman, Activist, and Reformer*. Lewiston, NY: Edwin Mellen Press, 2001.

Fillmore, Millard. Born in an upstate New York log cabin in 1800, Fillmore became the thirteenth president of the United States upon the death of Zachary Taylor in 1850. As a boy he received little formal education, and at fourteen was apprenticed to a textile maker. Unhappy, he paid off his term of service, then pursued an education that led him into the law. Soon after opening his own office in 1823, he entered politics and was elected to the New York legislature. Drawn toward the policies of Henry Clay and the emerging Whig Party, Fillmore denounced slavery but also objected to abolitionist tactics. In 1844 he lost the gubernatorial election and briefly served as chancellor at the University of Buffalo. In 1846 he became the state comptroller and two years later, in an effort by Whigs to balance their presidential ticket, he was elected vice president. As president after Taylor's death, Fillmore was responsible for signing into law legislation that became known as the Compromise of 1850. His stand opposing slavery helped to split the Whig Party and may have cost him the presidential nomination in 1852. He died the following year. *Bibliography*: Rayback, Robert J. *Millard Fillmore*. Buffalo, NY: Buffalo Historical Society, 1959. Scary, Robert. *Millard Fillmore*. Jefferson, NC: McFarland, 2001.

Fuller, Margaret. Born in 1810 and blessed with a brilliant and probing mind, Margaret Fuller became one of the leading intellects of Jacksonian America. After teaching school in Providence, she moved to Boston and became part of the transcendentalist movement. She also became involved in the anti-slavery campaign as well as the women's rights movement. Publishing poetry, philosophy, fiction, and some political tracts, she accepted an offer from Horace Greeley to become a foreign correspondent for the *New York Tribune*, thus becoming the first American female to serve in such a capacity. In Europe she met, had a child with, and married an Italian nobleman. Upon her return home in 1850, her ship was caught in a storm just off the New York coast. The ship sank, and Fuller's body was never recovered. *Bibliography*: Allen, Margaret V. *The Achievements of Margaret Fuller*. State College: Pennsylvania State University Press, 1979. Blanchard, Paula. *Margaret Fuller: From Transcendentalism to Revolution*. New York: Delacorte Press, 1978. Myerson, Joel. *Margaret Fuller: A Descriptive Bibliography*. Pittsburgh, PA: University of Pittsburgh Press, 1978.

Grundy, Felix. Born in Virginia in 1777, Grundy moved to Kentucky and began a political career in 1799. Quickly rising to prominence, he soon became entangled with another ambitious Kentuckian, Henry Clay, over the state's banks. The debates between the two men provided a preview of the future controversy surrounding the rechartering of the Second Bank of the United States (BUS). An able orator who opposed the bank, Grundy in most ways proved Clay's equal. Afterward, despite losing the bank campaign, he was appointed chief justice of the state. A year later he moved to Tennessee, where he built a reputation as an outstanding criminal lawyer. He reentered politics in 1811 by winning election to Congress. A champion of relief laws, states rights, and defender of the small farmer, he cautiously allied with Andrew Jackson. Although he often disagreed with Jackson, he usually supported the administration's policies. Serving in the House, the Senate, and briefly as attorney general during Van Buren's presidency, Grundy died in 1840 shortly after being reelected to the Senate.

Bibliography: Parks, Joseph Howard. *Felix Grundy: Champion of Democracy*. Baton Rouge: Louisiana State University Press, 1940.

Hawthorne, Nathaniel. The son of a sea captain, Hawthorne (1804–1864) was born in Salem, Massachusetts, and became one of the nation's preeminent novelists during his lifetime. After graduating from Bowdoin College, where he studied with William Henry Longfellow, he began contributing stories and articles to various periodicals. Though friendly with many transcendental leaders, including Ralph Waldo Emerson, Hawthorne nevertheless was skeptical of the movement. A growing family and debts forced him to curtail his literary endeavors temporarily during the mid-1840s and work as a surveyor of the Port of Salem. After three years, he again began to concentrate on his writing and in 1850 published *The Scarlet Letter*, one of his most popular works. The following year he published *The House of Seven Gables*, another very popular book. In 1853 he was appointed American consul in Liverpool, England, by President Franklin Pierce, a classmate of Hawthorne's at Bowdoin College. Afterward his production declined, but he continued to write. He died in 1864 while vacationing with former President Pierce. *Bibliography*: Turner, Arlin. *Nathaniel Hawthorne: A Biography*. New York: Oxford University Press, 1980. Wagenknecht, Edward. *Nathaniel Hawthorne: The Man, His Tales and Romances*. New York: Oxford University Press, 1989. Whitelaw, Nancy. *Nathaniel Hawthorne: American Storyteller*. Greensboro, NC: Morgan Reynolds, Inc., 1996.

Hayne, Robert Young. Member of a prominent South Carolina family, Hayne (1791–1839) built his political career by advocating traditional Jeffersonian principles. Elected to the South Carolina state house in 1814, he became speaker in 1818 and soon after attorney general for the state. Elected to the U.S. Senate in 1822 and again in 1828, he proved an outspoken opponent of protective tariffs and a defender of states' rights and slavery. His most notable encounter came in 1830 during the nullification crisis when he debated Daniel Webster. A fine orator himself, he proved a worthy opponent for Webster in one of the more famous Senate confrontations. Though a leading supporter of the South Carolina nullification ordinance, he nevertheless readily accepted Henry Clay's proposed compromise. In 1832 he resigned from the Senate to provide former Vice President John C. Calhoun the seat. Hayne instead was elected governor of South Carolina. After his term as governor, he became involved in developing an early railroad company. *Bibliography*: Jevey, Joseph. *Robert Young Hayne and His Times*. Charleston, SC: The Hayne Family, 1904.

Irving, Washington. The youngest of eleven children, Irving (1783–1859) grew up in New York City. His father was a successful merchant, and

Irving received a fine formal education as a result. From an early age he was an avid reader, and although trained as a lawyer his passion was story telling. After writing for several journals and newspapers and taking a tour of Europe, he wrote a fictional history of New York. The work became the source of the first American school of writers, The Knickerbocker Group. Soon after he wrote *The Sketch Book of Geoffrey Crayon, Gent.*, which included the tales "Rip Van Winkle" and "The Legend of Sleepy Hollow," two of Irving's most popular stories. The success of *The Sketch Book* enabled Irving to write full time. During the 1820s, he lived in Europe and for a while worked in the American embassy in Madrid and as a secretary to the American Legation. He returned to New York as an internationally acclaimed writer. Writing entertaining travel accounts, his popularity continued to grow. In 1842, with encouragement from Daniel Webster, he was appointed as the American ambassador to Spain, a post he held for three years. During the last decade of his life, Irving published numerous works, including a five-volume biography of George Washington. He died in 1859. *Bibliography*: Leary, Lewis Gaston. *Washington Irving*. Minneapolis: University of Minnesota Press, 1963. St. John, Edward. *Washington Irving: The Father of American Literature*. New York: Moses King, 1904. William, Stanley Thomas. *The Life of Washington Irving*. New York: The Grolier Club, 1935.

Longfellow, Henry Wadsworth. Longfellow (1807–1882) was born in Portland, Maine. Even as a child, he demonstrated a keen interest in literature and academic endeavors. He was sent to school at age three. Later, when he was just nineteen, his father encouraged him to become a lawyer, but he instead chose to become the first professor of modern languages at his alma mater, Bowdoin College, with the understanding that he would first spend time traveling in Europe. Upon his return, he prepared texts that brought the European masters to his students. In 1834 he accepted a professorship at Harvard and after a second European tour, embarked on a long career as a teacher at that school. It was while at Harvard that he published many of his most popular works, including "The Song of Hiawatha" and "Evangeline." A beloved teacher, he became the most popular poet of his day. Combining a gift for rhyme with numerous popular historical themes, his work encouraged both optimism and pride in his readers. Although an anti-slavery advocate, his political attitudes were rarely reflected in his poetry. During the last two decades of his life, he received many international awards and honors for his uniquely American poetry. He died in 1882. *Bibliography*: Arvin, Newton. *Longfellow: His Life and Work*. Boston: Little, Brown and Co., 1963. Lukes, Bonnie. *Henry Wadsworth Longfellow: America's Beloved Poet*. Greensboro, NC: Morgan Reynolds, 1998. Robertson, Eric S. *The Life of Henry Wadsworth Longfellow*. Port Washington, NY: Kennikat Press, 1972.

Mann, Horace. Born in 1796, Mann spent his youth on his parents' small farm in Franklin, Massachusetts. Despite a limited formal education, Mann was admitted to Brown. Upon graduation, he studied law and in 1827 began a political career in Massachusetts. Ten years later, he abandoned his political career, focusing upon public education within the state. During the next twenty years, Mann successfully worked to reform public education within Massachusetts. Among his achievements was the institutionalization of standard educational materials, the establishment of normal schools designed to train teachers, and the creation of free libraries throughout the state. His reforms became a model for many other states and significantly enhanced public education throughout the nation. In 1848 Mann served briefly in Congress. His final post was as president of Antioch College in Ohio, where he remained from 1853 until his death in 1859. *Bibliography*: Culver, Raymond B. *Horace Mann and Religion in the Massachusetts Public Schools*. New York: Arno Press, 1969. Downs, Robert Bingham. *Horace Mann: Champion of Public Schools*. New York: Twayne Publishers, 1974. Mann, Mary Tyler Peabody. *The Life of Horace Mann*. Boston: Lee and Shepard, 1891.

Marcy, William L. Born in Southbridge, Massachusetts, in 1786, he settled in Troy, New York, where he practiced law. After serving in the War of 1812, he began a political career aligning with Martin Van Buren's Democratic organization. While holding several key positions, Marcy soon became a dominant figure in New York's Albany Regency. An ardent supporter of Van Buren, he helped assure state support for the Jackson administration. His association with Van Buren helped to pave the way to a spot in the U.S. Senate in 1831. Two years later, he was elected governor of New York, a post he held for three terms. As secretary of state in the Polk administration, Marcy split with Van Buren. He again served as secretary of state under Franklin Pierce and assisted in the Gadsden Purchase. He died in 1857. *Bibliography*: Learned, Henry Barrett. *William Learned Marcy, Secretary of State, 1853–1857*. New York: A. A. Knopf, 1929. Spencer, Ivor D. *The Victor and the Spoils: A Life of William Learned Marcy*. Providence, RI: Brown University Press, 1959.

Marshall, John. Born in Virginia, young Marshall (1755–1835) was greatly influenced by his father's good friend George Washington. During the Revolutionary War, Marshall served under the general, rising to the rank of captain. After the war he briefly studied with George Wythe at William and Mary, then established a law practice in Richmond while also serving in the Virginia House of Delegates. His reputation as a lawyer and his commitment to a strong central government soon brought him to the attention of President John Adams. In 1797 Adams asked him to serve as an envoy to France in what became known as the XYZ Affair. Upon his return, he won election to Congress. In 1800 he was appointed secretary of state, and the following year Adams appointed him as chief justice of the Supreme Court. During the next thirty-four years, Marshall left his mark on the federal courts as no other justice has. His decisions established the federal judiciary as the nation's ultimate legal authority and brought significant new power to the national government. Despite confrontations with both Jefferson and Jackson, Marshall's reputation for fairness and justice remained unchallenged. *Bibliography*: Baker, Leonard. *John Marshall: A Life in Law*. New York: Macmillan, 1974. Hobson, Charles. *The Great Chief Justice: John Marshall and the Rule of Law*. Lawrence: University Press of Kansas, 1996. Stites, Francis. *John Marshall: Defender of the Constitution*. Boston: Little, Brown and Co., 1981.

Owen, Robert Dale. The son of a wealthy Scottish industrialist, Owen (1801–1877) came to the United States in 1825 and established a utopian community in New Harmony, Indiana. The community was founded upon socialist principles and promoted various social reforms including anti-slavery, women's rights, and educational reform, which was a particular passion of Owen's. In 1832 he was elected to the Indiana state legislature and in 1845 he was elected to Congress. In both cases, he proved an avid supporter of publicly funded education. He died in 1877. *Bibliography*: Leopold, Richard William. *Robert Dale Owen: A Biography*. Boston: Harvard University Press, 1940.

Porter, Peter. A graduate of Yale, Porter (1773–1844) in 1801 was elected to the New York legislature, where he served one term. Eight years later, he again ran for office. Elected to Congress amidst deteriorating relations with Great Britain, he joined Henry Clay and his "War Hawks" in advocating war. Porter's particular interest was the acquisition of Canada. After war was declared, Porter served in both the New York militia and the regular army, fighting Indians in upstate New York and along the Canadian border. In 1814 he was defeated by DeWitt Clinton for governor of New York. During the years that followed, he assisted Henry Clay in organizing the Whig Party and promoting Clay's political agenda. Porter briefly served as secretary of war under Adams before returning to private endeavors. *Bibliography*: Grand, Joseph A. *Peter Porter and the Buffalo-Black Rock Rivalry*. Buffalo, NY: Buffalo Historical Society, 1982. Steele, Peter. *Peter Porter*. New York: Oxford University Press, 1992.

Skidmore, Thomas. Skidmore (1790–1832) was a New York City carpenter and teacher who became an outspoken advocate for laborers during the 1820s. Interpreting Thomas Paine's *Rights of Man* from a laborer's perspective, he called for a ten-hour work day among other reforms. He saw a contest between capitalists and workers and argued that workers regardless of race, gender, and ethnic heritage had to unite if property was to be equitably distributed. One of the organizers of the Workingman's Party, he was almost elected to the New York Assembly. Soon afterwards the party split into factions that undermined Skidmore's efforts. Still an influential labor leader though considered too radical by some, he contracted cholera during an epidemic that swept through New York City in 1832 and died that same year. *Bibliography*: Franklin, Burt. *Thomas Skidmore: The Rights of Man to Property*. New York: Burt Franklin, 1964.

Smith, Gerrit. The son of a wealthy New York speculator and entrepreneur, Smith was a committed and active social reformer throughout his life. In addition to his own inherited wealth, he married the daughter of a prominent Rochester family. With his money, he supported causes ranging from temperance to women's rights and the Sunday school movement, but his most important crusade was anti-slavery. Among the recipients of his contributions was John Brown, who used Smith's money to establish an anti-slavery community in Kansas Territory. He was also a close friend and sponsor of Frederick Douglass. Smith ran for the presidency in 1848, 1856, and 1860 on the Liberty Party ticket. He died in 1874. *Bibliography*: Frothingham, Octavius Brooks. *Gerrit Smith: A Biography*. New York: G. P. Putnam's Sons, 1879. Hammond, Charles. *Gerrit Smith*. New York: Press of W. F. Humphrey, 1939. Harlow, Ralph Volney. *Gerrit Smith*. New York: H. Holt, 1939.

Taney, Roger B. In 1799, Taney (1777–1864) opened a law practice in Maryland, eventually moving to Baltimore. The same year he was elected to the state legislature as a Federalist. A successful lawyer, he was remained active politically though not as a candidate. As a result of Federalist opposition to the War of 1812, he broke with the party and by 1824 had become an energetic supporter of Andrew Jackson. As Maryland state attorney general, Taney used his influence to promote Jackson's candidacy in 1828. Three years later Jackson selected Taney as secretary of the treasury because of the Marylander's opposition to the Second Bank of the United States (BUS). Originally Taney had endorsed the bank, but because of what he considered unfair bank policies and the aristocratic director, Nicholas Biddle, he reversed his stand. As secretary of the treasury, Taney implement Jackson's controversial bank policy, withdrawing government funds from the BUS and depositing them into state banks. In 1836 Jackson nominated him as chief justice of the Supreme Court, a position he held until 1864. Taney's most controversial ruling as chief justice was the momentous Dred Scott decision, which significantly contributed to the split between the North and South. *Bibliography*: Swisher, Carl B. *Roger B. Taney*. New York: Macmillan Company, 1935.

Tappan, Arthur and Lewis. Brothers (Arthur, 1786–1865; Lewis, 1788–1873) from Northampton, Massachusetts, they became wealthy operating a dry goods business in New York City. Both were committed reformers. Among their early efforts, they used their wealth to bring evangelist Charles Grandison Finney to New York City in an effort to purge the city of the vices associated with early urbanization and industrialization. Soon they became leading antislavery advocates. Giving generously to the crusade, they disagreed with the more radical methods of William Lloyd Garrison and formed the American and Foreign Anti-Slavery Society as an alternative to Garrison's organization. The Tappans were also instrumental in establishing both Kenyon and Oberlin Colleges in Ohio with hopes of further advancing reform within American society. Arthur died in 1865 and his brother eight years later. *Bibliography*: Tappan, Lewis. *The Life of Arthur Tappan*. New York: Hurd and Houghton, 1870. Winter, Rebecca J. *Night Cometh: Two Wealthy Evangelicals Face the Nation*. South Pasadena, CA: William Carey Library, 1977.

Thoreau, Henry David. Born in Concord, Massachusetts, Thoreau (1817–1862) graduated from Harvard. While a student, he met Ralph Waldo Emerson who encouraged the young man intellectually. Rejecting materialism, he worked a variety of low-wage jobs and as a carpenter and eventually became an important part of the transcendentalist movement. For several years he was largely supported by Emerson, who genuinely admired his intellect. In 1845 Thoreau moved to a hut on Walden Pond near Concord and spent a solitary year there, observing, pondering life in general, and recording his thoughts in what later became one of his best-known works, *Walden*. Though most of his works were not published until after his death, his philosophical proposals, including "Civil Disobedience," written to protest a tax designed to help pay for the Mexican War, inspired many in his generation as well as since. He died in 1862. *Bibliography*: Sanborn, F. B. *The Life of Henry David Thoreau*. Boston: Houghton, Mifflin, 1917. Smith, Harmon. *My Friend, My Friend: The Story of Thoreau's Friendship with Emerson*. Boston: University of Massachusetts Press, 1999.

Weed, Thurlow. Born in 1797, Weed, despite minimal formal education, became one of the most powerful men in New York state government. After brief service during the War of 1812, he began working in a printer's shop. By 1820 he had become the foreman of the *Albany Register*. Increasingly active and influential in local and state politics, he supported DeWitt Clinton for governor and helped to engineer John Quincy Adams New York in 1824. The following year, he was elected to the New York Assembly. Operating several newspapers and cautiously maneuvering, he consistently opposed Martin Van Buren and the Jackson Democrats in the state.

Instead he lined up behind Henry Clay and the emerging Whig Party. He was an opponent of slavery and generally embraced Whig policies. At the height of his power, he helped to elect William Seward governor and swing New York's support behind William Henry Harrison in 1840. Through his long career as a political manager, Weed emerged as the most powerful New York State Whig. *Bibliography*: Van Deusen, Glyndon. *Thurlow Weed: Wizard of the Lobby*. New York: Da Capo Press, 1947. Weed, Thurlow. *The Life of Thurlow Weed*. New York: Da Capo Press, 1970.

Weld, Theodore. Weld was born in Hampton, Connecticut, in 1803 and moved with his family to upstate New York. While a student at Hamilton College, he became a disciple of evangelist Charles Grandison Finney. Traveling throughout the region, Weld promoted various social reforms including temperance and educational reform. By 1830 he was recognized as one of the leaders of the antislavery movement. Tirelessly pursuing his causes, he enrolled in Lane Seminary in Cincinnati for ministerial training but was dismissed from the school after leading a student anti-slavery protest. In 1838 he married abolitionist and women's rights advocate Angelina Grimke. During the years that followed, he edited and contributed to the abolitionist paper, the *Emancipator*, while also organizing numerous other anti-slavery activities. Because of both financial and physical problems, he withdrew from his reform efforts until after the beginning of the Civil War and, along with his wife and sister-in-law, opened an experimental school in Raritan, New Jersey. He died in 1895. *Bibliography*: Lerner, Gerda. *The Grimke Sisters: From South Carolina Pioneers for Woman's Rights and Abolition*. New York: Houghton, Mifflin, 1971. Thomas, Benjamin. *Theodore Weld: Crusader for Freedom*. New Brunswick, NJ: Rutgers University Press, 1950.

Whittier, John Greenleaf. The son of a poor Quaker farm family in Massachusetts, Whittier (1807–1892) had minimal formal education. Nevertheless, he demonstrated an unusual talent for writing. As a young man, he submitted a poem to a paper published by abolitionist William Lloyd Garrison, who afterward aggressively encouraged Whittier to develop his literary skills. Over the next two decades, Whittier wrote many poems denouncing slavery and became active in the abolitionist movement. In the 1840s, troubled by the increasingly confrontational tactics of the abolitionist leaders, he parted company with Garrison and became a founding member of the Liberty Party. For a while he edited the *Liberty Party* newspaper, but constant health problems forced him to resign form his publishing duties. However, he continued to write poignant and influential anti-slavery poetry and to support the movement to end slavery. *Bibliography*: Pickard, Samuel T., ed. *The Life and Letters of John Greenleaf*

Whittier, 2 vols. New York: Barnes & Noble, 1961. Pollard, John A. *John Greenleaf Whittier: Friend of Man*. Boston: Houghton, Mifflin, 1949.

Wirt, William. Wirt (1772–1836) was born on a Maryland farmstead. Though from meager beginnings he was blessed with an exceptional mind, and despite limited formal education he became an accomplished lawyer. After opening a practice in Richmond, he entered politics in 1802 when he was elected to the Virginia legislature. As a federal prosecutor, he was part of the government's team that put Aaron Burr on trial. In 1817 he became attorney general for James Monroe and retained the post during the Adams administration. In 1831, concerned about a split among Jackson opponents, Wirt reluctantly agreed to become a third-party candidate for the presidency. However, he soon regretted his decision and unsuccessfully attempted to pull out of the campaign. Afterwards he retired from politics and instead became involved in an attempt to create a German settlement in Florida. *Bibliography*: Wirt, William. *William Wirt Papers*. Baltimore: Maryland Historical Society, 1971.

Wright, Frances. Born in Scotland in 1795, Wright came to America in 1818. Bright and well read, she published several works advocating social change. She helped to influence transcendentalists, including Ralph Waldo Emerson. An active opponent of slavery, she attempted to create a community for manumitted slaves first in Tennessee and then in Haiti, but both efforts failed. Later she became a member of the New Harmony, Indiana, utopian effort, advocating the necessity for universal public education. She also lectured about women's rights and criticized organized religion for limiting women with the church. She died in 1852. *Bibliography*: Perkins, A.J.G., and Theresa Wolfson. *Frances Wright, Free Enquirer: The Study of a Temperament*. New York: Harper & Brothers, 1939.

Young, Brigham. Born in Vermont, Young (1801–1877), his ten siblings, and his parents moved to upstate New York when he was three. As a young man, he joined the Methodist Church but several years later, after reading Joseph Smith's Book of Mormon, was baptized into Smith's Church of Latter Day Saints. Immediately afterward, he began doing missionary work in Canada for his new church. The following year he joined Smith in Ohio, where a Mormon settlement was planned. During the next five years, public pressure forced the church to move repeatedly. Meanwhile, Young rose to become Smith's immediate subordinate. In 1844, Smith was murdered by an angry mob and Young became the church's new leader. Rather than endure continued attacks, Young moved his followers first to Nebraska and then to the Great Salt Lake, Utah, where a Mormon community, Salt Lake City, was organized. Protected by the remote location, Young's community was built upon strict Mormon principles as well as self-sufficiency. Young also directed the creation of satellite communities throughout the region. Further strengthening the church, Young was appointed governor of the territory by President Buchanan. Despite threats from Indians and the railroads, as well as controversial customs including the practice of polygamy, Young's church and community prospered and became an important part of the American social landscape. Young died in 1877. *Bibliography*: Arrington, Leonard. *Brigham Young: American Moses*. Urbana: University of Illinois Press, 1985. West, Ray B., Jr. *Kingdom of the Saints: The Story of Brigham Young and the Mormons*. New York: Viking Press, 1957. Hirshorn, Stanley. *Lion of the Lord: A Biography of Brigham Young*. New York: Knopf, 1969. Hunter, Milton. *Brigham Young the Colonizer*. Santa Barbara, CA: Peregrine Smith, 1973.

INDEX

INDEX

About the Author

PAUL E. DOUTRICH is Associate Professor of History at York College.